MIME
SPOKEN
HERE

**The Performer's
Portable
Workshop**

MIME
SPOKEN
HERE

The Performer's Portable Workshop

By Tony Montanaro
with Karen Hurll Montanaro

Tilbury House, Publishers
Gardiner, Maine

Tilbury House, Publishers
132 Water Street
Gardiner, Maine 04345

Library of Congess Cataloging-in-Publication Data

Montanaro, Tony, 1927–
Mime spoken here : the performer's portable workshop / by
Tony Montanaro and Karen Hurll Montanaro.
   p. cm.
Includes index.
ISBN 0-88448-178-6 (hardcover : alk. paper). —ISBNB 0-
   88448-177-8 (pbk, : alk. paper)
1. Mime. 2. Mime—Study and teaching. I. Montanaro, Karen Hurll,
1960- II. Title.
PN2071.G4M66 1995
792.3'028—dc2095-18963
   CIP

Text and jacket designed by Edith Allard
Editing and production: Mark Melnicove, Nina Medina,
Val Cope, Ruth LaChance, and Jennifer Elliott
Printing and Binding: Maple Vail, Binghampton, NY
Printing (jackets and covers): The John P. Pow Company, South
Boston, MA

10 9 8 7 6 5 4 3 2 1

•   •   •   •   •   •   •   •   •   •   •

This book is lovingly dedicated
    to my children,
who kept me awake in more ways than one:

    Jovin,
    Raman,
    Christopher,
    Kavi Sean
    Adam,
    Gabriel,
    Lisa,
    and Lara.

CONTENTS

Note to Teachers and Students:
When a subtitle begins with the heading "The Class," this indicates that an actual class exercise is described in this particular section. In the chapter entitled "Improvisation," class exercises are indicated by the heading "First Exercise," Second Exercise," etc. I have done this to make it easier for you to quickly isolate the class exercises from the rest of the book.

I NTRODUCTION

E arly in Tony's career, he was hired to do a commercial, selling carpet deodorant. The producers were looking for "a mime," and Tony's reputation preceded him. He was hired without an audition.

In this commercial, Tony was supposed to walk into a carpeted room and do a mime of someone repulsed by the odor of the carpet. He showed them a few exaggerated gestures and everyone laughed—the producers were delighted. Everyone who has ever seen Tony perform has been thrilled. Even the professed "mime-haters" have been converted, instantly.

Everything was running smoothly until Tony was directed to the wardrobe department. There, someone handed him a blue-striped shirt, high-waisted white pants, black shoes, and suspenders—Marcel Marceau's costume. Tony objected, "You don't want me. You want Marceau!" He explained that Marceau was certainly a brilliant mime but, "There's only one mime out there who looks like Marceau, and that's Marceau." Tony ended up not shooting this commercial, but this was only one of the many jobs he lost by refusing to cater to Hollywood's definition of mime.

• • •

Tony and I drove up to a school where we were to perform that day. It was recess time, and the seventh and eighth graders were loitering in the parking lot. When they saw our car, they ran to greet us with their own silent renditions of the wall-mime. The more extroverted students even added the "appropriate" facial expression: eyebrows lifted and lips pursed into the classic "I'm-a-jerk" look. "So that's what they think mime is...." Tony's lament was just loud enough for me to hear.

• • •

A clerk in one of our local stores recognized Tony's name on his credit card. "Hey! You're the mime!" Tony replied in the affirmative. "Then why are you talking to me??!!" With that, the man cocked his head and grinned at Tony askance as if to say, "You made a boo-boo! Mimes don't talk!"

• • •

It's sad but true. Most people, if they think of mime at all, think of a white-faced man wearing a blue-striped shirt, palming an invisible wall and, of course, remaining absolutely silent. This is like saying that ballet is a lady in a pink tutu twirling in a music box. How would Babe Ruth have felt if everyone around him equated baseball with men in knickers, swinging wooden clubs, and chasing balls?

What exactly is mime? For the sake of brevity, Tony defines mime as *physical eloquence.*

For many years, it satisfied him to leave it at that, but with the upsurge of misconceptions regarding this art form, he recognized the need to define his work more thoroughly. This book is an in-depth study of Tony's unique understanding of mime as a technique—as entertainment—as art.

Tony's motivation for writing a book was similar to that which any artist experiences after forty-five years at the top of a trade. He wanted to share his experiences and revelations with the next generation to spare them a few mistakes, maybe—to inspire and instruct.

My motivation for writing Tony's book was, I think, more convincing than Tony's motivation. Tony has been doing mime all his life and doing it with extraordinary skill, even before he studied with Marcel Marceau and Etienne Decroux in Paris in the late 1950s. I, on the other hand, had no idea what mime was until I met Tony. During the past five years of our working together, I acquired a profound and life-changing appreciation for this art form—specifically Tony's unique approach to it.

Tony's approach to mime is more than an invaluable lesson in theatre; it's a lesson in problem solving. Some performers have the problem of not knowing what to say. They may have lots of technique but don't know how to write sketches. Other performers have lots to say but lack the technique to carry these ideas across. Knowing what you want to say, sensing what the audience hears, and having the skill necessary to bring the two together with eloquence and personal style— these are latent skills in all of us which Tony's exercises and instructions serve to uncover. For this reason, the benefits of learning mime (as Tony teaches it) extend far beyond the stage; Tony teaches the art of communication.

Between Tony's fatherly affection for the next generation of mimes and my firm conviction that Tony's approach to mime is revolutionary, we found more than enough enthusiasm to see this book through to completion.

—Karen Hurll Montanaro

INTRODUCING TONY MONTANARO

In the early part of our friendship, I accompanied Tony to Augusta, Maine, to watch him perform for a Jewish ladies organization. The sponsor, looking rather harried and troubled, met us as we pulled in. Apparently their advertising campaign had run into some trouble and there wouldn't be a large audience for the show. The auditorium was only a third full, but that didn't dampen Tony's spirit. The show went on and what a show it was!

As a finale, Tony performed his one-word improvisations. Someone in the audience would shout out a word. As soon as he heard the word, Tony would repeat it to let the audience know that this was to be the theme of his improvisation. He then proceeded to show us what that word "did to him." (A thorough description of this exercise is found on page 181.)

I remember that one word was "wind." Tony paused for a second, lifted his arms above his head as if clearing the air to receive inspiration from Above, and then started walking against the wind—but it wasn't an ordinary wind. The debris that whipped past him consisted of dates and memories. A snippet of a memory flew by and Tony shouted out a year or a shard of a recollection, but the wind was blowing too furiously to hold onto one particular year or memory for long. There were other one-word improvs that evening; each one more provocative than the last.

When Tony took his final bow, we all stood up at once and clapped until our hands were tired. As the audience filed out, a well-dressed woman from the audience approached Tony and without a word, kissed him gently on the cheek and walked away.

Now as I attempt to recapture Tony's life in a list of accomplishments and awards, I realize that this list of accomplishments, though impressive, does not accurately portray Tony's major accomplishments as a human being, philosopher, and truth-seeker. Tony's humanity may go unsung by critics, but it comprises the soul of his performance. His show has a long-lasting, sometimes life-changing effect on people.

• • •

Tony, the eldest son of working-class Italian Americans, grew up in the small New Jersey town of Paulsboro. His first stage experience was in school productions. From the "Nickle Club" in grade school to high school musicals, to college productions, Tony's talent was apparent. At that time, no one in

Little Tony.
(Courtesy of the
authors)

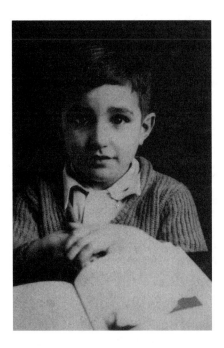

Paulsboro knew what "mime" was, but everyone noticed
Tony's uncanny ability to make the invisible world, visible.
One director watched in amazement as Tony pushed an invisible lawnmower across the stage, "You make people see things
that aren't there!" he said.

Tony studied romance languages and theatre arts at Rutgers
University and Columbia University. He received a bachelor's
degree in drama from Columbia University in 1952. While still
a sophomore at Rutgers University, Tony saw the film *Les
Enfants du Paradis* or *The Children of Paradise*. The story is set
in Paris in the early 1800s, just as the mime movement was
gaining momentum and prestige. Some of the world's top
mimes, including Jean-Louis Barrault and Etienne Decroux
performed in the film. (Little did Tony realize that he'd be
studying mime with Decroux in Paris a few years later.)

This film marked a turning point in Tony's life. He was
transfixed by the story, the mime, and the climate in which
the story takes place. When the film was over, he left the
theatre and performed the illusionary walk on the sidewalk.
His technique was perfect even without having seen the illusion before.

In the years following his graduation from Columbia, Tony
spent three summers with the Grist Mill Playhouse, a profes-

sional summer stock company in Andover, New Jersey, and worked professionally as a puppeteer with Suzari Marionettes for two of their performing seasons. But the attraction toward mime became more and more powerful. When Marcel Marceau made his debut appearance at the Phoenix Theatre in New York City in 1956, Tony was in the audience; this performance became the deciding factor in Tony's becoming a mime. He recalls being impressed with Marceau as a performer, but he also remembers thinking, "I can do that!"

Determined to study with Marceau, Tony went backstage at the Phoenix Theatre to talk business. Marceau was pleasant, but had no time for auditioning young mimes. Tony followed him to Philadelphia. The master must have been impressed by Tony's impetuosity and persistence because he told him to get up on the stage, "Show me what you can do." That was that. Tony was suddenly on stage auditioning for Marcel Marceau.

During this audition, Tony did a brash and innocent thing—he performed one of Marceau's sketches, "The Butterfly." If Marceau had any objections to this, it was now too late to voice them; he sat back to watch. At the end of the sketch, Tony could see that the master was genuinely moved. He had tears in his eyes, then told Tony that he must never perform that sketch in public again. He quickly added, "There is only one mime in the world who can teach you." Tony received a scholarship to study mime with Marceau in Paris and he was on a boat a few months later.

Paris was harsh on Tony. He had a difficult time with the language and lived in abject poverty for about six months. During this time, he studied with Marcel Marceau and with Marceau's teacher, Etienne Decroux. He learned a lot from these masters, but the survival instinct was his most demanding taskmaster. A few "guardian angels" appeared to help Tony out of dire circumstances. Louis Thomas, Marceau's stage manager, let Tony stay in the *Chambre de Bonne* of a building he rented. For heat, he told Tony to burn the bed that was stored up there. A few other people gave Tony a meal here and there, and Marceau himself loaned him the equivalent of $10 one day. (When Tony tried to pay it back later, Marceau wouldn't accept it.)

The day arrived when Tony realized his stay in Paris was over and decided to travel to Italy to see relatives. He had never been to Italy before, but both of his parents had been raised there and as soon as Tony set foot on the soil, he felt at home. Tony's fortune shifted in Italy. Every door opened to him and his pockets were always filled with money. He taught American English at a language school and earned a sizeable weekly wage. He also quickly became the darling of Italian TV when he was hired to create and perform in a series of Colgate commercials.

He wrote at least twenty-six different commercials for Colgate, all with a similar theme. Tony would be an adventurer going through some jungle or crypt or ghost ship, and just as he was opening a mummy's tomb or a treasure chest, his glamorous sidekick, Lily Cerasoli, would walk out of the tomb or treasure chest smiling and flashing her dazzling white teeth. Tony's eyes would pop out of his head in amazement and he'd say in Italian, "What a beautiful smile!" She'd say, "*Si Colgate con Gardol.*" ("Yes, Colgate with Gardol.") The commercials were famous throughout Italy.

Whereas Tony had feared for his life in Paris, he suddenly found himself experiencing a more elusive fear in Italy—the fear of his accelerated speed toward stardom. He didn't feel he was "ready" for Easy Street and decided to go back to the United States. He secured a performing job on the cruise ship *Isle de France* and set sail for home. On the ship, he met his future bride, Lahiila lai Cohane, and the next chapter of Tony's life commenced.

Tony and his wife had two sons and although they were never well off, he supported his family almost entirely through performing and teaching mime.

In the late '50s, early '60s, Tony designed his one-man show entitled *A Mime's Eye View*. For almost thirty years he kept this show alive, designing new sketches and perfecting the old. One of his first appearances took place at the Gramercy Arts Theatre in New York City. A critic from the prestigious *Show Business* newspaper wrote:

> *Tony Montanaro's "A Mime's Eye View" is a wholly delightful evening. He is a young artist with a broad range of movement and gesture, a warm stage presence, and his ideas are original, well thought out and developed, and not at all derivative—a difficult accomplishment for any mime.*

Kenn from *Variety* wrote:

> *Tony Montanaro, a student of Marcel Marceau, proves in his new one-man show that he is a talented mime. He is an ingratiating performer with fine control of his body and putty-like*

face and a keen sense of the humorous aspects of everyday life. He is a talent worth watching.

As his fame grew, so did the opportunities. In the early 1960s, Tony performed on *Captain Kangaroo*. He also designed and hosted a children's television show for CBS in Philadelphia. He and the producers had differing ideas as to how the show should be approached. The producers, naturally, wanted to control the script and camera angles, etc. As was typical of Tony, he balked at the prospect of being told what to do and pleaded with the producers to let him do it his way. For once, television complied and let Tony have almost total freedom on camera. The result was the award-winning *Pretendo*.

The instant success of *Pretendo* surprised and delighted Tony's producers. But Tony became disillusioned when the pressures of commercialism closed in on him. Companies wanted to air their commercials during *Pretendo* and in those days, the hosts of the shows had to act in the commercials. Tony didn't want to do this. He resented the thought of the "deep pockets" owning and manipulating his creativity. After two years, he left CBS and moved on to the next chapter of his career.

Tony hosting his children's show, "Pretendo," for Channel 10 (CBS) in Philadelphia, in the early 1960s. (Courtesy of the authors)

In the meantime, Tony's first marriage had ended and he married Pamela Walbert. Desiring to escape the big city, he and Pam moved to Bearsville, New York, where three more sons were born. It was soon apparent that this was not the ideal place to raise a family. The drug craze was moving into nearby Woodstock and Tony didn't want his family growing up around this peer pressure. In 1970, the Montanaros relocated to South Paris, Maine.

Tony had been intrigued by a huge, dilapidated farmhouse and barn on the end of a dirt road. The house looked like a ghost house and the barn was piled high with horse manure. Within two years, the barn was transformed into a theatre and Tony named it The Celebration Barn Theatre. He began holding six- and eight-month workshops in mime, storytelling, and improvisation. These workshops inevitably produced performing troupes. The first troupe, consisting of eleven or twelve people, eventually evolved into the six-member Celebration Mime Theatre. The company toured nationally and received rave reviews wherever it performed.

> This bounding band of zanies came from nowhere—well, South Paris, Maine—and were as quickly gone. Five performances at New England Life Hall, then back to the wagon, the road, and the tambourines, like the nomadic mimes of the Middle Ages...their work is delightful...these kids can convince their bodies that they're just about anything.
> —Carolyn Clay, The Boston Phoenix

> In the Celebration Mime Theatre concept of mime, actors pass effortlessly between the animate and the inanimate, being for one moment a person and at the next, his environment. The striking thing about their performance that makes it so unique is their ability to find the simple essence of the situation they are portraying. After this they seem to uncannily find a way to achieve their illusions that is so simple no one else would think of it. Simplicity is the hardest state to arrive at in art....
> —Frances Wessells, Richmond Times-Dispatch

> ...the most thrilling moment came with the recognition that Montanaro has created a modern "Commedia dell'Arte". "Commedia dell'Arte," an outgrowth of ancient Roman mime theatre, did not confine its performers to mute expression. Rather it allowed the players to make sounds, to say words, to elaborate on action with musical and spoken accompaniment.

The South Paris group,...displaying elastic virtuoso style, has created a unique stage image, a refinement of "Commedia dell'Arte" that at once establishes it as an important addition to American theatre. There is nothing like it I know of in the country today.

—John Thorton, *Portland Press Herald*

Tony ostensibly teaches mime, but essentially he promotes the art of self-expression. Consequently, many of Tony's students realize that the stage is not the best place for them to express themselves. Former students and troupe members have joined human rights movements, monasteries, ashrams. Some have become teachers, homemakers, therapists, but all of these people confront life as if it were an extension of Tony's class: a lesson in problem solving and personal style.

The Celebration Barn became a metropolis for personal style theatre. At one time, "The Barn" was home base for three performing troupes: The Celebration Mime Theatre, Razzmatazz!, and Garbo and Jillian. In addition to this, the Celebration Barn "family" published a quarterly newspaper, *The Mime Times*. The paper was informative and educational, a scintillating collection of reviews, current events, and discussions on mime, gesture, expression, and the art of perform-

The Celebration Barn Family of Performing Troupes. From left to right: Fateh Azzam, Bob Dillard, Claire Sikoryak, Nat Warren-White, Brian Meehl, Douglas Leach, Carolyn DeNigris, George Sand, Jane Crosby, Fred Garbo, Gillian Hannett. Tony is seated in front. (Courtesy of Brian Meehl)

ing. The paper went out to subscribers for five years, but when the running costs exceeded the profits, the press stopped.

Tony's students formed new alliances. Many of them went solo or teamed up with other members of the Celebration Barn family and began designing new sketches. Meanwhile Tony and Pam adopted two daughters and had another son (Tony's sixth).

In the early '80s, four of Tony's students who had participated in a six-month workshop asked him to form another troupe. By now, Tony was not sure he wanted to invest so much time in yet another directorship position, but their enthusiasm won him over and The Celebration Theatre Ensemble was born. Another hugely successful performing company, the Ensemble performed in theatres all over the world from New York's Lincoln Center, to Washington's Kennedy Center to Stockholm, Sweden, and Canada.

In between jobs as a teacher and director, Tony returned to solo performing. Sometimes, he asked one or two of his students to join him on stage and share some of the load. He continued to receive accolades for his performances.

In 1984, William Collins of *The Philadelphia Inquirer* wrote:

Life is what the best of mimes shed light on. They are corporeal poetry, walking insights into the human condition.
Montanaro's work with the masks and stock characters of the Commedia dell'Arte was like a street scene by Callot. When he showed people turning into animals they resemble—a rooster, a monkey,—the suggestive power in mime took on the aspect of sorcery.

George Jackson of *The Washington Post* also admired Tony's work:

Tony Montanaro has a face with those big, distinctive features whose slightest move can change his mood, his age, his very character. His spacing of motions, timing of steps, and levels of energy have the clarity one can expect of a performer in the classic French mime tradition who has studied with Decroux and Marceau. Yet he's also a clown, a dancer, and storyteller.

After seventeen years of marriage, Tony and Pam decided to divorce and in 1988, he sold "The Barn" to Carolyn Brett (former agent and manager for the Ensemble) and Leland Faulkner (Tony's friend, partner, and former student). In 1992, Carolyn Brett became the sole owner. Tony continues to offer summer workshops at The Barn every year and is gratified to

Tony and Karen in "Paper Doll," 1993.
(Photo by C.C. Church, courtesy of Marge Ghilarducci Agency)

see the evolution and continuing success of "his" school and theatre.

Tony and I met in 1987 during rehearsals for the Portland Ballet's *Nutcracker.* (Tony played the part of Uncle Drosselmeyer and I danced the Sugar Plum Fairy.) A professional ballet dancer for over ten years, I was delighted to see how perfectly the mime and ballet disciplines harmonized and supported each other. More than this, I fell in love with Tony's unique approach to mime and movement. He gave me a new perspective on my work and cured me of the "bunhead" syndrome. We were married in 1989 and began designing our two-person show, The Montanaro-Hurll Theatre of Mime and Dance. We performed together for five years before deciding that it was time to pursue other interests. I still dance with the Portland Ballet. Tony recently discovered a passion for art, monotypes, etching, and watercolor. We have been getting into the studio more often lately to improvise and try new things. Perhaps we'll write a new show soon.

—Karen Hurll Montanaro

1

DEFINITION AND HISTORY OF MIME

If you're looking for a date when mime began, you'll never find it. Mime "began" with the first gesture, the first time someone or something moved in response to a need, a thought, an instinct. It is accurate then to say that the "beginning" of mime is not a static, chronological date but a dynamic, timeless imperative.

The Beginning of Mime

Every art form has evolved to satisfy the human need for self-expression. The thoughts, ideas, and feelings expressed through art are universal; only the medium is specific. The more specific the medium, the easier it is to define the art form.

Here we come to the problem with defining mime. Many art forms are defined by an instrument or a set of rules. Ballet, for example, is defined by turn-out, stretched feet, square hips, etc. Mime has no specific rules to distinguish it from the other art forms. The medium for mime is "whatever works," whatever gets the point across. Mime is simply self-expression. For this reason, I call mime the "common ground" of theatre.

While other art forms have become more clearly defined through time, the definition of mime has blurred. This has happened because by its very nature mime is an iconoclast. Nothing is sacred except the message. For most art forms the medium is the message. For mime, it's the other way around: the message is the medium.

I have listened to many heated (and some unpleasant) discussions as to the correct definition of the word "mime." This is only indicative of human nature. We want to have names for things. Artists need to label themselves for publicity reasons. Agents need words and short phrases for their "products." Audiences like to refer quickly to the art forms they like or don't like.

The Definition(s) of "Mime"

Words with clear-cut definitions save us a lot of time. But often they save too much time. For example, many people don't go to mime performances because they hate mime. But what if that show is really fantastic? They miss a wonderful experience just because they defined mime incorrectly.

Some people think that mime is the "charade" section of the

ballets. This mime is simple sign language (i.e., two hands over the heart means "love." Pointing to your eyes means "I saw.").

Other people equate mime with the mime *illusions.* Anyone who palms an invisible wall is a mime, according to this definition.

Then there are those who define mime as silent acting. It's true: anyone who is capable of "speaking" without the use of words would have to be a mime. But all mimes don't have to be silent, at least not in my book.

My definition of "mime" is "physical eloquence."

Mime is the eloquent and efficient delivery of a mood or a message in which the body is the primary instrument. That message doesn't have to be a story! The theme may be abstract or literal, but if the artist delivers that theme *eloquently* he/she is a mime as far as I'm concerned.

You will find that the more you learn about and practice mime, the broader your own definition of the word will become, until you see mime everywhere.

Who is a "Mime"?

According to my definition, José Limón was one of the greatest mimes of all time. The first time I saw him on stage, he was performing a piece he choreographed called *The Traitor.* This was the story of the betrayal of Jesus, danced by eight men. Lucas Hoving danced the role of Jesus, José Limón played Judas. The other dancers were Jesus' disciples.

Many times during the piece, Judas (Limón) moved independently of the music. Whether someone moves *with* the music or *against* it doesn't mean anything. What impressed me about Limón's performance was not *what* he did but *how* he did it. When he moved across the stage (against the music), he sidled across, like a serpent. When he kissed Jesus, the audience groaned.

He had such a knowledge of movement! When he moved, all I could see was Judas. The dancing never got in the way. The movement was certainly impressive, but it never took the audience's attention away from the story or the theme of the piece.

The dancers used a prop: a white sheet of cloth, that served to create different scenes, different effects. At one point, the dancers snapped the cloth taut: it became a tablecloth over which Jesus laid his hands. Another time, the cloth became a robe and people stepped on it. The dance was mimetic: you could see tablecloths, robes, stones, the cross; you could see the human and the divine meeting in the betrayal of Jesus. That's why I thought, "This guy's a mime!"

Later, I enrolled in a couple of dance classes at Limón's school, but I soon realized that I wasn't interested in learning a dance technique; I wanted to see and work with Limón personally. This never happened, but I watched him in rehearsal one day and the details of this day are still crystal clear in my memory.

Limón was a formidable figure. I don't remember if he was actually tall, but he seemed immense. He had a gaunt, powerful, chiseled face with high cheekbones and feet like clubs. All his dancers had feet like clubs—massive bunions, huge callouses—these feet would hit the floor and stay there. No wobbling on those feet.

I remember he grabbed an orange and ate the whole thing, skin and all. It was a hot day. Everyone was sweating and thirsty. Limón took the orange and devoured it whole. That was the kind of guy he was—frightening, almost.

When he came out of the rehearsal and sat down next to me on the bench, his breathing was heavy and his face was sweaty. I was beside myself with awe and admiration. More than anything else I wanted to say something to him. After all, I might never get the chance to speak with him again. I said, "Mr. Limón?"

He turned, looked at me, and said, "Yes?"

I was struck dumb by the intensity of this moment. It was as if he were saying, "If you talk to me, we're locked together for life." He expected the profound. Idle talk at that moment was simply not appropriate.

Feebly, I said, "I enjoyed watching the rehearsal." He said, "Thank you" and smiled, I think. But I turned away, stunned, and that was that.

As Providence would have it, I did meet this giant of a man later. My friend Tom was the stage manager at Julliard. Limón was performing there and I went backstage to see Tom.

Limón was in Tom's office and we were introduced. Then Tom went off to do something. I was alone with Limón.

This time I had more of my wits about me and opened a conversation. "I watched you in rehearsal a long time ago."

"Oh?" He was relaxed and personable.

"You know, I think you're one of the greatest mimes I've ever seen," I said.

He corrected me. "Oh no, I'm not a mime; I'm a dancer."

"No sir, you're a mime. You may be a dancer as well, but you are a mime."

He studied my face for a second and said, "Define your terms."

I gave him a brief description of what, at the time, I thought mime was. I must have said something to the effect that mime is more than the mime illusions; it's character work, the ability to create a mood or tell a story through movement.

Limón listened carefully and said, "On *those* terms, I'm a mime."

My meeting with José Limón was brief but satisfying. We shook hands and parted friends.

I once told a friend of mine, Kurt Records, about my two meetings with Limón. A few days later, he gave this poem to me as a gift. It's a description of the first, very brief exchange that took place outside the rehearsal studio.

THE MEETING
Too quickly to retrieve it
my mouth
tossed out his name.
As it fell on his lapel
the distant profile turned
into the fullness of his sculpted face,
all eyes and close
as breath. Someone whispered
"yes?" but the face demanded more
than mindless greetings could endure so
we called the whole thing off
right there.

—Kurt Records

The History of Mime as a Silent Art Form

Before mime was defined as a silent art form, it was simply the art of telling a story using the body, the voice, and "whatever else" to carry the point across to the audience. The term "mime," therefore, included dancers, poets, clowns, actors, singers, and musicians.

The idea of telling a story without using the voice came up originally as a solution to a problem. According to mime history, there were at least three separate occasions in which performers encountered a problem with speaking on stage. The solution was to use the body and facial expressions to get the message across.

It is recorded that an early Roman mime, Livius Andronicus, lost his voice one evening. Rather than cancel the upcoming performance, he chose to perform silently while a chorister delivered the lines. The results were so impressive that Andronicus decided to use silence as his own personal style of performing.

Some historians cite this as the birth of mime. Yet, in the early 1700s, the popular English pantomimist[1] John Rich came up with the idea of silent acting independent of Andronicus's example. On this occasion, John Rich was to play the part of Harlequin in the English Harlequinade. He chose to make his character mute "for the simple reason that, though a clever actor, he could not speak well enough for the stage."[2]

The success of Rich's performance gave rise to a sweeping reform on the English theatre scene and marked the beginning of the true wordless English Harlequinade. Prior to this, the Harlequinade had relied heavily on voice and dialogue.

Another story of silence being used on stage takes us back to the days of Louis XIV (King of France, 1643-1715) and the Commedia dell'Arte. The Commedia dell'Arte was a theatre of improvisation that originated in Italy in the 1500s. It consisted of a cast of wildly exuberant and irreverent Italian actors. This theatre traveled throughout Europe and, for a while, made a home for itself in France, where it enjoyed un-precedented popularity. Louis XIV was one of its greatest fans.

In 1668 Louis XIV gave the Italian actors permission to sing and speak in French.[3] This was like a death sentence for the French theatre (the Comédie-Française), which could not pos-sibly sustain public favor in the face of such competition.

The Italian theatre became more bold, more satirical, more witty, and more popular. The French government finally stepped in to check the comedians' increasing favor and to give the French actors a chance to recover "their" audience. The French government prohibited the Italian mimes from speaking on stage. They were legally forced to stop talking.

Undaunted, this group of Italian comedians devised means for getting their point across without using audible speech. Among other ploys, the Italians used placards. When the time came for an actor to deliver his lines, two cupids bearing the written version of the forbidden dialogue might suddenly

---

[1]The difference between "pantomime" and "mime" is an issue for the lin-guist; almost everyone I know in the mime business uses these two words interchangeably. "Pan" is a prefix meaning "all" or "everything." Therefore, the literal meaning of "pantomime" is "one who mimes everything." This is redundant; all mimes "mime everything."
[2]Perugini, Mark, *The Art of Ballet*, (London: Martin Secker, 1915), p. 123.
[3]Storey, Robert F., *Pierrot: A Critical History of a Mask*, (Princeton, New Jersey: Princeton University Press, 1978), p. 29.

appear over the actors' heads.[4] The actors also wrote their dialogues on scrolls and unfurled these scrolls on cue. Scrolls unfurled out of their pockets or from off-stage. The Italian comedians were always devising new ways of revealing their lines. Meanwhile, they became more and more adept at expressing the feelings, thoughts, and words of their characters solely through gesture and facial expressions.

Livius Andronicus, John Rich, and the Commedia dell'Arte each employed silence as a solution to a particular problem. These events occurred independently of each other and ended up being serendipitous. The use of silence "stuck" as a means of incorporating originality and innovation into the artist's work, while satisfying the audience's need for entertainment. Artists are forever solving problems; some of these solutions survive history, some don't.

• • •

The creative use of problems and limitations is vital to the evolution of art. The piano, for example, is an obstacle to self-expression until the pianist masters the technique. The piano limits the venue for self-expression—only the fingers are used. But there is no limit to what may be expressed through the virtuosic mastery of the fingers.

By the early 1800s, the self-imposed elimination of words and sounds from one's performance had created a new and provocative art form. One of the earliest silent mimes was Jean-Gaspard Deburau (1796–1846) also known as Baptiste Deburau. Deburau's strength as a silent actor not only defined mime as a silent art form, it also immortalized the character of Pierrot. Deburau made his Pierrot "Everyman"—someone everyone could relate to. Prior to this, Pierrot (a stock character of the Commedia dell'Arte) had been a scapegoat, the butt of jokes and ridicule. Pierrot never would have survived history as his former self. Deburau is also credited with changing mime from slapstick to theatre.[5]

Etienne Decroux, considered the father of modern mime, reached a pinnacle of influence and expertise in the mid-1900s. He created many of the now-classic mime illusions, such as the illusionary walk, and promoted the illusions as a central feature of mime as we know it today. Not all of the mime illusions were invented by Decroux; many of us have

[4]Ibid, p. 38.
[5]Shepard, Richmond, *Mime: The Technique of Silence*, 2d ed., (New York: Drama Book Specialists, 1971), p. 13.

Etienne Decroux, 1973.
(Photo by Claude Perrain, Visages de France, Paris, courtesy of Thomas Leabhart)

invented our own, but Decroux is recognized as the originator of the *concept* of the mime illusions.

Toward the end of his career, Decroux became a purist. He had invented many exercises to enhance the mime's control and clarity of movement. In those latter days, he stressed the importance of discipline and technique above all else. Many of Decroux's disciples systematized the master's style and evolved a highly refined technique. This technique is now called "corporeal mime."

Decroux was Marcel Marceau's teacher, and Marceau was Decroux's prize pupil. Such a relationship is fraught with tension. The teacher's temptation is to control the student, to direct his/her career and claim partial ownership of the student's prowess and finesse. The student's dilemma is one of having to separate from the teacher in order to find his own style and tastes. These were the tensions that eventually divided these two artists. By the time I went to Paris to study mime, the animosity between Decroux and Marceau had reached unfortunate proportions. I studied with both masters but never breathed a word of this to Decroux. If Decroux had known I was studying with Marceau, he would have kicked

19

me out of his school. Marceau, on the other hand, advised me to study with Decroux, but warned against mentioning his (Marceau's) name.

Marcel Marceau's contribution to defining mime as a silent art form cannot be over-estimated. As one of the world's greatest mimes, Marceau put mime on the map. He was rising in stature just as television was reaching a broader audience. Television brought the finest and most current trends in art and entertainment into people's living rooms, and Marcel Marceau became a household word.

Marceau is a brilliant performer with impeccable technique and a personal style. When he first appeared in the United States (the Phoenix Theatre in the '50s), no one in this country had seen the mime illusions or silent mime before. He was an overnight success. Because he had no competitors, the public soon considered "Marceau" and "mime" to be synonymous

Marcel Marceau as "The Lion Tamer," with Tony's friend Pierre Verry carrying the sign. (Photo courtesy of Archive Photo/Express Newspapers)

terms. But Marceau's style is his own; it should not be considered the precedent for all mimes.

Marceau's style is characterized by highly refined and classical gestures. His fingers are wonderfully lithe, delicate, and deliberate. His facial expressions are broad and explicit. When he moves, the air around him vibrates and time appears to suspend itself. In this magical atmosphere, the audience appreciates the remarkable clarity of Marceau's gestures and the emotional subtleties of his sketches. His reputation is well-deserved. With his performance at the Phoenix Theatre, Marceau started a rage that has not stopped, even though that rage has often turned to ridicule and disdain as so many mediocre mimes have attempted to imitate him.

Mediocrity and derivative mime (Marceau imitations) have set an unfortunate precedent in the mime business today. When mimes attempt to imitate Marceau, they are missing the point of mime. Mime is not imitation; it is originality. It is not simply the mastery of certain exercises and illusions; it is the study of the mental, emotional, and spiritual *origins* of movement, itself.

Because I emphasize the importance of *self*-expression through mime, I have evolved an approach to teaching that departs from many other approaches. I use what I have learned from my teachers, Louise Gifford, Etienne Decroux, and Marcel Marceau, but I do not emphasize the use of silence. I have designed exercises that develop certain elusive skills such as attentiveness, spontaneity, timing, and empathy. These skills are essential to physical eloquence and honest-to-God self-expression.

Mime was originally the art of telling a story or creating a mood using the body, the voice, and "whatever else" to carry the point across to the audience. I would like to see mime restored to its original meaning. It is a great challenge to deliver a message *without* the use of words and props, and I believe all performers should learn how to do this. If you are a brilliant, silent mime, by all means continue in this noble tradition—but don't be afraid to broaden your horizons and find how many venues of self-expression are constantly open and available to you.

The study of mime is a lesson in economy. Very often in mime, there are no props, no special effects, no dialogue and yet, the audience never feels starved for information. This is because the mime understands just how much to do and how

Mime: The Art of Doing More with Less

much to leave undone; how much to show and how much to leave to the imagination.

This makes mime one of the most esoteric art forms. It delights the spirit in a novel way. Watching a good mime at work, you are not initially impressed with the mime's skill, but rather you are totally absorbed by your own mental images. You "see" objects. You follow events. You empathize with various characters. Yet there are no objects, no events, and no characters on stage; there is usually one person on stage using impeccable skill to activate and direct the imagination.

Every mime dreams of generating the most powerful emotional response using the bare minimum of effort. Often the mime designs an entire sketch around a simple gesture or phrase.

Marcel Marceau is famous for such moments. In his "Butterfly" sketch, he masterfully sets his audience up to believe his character ("Bip") has befriended an exquisite butterfly. (Of course, the "butterfly" is Marceau's hand.) Bip's adoration for his friend is contagious and the whole audience is devastated when the butterfly dies. Bip holds his hand out as if he is cradling the corpse of the butterfly. And then, almost imperceptibly, the butterfly begins to "breathe."

In fact, Marceau's *hand* is moving, bending and opening at the joint where the fingers meet the palm. But the audience doesn't notice Marceau's hand moving; they "see" the butterfly reviving. Everyone watches with bated breath as the feeble fluttering grows stronger and stronger until the butterfly is well again. This simple hand gesture has a tremendous impact on the audience.

Another of mime's brilliant moments occurred in a sketch by Gilles Ségal. Gilles was an inspiration to me. I met him when I went to Paris to study with Marceau. He was performing with Marceau's mime company at the time and, as a scholarship student, I was fortunate to be included in many of the company's drills and scene studies. Gilles intrigued me from the beginning. He was a loner, never talked much with anybody—but he was a tenacious mime. He worked all the time. Even in the restaurant after a full day of rehearsals, Gilles practiced bits of his sketches to see if a hand gesture or a facial expression "worked."

One of Gilles' ambitions was to bring an audience to tears with the simple movement of a thumb. He wanted to get the biggest reaction from the smallest gesture. This personal challenge was, I think, the starting point of his "Puppeteer" sketch.

At the end of this sketch, Gilles simply moved his right thumb up and down and the audience cried. This was how he did it:

Gilles played a puppeteer, and on his right hand he wore a crude little hand puppet. There was nothing special about the puppet. It had a head and two sleeves for Gilles' fingers.

As the sketch opens, we see the puppeteer performing and realize that he is a failure in front of the crowd. No one is interested in him, he doesn't make any money. The puppeteer is dejected, and he starts to drink. As he brings the glass to his lips, the puppet (Gilles' right hand) takes on a life of its own and tries to shove the glass away from his master's mouth. Each time the puppet master tries to drink with his left hand, his puppet—on his right hand—interrupts him.

This is already very beautiful minimal work. Gilles is showing a conflict between his right hand and his left hand, but the audience sees a puppet trying to keep his master from destroying himself.

At the end of the sketch, the puppeteer puts the glass down. He's dejected and distraut. He drops his head and begins to sob. At this point, the puppet slowly crosses over, hugs his master's left shoulder, and begins patting him softly.

The patting was simply the up-and-down motion of Gilles'

Gilles Ségal in the early 1960s, performing "The Puppeteer." (Courtesy of the authors)

thumb, but even the most sophisticated audiences melted when they saw this. I remember being in the audience when Marceau opened at the Phoenix Theatre in the late '50s. Gilles performed this solo sketch, and there was an audible sigh through the house when the puppet patted his master's shoulder.

This is the impact mime can have on an audience. When reality is stripped down to its bare essentials, very minimal gestures evoke profoundly moving images.

2 • • • • • • • • • •

WARMING UP

Technique is impressive. Artistry is interesting.
"Impressive" alone does not stand the test of time.
The next guy comes along and is taller than you, more accomplished, quicker, wealthier, busier. "Impressive" is based on relatives: more or less, better or worse, etc.

"Interesting" stands alone. When something is interesting, time stops, comparisons are irrelevant.

Technique and artistry evolve together as long as the primary motivating force behind one's effort is enthusiasm. Enthusiasm overrides the lesser motives that might hamper progress. (Incidentally, the word, *enthusiasm,* is derived from the Greek *[en,* in + *theos,* god]. *Enthusiasm* means "in God.")

Only the ego can interfere with enthusiasm. Emotions such as frustration, doubt, envy, anxiety, resentment, and blind ambition are offspring of the ego; even the most subtle hint of these emotions undermines progress and divides the artist against him- or herself. Technique may still improve under ego-stress, but artistry is absolutely blocked. The schism between technique and artistry begins here.

The finite ego is that which believes it is separate—separate from the other students in the class—separate from the teacher—separate from the audience—separate from one's subject matter. These separations are illusions. The finite ego also uses technique as a short-cut to greatness and neglects the issue of artistry altogether. In fact, technique and artistry are not separate issues; they are two sides of the same coin.

• • • • • • • • • • • • • • • • •

"Something there is that doesn't love a wall,
That wants it down...."
                    —from "Mending Wall," by Robert Frost

Over the past forty years, I have developed a style of teaching that stresses the importance of watching and training the mind. The body is used as a monitor to check whether one's thoughts are correct, but the external appearance of the body is *never* considered the ultimate authority in determining whether something is "good" or not. I teach this way because early in my career, I noticed that the body lies quite a bit. For example, I'd see mimes doing beautiful, impressive work with their bodies, but I couldn't *believe* their performances. Or I'd see mimes with remarkably *un*aesthetic bodies doing wonderful, convincing characters. These performances were so captivating that the physical "flaws" disappeared within seconds of their opening moves.

I found that I much preferred watching the unaesthetic body as long as I could *believe* the work and *identify* with what I was seeing. Instinctively, I decided that honesty and believability were the most important elements comprising the art of mime. But the raw elements of artistry are worthless if the mime lacks the technique to carry them across to an audience. Therefore, since my first day of teaching, my objective has always been to develop the elusive qualities of believability and honesty in my students and to treat technique as a vehicle rather than an end in itself. My exercises and my style of teaching have evolved from this main objective, and my students (a great many of whom now have successful performing careers) attest to the effectiveness of this approach to the art and technique of mime.

The Class: Sun Salutation

I begin all classes with the sun-salutation from Hatha Yoga. Although I give a few instructions as to the correct body positions, I stress the most important instruction: "Let the movement get to you."

The sun-salutation is ages old. No one knows exactly how old it is, but certainly it goes back to prehistory, when worship and ritual were born. When one stands in the opening pose (feet together, hands in a prayer position, head bowed) the mind wanders through history and lights on certain feelings. These feelings are unique to each individual. When I stand in this position, I feel devout, thankful, penitent—it all depends on the day and what I'm going through at the time.

From the opening pose, one rises slowly up on the toes with the arms extended heavenward, palms lifted, chest and eyes focused upward. (The rising up on the toes is my personal addition to the exercise.) This position suggests other feelings. These feelings are not the "right" ones or the "wrong" ones. Each individual is exploring his/her own mind and discovering private and personal information there. The sun-salutation performed in this way is a private and personal communication with our history—our ancestry.

Our ancestors are not necessarily sun-worshippers, rather, all of humanity is spawned by the same emotions. Our

All sequential photos by Marc Peloquin

The Salutation

"ancestors" are the beatific emotions that dictate our behavior. These emotions engender sun-worshippers, priests, astronauts, mountain climbers, mothers—all people at one time or another.

People have asked me if I believe in "past lives." No, I don't believe in *past* lives. Life is never past; it's always present. And I believe that every living person is a composite of every so-called *past* life. Mime is a physicalization of primordial memories.

The ideas of Michael Chekov have played a crucial role in shaping my approach to performing and teaching. In his book *To The Actor*, he discusses the "psychological gesture." I teach this in all my classes.

The "psychological gesture" maintains that every gesture or pose is psychologically based. In other words, every gesture or pose embodies a specific feeling, attitude, or memory—a specific mentality or temperament.

When the actor/mime is unsure of a character's temperament, it is often helpful to assume a body position that the character would take. Once in the position, the actor/mime *yields* to that position. I tell my students, "Let the movement get to you " or "Buy it."

Michael Chekov and the Psychological Gesture

29

The following story illustrates what I mean. In the early '70s, I was hired to teach mime to university students in Bridgewater, Connecticut. We came to the subject of the psychological gesture. I told them to assume a position similar to the second pose from the sun-salutation: arms outstretched, palms lifted, and gaze heavenward. I told the students to walk slowly around the room and "let the position get to you." One boy could not keep his palms facing upward! He would start out fine and then, as he began walking, the palms would slowly turn to face the floor. The class was amused but the boy was perplexed and frustrated. He simply could not "open up" to the gesture. I stopped the class for a few minutes, and we talked about the deeper implications of the psychological gesture.

Suddenly, the class was interrupted by a bellowing, angry intruder. This intruder turned out to be the boy's father. The man was livid. His son had neglected some duty or other, and the father was not going to postpone disciplinary action. He stormed his way onto the stage and yanked his son out of class. The father didn't introduce himself to me or appear to notice anyone else in the class; he bellowed incessantly at his son, who was mortified. The two disappeared through the front door, and the rest of the class stood still in shocked silence. We were horrified.

Two years later, I went back to the same university for another residency. When I walked into the class, I recognized the student from two years ago. We greeted each other and class started. When we came to the subject of the psychological gesture, the young man spoke up; "Mr. Montanaro, may I show you that exercise we did last time?" I recalled the whole ugly scene as if it were yesterday, but I agreed—reluctantly. With that, the young man assumed the salutation position (arms outstretched, gaze upward) and began to circle the room. Slowly a transformation took place. I saw that he was "buying it." His steps became firm and decisive. His chest swelled and his gaze seemed to penetrate infinity. Needless to say, his palms maintained their solidly upright position. I couldn't help wondering what that father and son must have gone through in the intervening years.

3

PREMISE WORK

Tony wearing a Harlequin mask on his head, 1988. (Photo by Walter Nelson)

Crosses

After the sun-salutation, the class moves ahead to what I call *crosses*. This exercise is so-named because each movement travels across the floor. I designed this exercise to introduce students to the concept of *premise*. After the student has traveled across the floor a few times, the concept of premise dawns as a practical tool for understanding and perfecting mime technique.

Premise and Priming

I often define premise as *the invisible "cause" governing the visible "effects."*

Premise is also an instruction or a mission that remains consistent and unbroken during the various states and stages of your work. For example, a missionary's premise is philanthropy. The love of humanity must prime all of the mission-

Crosses, Premise, Priming, Blending

ary's activities, whether he/she is cleaning a latrine, opposing legislation, or nursing a child. When the missionary's attention strays from the cause of his or her efforts, those efforts become pointless, nonsensical, vain. The person who acts without knowing why is vulnerable to the despotism of ignoble motives.

In art, the same principle applies. When a performer loses touch with the premise, the performance succumbs to cross-purposes and confusion. Losing touch with the premise also means losing touch with the audience. The audience, however, is always in touch with the performer; they are keen to the logic and causality behind the performer's behavior, and they willingly suspend disbelief—until the performer lets them down.

The audience will be with you as long as your actions and gestures are justified. This means that everything you do on stage must be motivated. All effects must have a cause.

Blending

In crosses, we start with one or two simple premises and progress toward more complex missions. Eventually, the student can work with many premises. When one's behavior originates from a complex personality (Hamlet for example), one must work from several premises simultaneously. I call this *blending*.

Blending is the process of working with several premises simultaneously. Suppose, for example, you just received news that you won the lottery. You invite all your friends over to celebrate and all of you are reveling in big dreams, when suddenly the neighbor bursts into the house to tell you that your dog has just been hit by a car. In life, these two polarities (joy and sorrow) would combine to form one state of psychological turmoil. Likewise, if you were to act this out on stage, you wouldn't be purely joyful for a few seconds and then purely sorrowful for another few seconds. Even if one emotion gained top priority in your attention, the other emotion would always be there, tempering the effects of the dominant emotion. In other words, two unlikely bedfellows, joy and sorrow, would *blend* to form a singular psychological state.

To play Hamlet or any character convincingly, you would have to understand, and be able to reenact the blending process that takes place naturally in life. Premise work leads to this understanding and mastery.

Motivation is an advanced concept in most mime classes. But I teach crosses before I teach anything else. This exercise

calisthenics, but it introduces
motivation to students more
rcise or lecture I know.

imply. The first cross, the "dead-
ises:
elaxed)
floor without veering off at an

oll lying flat on the floor, arms
your attention must remain fixed
(or premises). The premise
ention.
a two premises, you are already
ocess. When this exercise is done
you don't have to divide your
ses. You don't have to concentrate
onds and then break your con-
th premises *blend* in your attention to of mind. This, in turn, produces
one effect—a ly roll across the floor. Therefore,
even when we are working with two or more premises, I often
refer to premise in the singular.

The distinguishing feature of the dead body is that it has no
mind of its own. If this body is to be rolled, it must be pushed
from the outside. Therefore the first premise means that the
cause of your movement is *outside* of your physical body. As
you move, you must remain constantly aware of that first
premise (i.e., that force coming at you from the outside) and
constantly aware of your second premise (i.e., the direction of
your roll).

Students unfamiliar with this work may require a few
moments of repose in order to prime themselves. Also, the
premise becomes easier to assimilate as the cross progresses.
With each roll, your clarity is sharpened as the premise
absorbs more and more of your attention. The mind turns gently toward the premise and away from external distractions
such as self-consciousness and physical sensations.

The Crescent Roll
The two premises in this roll are:
1) Crescent shape
2) Roll straight across the floor without veering off at an
angle.

The Crescent Roll

In the crescent roll the body assumes the shape of a crescent. In the starting position the body is curved in the shape of a half-circle. As you roll, the mid-section of the body "leads" while the limbs or extremities drag behind.

Your physical sensations will tell you that you are going through myriad contortions. They're lying. In fact the body is maintaining one shape. If you were to view yourself from above, you would see only a crescent shape maintaining itself as it glides across the floor. (In fact, it may help you perform this exercise correctly if you see yourself from the outside—envision how you look from above.)

Also, the temptation to be confused, lost, dizzy, awkward, and frustrated may plague you in the beginning of this exercise. But don't give in to this temptation (these are only old personal premises trying to hang on to you!). Hold the idea of crescent in mind. Rise above all other thoughts and sensations. Be comfortable and serene in this idea, and move (slowly at first) until you are aware only of the idea.

The Reverse Crescent

Here, the extremities (arms and legs) *precede* the mid-section. The mid-section lags behind the limbs. But the premise is the same as for the first crescent:

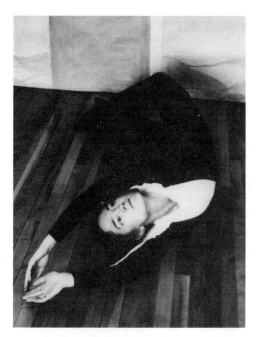

1) Crescent shape

2) Roll straight without veering right or left.

When you master the technique of premise there is literally no limit to your progress. Premise puts the horse back in front of the cart; the mind ahead of the body. The body is no longer an obstacle to expression. Rather, the body reflects the mind (the premise) as naturally as a mirror reflects the object in front of it.

Premise has a way of elevating the attention above the body—above physical sensations, commentary, and self-consciousness. During these exercises you experience a shift of attention from the external, visible world of effects to the internal, invisible world of cause. This ultimately (and paradoxically) makes your work more "external"—more accessible, more believable, more convincing to your audience.

Premise

Since premise work is one of the cornerstones of my method of teaching, I don't want to go on describing crosses until I have defined premise to my (and your) satisfaction.

As I wrote earlier, the premise is the invisible cause governing the visible effects. Synonyms for premise are: model, objective, desire, reason, belief, assumption, mission, etc.

Premise is also the mental cause—the impetus—that produces the physical effects.

Many beginning mime students are either shy, stiff, or self-conscious. They're not interested in hearing about invisible causes and visible effects. This is not a practical way to start a mime class, anyway. The mime student (particularly the young mime student) wants to *do* something. And this is how the class should begin. The student must feel, recognize, and *experience* a premise (an invisible cause) before a theoretical discussion makes sense.

Therefore I begin all classes with crosses. We start with simple, physical objectives. Among the first crosses we practice are the dead-body roll and the crescent rolls. Even a very shy person feels safe in these exercises because you can *see* these objectives. We're not ready to tackle invisible objectives yet.

Take, for example, the crescent roll. Even though the cause and effect are both "crescent," the person performing the cross becomes (privately) aware of a critical difference between crescent-as-cause and crescent-as-effect. Once the person is aware of the difference, he or she is also aware of the *relation-*

ship between the two. This is one of the most important moments for the student. He or she can actually feel how the idea of crescent creates and controls the physical crescent. The student notices that the clear idea of crescent guides him or her through all the confusing signals coming from the body. This is the power of the premise: The *premise* produces its own conclusions naturally as long as it holds the center of your attention.

From this moment on, the student understands me when I say, "You cannot get rid of confusion by addressing the confusion; you must rise above confusion by becoming more attentive to your premise."

"Assume a virtue if you have it not."
—From *Hamlet* by William Shakespeare

• • •

Once you have experienced the difference between crescent-as-cause and crescent-as-effect (and you can't experience this simply by reading this book!), the next step is to become more attentive to cause and less attentive to effect. A remarkable thing happens when your attention is fixed on premise: your mind doesn't contract, it *expands!* You become acutely aware of effects but they do not distract you.

Effects are always late; they *follow* the cause. Conclusions come after the premise. Therefore if you are primarily concerned with effects, you'll be late. You'll feel as if you are constantly struggling to "catch up" to something. On the other hand, when your attention is centered on the premise, you are in the present. You are acutely aware of the effects because you are ahead of them. Your premise anticipates and directs its own conclusions or effects.

I have noticed the time lapse between cause (premise) and effect watching dancers. Many of them are just a tad behind the music. This is because they are dancing to what they *hear.* Their attention is therefore centered on effects. From this vantage point, they cannot dance *with* the music, they have to *follow* it. If, however, they were to attend to their *present* feelings, they would find the invisible cause of the music. The music has *already* informed their present feelings. Now the dancer needs honesty and vulnerability more than he/she needs a good pair of ears. When the dancer moves honestly and impulsively from *present* feelings, both the composer and the dancer meet in the same moment—the moment of inspiration. From here the appropriate effects happen naturally and effortlessly. The notes and the steps follow in the wake of undaunted self-expression. (Remember: The premise—not the body—produces effects.)

• • •

Another word for premise is "lodestar." The premise is a lodestar for your attention. While the mind is focused on the premise, it cannot be distracted by physical sensations or self-defeating thoughts. You will notice only those things which *serve* the premise.

The object of the crescent roll is not, exclusively, to maintain a crescent shape. Once the body maintains the shape, the work is just beginning. The object is to distinguish between two experiences—the mental and the physical—and to understand how these two experiences *relate* to each other.

The more attentive you are to the premise (the *idea* of crescent), the better your physical crescent will be. As your attention shifts from effects to cause, your effects *improve*. The body relaxes and follows your premise with perfect ease and fluidity. This is the beginning of physical eloquence.

What Premise Work is NOT

Premise work is not synonymous with visualization. It goes beyond it. Visualization often becomes an intellectual exercise in which the person remains detached from the process. Here the person holds an image in mind and thereby hopes to superimpose that image on an already existing condition. For example, many people practice visualization in order to lose weight. They picture a thin person replacing the fat person they see in the mirror. But this is as far as they go. This type of visualization concerns itself totally with effects and physical appearances. The cause of those effects is neglected.

Premise work, on the other hand, is primarily concerned with cause. If the overweight person were to practice premise work instead of visualization, he/she would have to *yield* to the *cause* of thinness. Rather than super-impose a thin body on a heavy body, premise alters the condition that *caused* fatness. The body does not shrink for no reason. The person loses weight because he or she has *become the person for whom thinness is natural.*

This is the primary difference between premise work and visualization: Visualization often does not include the person. It concerns itself with physical appearances and physical desires and thereby remains superficial, intellectual. Premise work involves the whole person. It is a visceral experience in which the person yields to an ideal and submits to the process of *becoming.*

Therefore, even in the crescent roll you may visualize the crescent, but the aim is not so much to form a perfect crescent; the aim is to *become* the person for whom the crescent roll is natural. As a matter of fact, anticipating the physical appearance of your premise often interferes with the success of premise work.

There are many self-help, self-improvement techniques in practice today that resemble premise work, but one of the major differences between premise work and the other types of work is that premise relieves the person of an exaggerated sense of responsibility.

Premise—not person—determines the success or failure of an endeavor. If you fail constantly, it's not your fault; it is the fault of the *premises* dictating your behavior. Likewise, if you succeed constantly, you know that this is proof of the fact that good premises work and bad premises don't.

Premise work is the assumption that the work is already done. ("Assume a virtue if you have it not.") And the more earnestly you believe this, the less you have to strain. The only effort (and this is a formidable task sometimes) is *yielding* to the premise—honestly believing that the premise does the work and that this work involves every part of yourself.

•   •   •   •   •   •   •   •   •   •   •   •   •   •   •   •   •   •

Premise doesn't say: "I will do this." Premise says: "This is done." Not: "I will be" but: "I am." Premise is a foregone conclusion.

Premise work is not physical labor; it is an exercise for the mind and develops mental acuity. For instance, I often see students sweating and straining to climb an illusionary ladder. They are concentrating so intensely on what the body is doing that their movements look awkward and unnatural. They need to be less concerned with the effects and more concerned with cause—less concerned with the hands, for example, and more concerned with the rungs. The rungs are the *cause* of the hand positions.

•   •   •

Premise work is also different from "positive thinking." Positive thinking is often directed outward. In other words, the person who engages in positive thinking hopes that the external world will change to suit his/her specifications. Positive thinking is exterior decorating. Premise work is interior structuring. One's desires and tastes and personality may shift as the ideal (the premise) assumes one's entire attention.

39

The pursuit of an ideal is self-correcting.
—Greek Thought

I feel quite strongly that all people should study mime, not necessarily to become stage performers, but to learn about themselves and the laws governing their behavior.

Crosses are simple movement exercises that teach advanced, psychotherapeutic concepts. For example, in the crescent roll, the constant idea of crescent governs the various contortions of the body. Likewise, in life, our constant sense of who-we-are governs our myriad reactions to circumstance.

Mime may have some advantages over psychotherapy, too. In life, stress and tension are produced by emotional turmoil, complicated personal affairs, etc. Talking about the problem is certainly a good idea, but often it's impossible to determine whether the problem produced the tension or the tension produced the problem.

Excess physical tension indicates a lack of flexibility in the "premise area." The person is not sublimely comfortable with the *cause* of his/her actions and behavior. Movement exercises that begin from premise help to reinstate the person's natural flexibility in this area. And this basic flexibility is a strong defense against psychological (and physical) tension.

Premise vs. Preconception

You do not know how your premise will manifest itself outwardly.

At the right is an example of premise-at-work. This player had no idea what his body was doing. His body was serving his premise with perfect agility and speed. His premise was, *catch the ball*. When the player saw his picture in the paper the next day, I'm sure he was surprised: "Did I do that?!!"

Premise at Work

Whether you're on stage or not, premise is always at work governing your thoughts and actions. Your personal premises are your reasons for doing the things you do. In life, as on stage, premise produces its own conclusions. In other words, your personal premise determines how well or how badly you hold up under pressure.

My strength as a teacher and performer comes from the fact that I love to solve problems. Nothing (no fear, doubt, or indifference) gets between me and a problem. And this is what I want to pass onto my students: fearlessness in the face of difficulty and an insatiable curiosity for what makes something *work*. My love of problem-solving and my desire to share this

penchant with my students is my premise when I teach. This premise conducts the class and embraces both the students and me as it operates. It has also seen me through some pretty hair-raising experiences.

Dave Hollins of the Philadelphia Phillies. (©1994 *USA Today*, reprinted by permission)

About thirty years ago (late '60s), I was hired to teach mime in upstate New York. My students were seriously delinquent teenagers from Harlem. I think many of them had spent time in detention centers. They were hostile and under a tremendous amount of stress.

The man who hired me (I knew him as Mr. Reed) was an angel—a true-blue humanitarian. He regularly brought teenagers out of Harlem for a weekend and gave them opportunities they wouldn't normally have in the slums. On this particular occasion, Mr. Reed hired me to teach two full days of workshops and to socialize (or whatever) with the "students" when the classes weren't in session. Mr. Reed knew that I had a spontaneous, improvisational approach to teaching, and he believed that I could handle this (tricky!) situation.

On the first day of class, I went in there as nervous as a cat and began teaching. I began by asking them to do the sun-salutation. They didn't move. I tried another exercise. They didn't move. It was clear to me that I would have to abandon my typical class structure to meet the specific needs of this class. The students were looking at me with tremendous defiance. They weren't going to do anything a white man told them to do—not willingly, anyway.

Mr. Reed was watching the class, making sure nobody hurt me, I guess. I was embarrassed. There I was: a short, white man in front of black, angry teenagers. I was wearing spandex pants and jazz shoes and hoping to teach *mime*, of all things.

I realized I had to do something rather desperate to make it all work. Suddenly, the word "freedom" came to me. Black people in this country have lived in captivity and under duress for centuries. They are naturally obsessed with the idea of freedom—freedom from slavery, freedom from oppression, freedom from the white majority....

I understand mime to be a freeing experience. In the theatre arts—in all the arts, actually—personal history and circumstances are tools rather than obstacles to self-expression. I looked at these people and realized that they were being stifled and manipulated by their own anger. They were, in fact, slaves in the worst way. It didn't matter what color they were at this point. They were just like the many students I meet who are bound by their own habits, shyness, peer pressure, etc.

This was the worst example of peer pressure I had ever encountered. The pressure was tremendous. No one was going to be the first to move—for a *white* man especially and a *tiny* one. (I was small—they all towered over me. One guy was over six feet tall!)

I settled down and said, "Look—I've come here to teach something kind of exciting. But, by looking at you people, I don't think you're free enough to understand this. You look like slaves to me. You talk about freedom all the time. But, I'm disappointed—you're not *free* enough to take this class."

That got a rise out of them. "Whadda-yu mean!?" "Whadda-yu talkin' about slaves!" "I can do anything I wanna do!"

I said, "No, I don't think you can do anything you wanna do. You're trapped. You're locked into something. Look at you! You're not even moving."

"We're not gonna do what you tell us to do." They looked big and tough.

"It's not a question of what I want you to do—it's that you're not free enough to try something! I'll bet you anything you can't do what you really want to do." That was my tack: "I'll bet that you're not free enough to do whatever you really want to do."

I walked over to the six-foot guy, "You're free, right? You can do whatever you want to do?"

"Damn right! I do what I want."

I felt OK now. I knew that while he said, "I do what I want," he *meant:* "No one tells me what to do."

I spoke to this belligerence—challenged him. "Could you hold a pose of a boxer, say, and freeze, like a stone statue while I try to make you move? Without hurting you or forcing you, I bet I'll make you move."

He said, "You can't make me move."

"I bet I will. I'll make you move." The class was really interested now. Everyone was watching us. Mr. Reed was leaning forward. They all came forward. The guy took the pose.

"Now I'm not going to hurt you. I'm not going to inflict physical pain on you or force you to do anything, but I bet I'll make you move."

Silently I asked myself, 'What can I do to make this guy move?' I tried a few jokes. I waved my hands in front of his face. I asked him, "Do you always have a sausage hanging out of your nose?" etc. The guy didn't move. He was tough. Then I "took the bull by the horns." I looked at Mr. Reed one last time and turned back to the guy. Then I rose up on tip-toe and kissed him lightly on the cheek.

The guy exploded. "Whadju do!! You...you *faggot!!!*" His fists were clenched and his mouth was spewing forth some pretty vile obscenities. I stepped back a little but the rest of the class was tickled. In one uproar, they pointed at the guy, "YOU MOVED! The man was right—you DID move!" It was a joke for them now.

The guy was about to hit me, and I said, "Look—please—don't get excited. I said I could make you move and you did. Now, in this class you can learn how to do whatever you want, *for real.* It's a form of freedom."

Then the class challenged me. "Can you do that?! Can you hold a pose and not move no matter what *we* do?"

I answered, "Yes, I can. Now you can do whatever you want with me. You can even pick me up and carry me. Just don't hurt me or *force* me out of the pose."

I took the pose and the class went to work. This one, beautiful girl began cooing, "Hey, you're cute—big ol' Italian nose—I like you." She kissed my face and leaned into me. The rest of the class laughed and waved their hands in front of my eyes. They tried to scare me and make me laugh. But I didn't move. They picked me up like a statue and walked around the room with me. Then I heard somebody ask, "When's he gonna come out of it?"

They put me down and said, "OK you can drop it now. Come on!" But I didn't move. They were laughing, "Hey, you won the bet. Now come out of it." I stood there motionless for at least thirty seconds. Suddenly I moved and made them all jump.

"Now, that to me," I said, "is a form of free-will. You can learn this. Now, we'll do a giraffe and some rolls on the floor. But whatever you do, you do it because *you* want to—not because I'm telling you to do it. You understand? It's not my will against yours. You decide to do it the way *you* want to do it." That broke the ice. Mr. Reed smiled and walked out of the room.

We had a wonderful time after that. They couldn't wait for class to begin and we worked the full three hours.

A few months later, I received a letter at my house in New York City. In broken handwriting, the person introduced herself as a student from that class. She wrote that she had been in a situation recently in which she could have physically hurt someone very badly. But, she continued, "I didn't do it because of what I learned in your class. Thank you."

The Class: Abstract Premises

Back to the crosses.

For the dead-body roll and the crescent rolls, the premises are obvious physical shapes and objectives. After this, the premises become increasingly abstract. In the next crosses, the premises are qualities of movement rather than shapes and "things."

The Ooze

In this cross, the premise is OOZE and the movement is a backward shoulder roll.

You begin the ooze sitting on the floor with your back facing the direction you will travel. Let your whole body go limp as you focus your attention on the premise: ooze. Your movement must have the viscosity of oil, flowing in one steady, slow tempo without jerks or interruptions.

The mechanics of the backward shoulder roll are: Gently roll onto your back. Keep your arms relaxed and close to the sides of your body as your knees fold up to your chest and over your right or left shoulder. Use your arms or whatever you need to assist the backward roll and preserve the integrity (i.e., the ooze-quality) of your movement. The hips follow the knees, lifting up and over your head until the knees are on the floor above your shoulder.

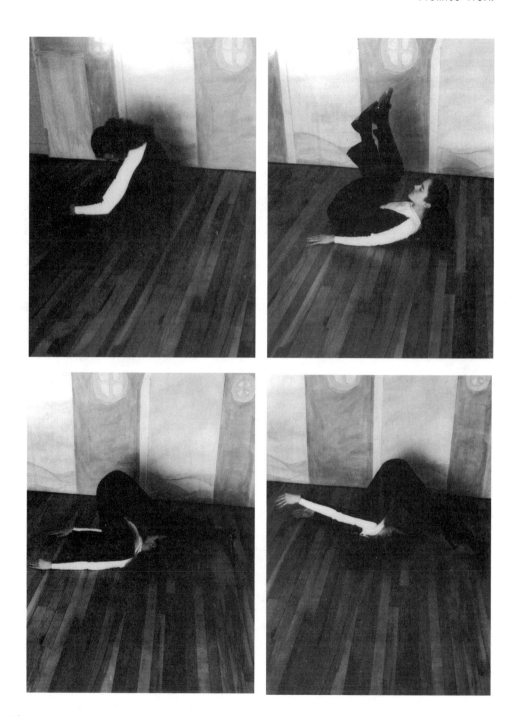

The Ooze

Transfer the weight of the body onto the knees and let your legs straighten out behind you as you lower your hips, stomach, and chest to the floor.

Your body spreads out into one big oil spill. Slowly gather your limbs together and begin the next ooze. This time the knees go over the other shoulder. All of this should happen in one steady, slow tempo according to your premise.

As I mentioned earlier, working from premise you soon realize that it doesn't much matter whether you are working from one premise or a thousand premises. All premises are embraced by one mind. As you are able to yield to more and more abstract premises, you will also be able to assimilate more and more instructions into one movement—one moment. In the case of the ooze, you must be sure to roll in a straight path across the floor. Even though your knees go over the right or the left shoulder, your premise (to travel in a straight path across the floor) will keep your hips from toppling over to the right or left and will prevent you from taking a wayward course.

The person performing this for the first time often looks and feels awkward and perplexed. This is a sign that an invading thought is usurping his or her attention—taking the mind away from the premise. When a student forgets or *leaves* the premise in order to indulge in distracting thoughts (i.e., "I feel awkward." "This is terrible." "No, that's not right." "Everyone's gonna laugh at me," etc.), this creates what I call the stuttering effect. The integrity of the movement is lost as soon as the premise is abandoned.

Correcting your body (your conclusions) is a very different thing from *judging* the body. It is important to correct your conclusions as you go along, but you should never lose touch with your premise as you do this. If you forget your premise in the process of correcting your conclusions, that means your corrections may be corrupted by other premises such as the need to impress or the fear of criticism, etc.

Remember, this is premise work—not calisthenics. Brute strength and willpower sometimes cause injuries and always produce lifeless mechanical movements. Never rely on brute strength and willpower; always rely on premise to produce the desired effects.

In the beginning, your movement may be choppy. You may bump and "skip a frame" every once in a while but even as you struggle, the premise is working to smooth out those rough, unconscious edges. When a choppy movement threatens to unnerve you, resist self-consciousness by focusing even more intensely on the premise.

· · ·

Other Crosses

Make up your own crosses. Whether the crosses are simple or complex, the premise will see you through every level of difficulty. The premise demands your whole attention. You should not squander your attention on frustration, discouragement, or physical strain. Remember: frustration, discouragement, and physical strain represent old, unconscious premises interfering with (rather than promoting) progress.

Forward Roll
Premise: Smooth, unbroken movement.

Mechanics of the movement: From a standing position, allow your knees to bend easily as you rest your hands on the floor. Lower the head between the hands and curl the chin to the chest. Now be careful: you must lower the nape of your neck to the floor without any bumps. In the beginning, you might want to use a mat to soften the blow of the initial "bumps." (A mat is not absolutely necessary, and you shouldn't depend on it longer than you have to.) Once the nape of the

The Forward Roll

neck is safely on the floor, continue the roll maintaining a fluid, slow and even tempo. Carry that tempo into the second, third, and fourth rolls until you are across the floor.

Shoulder Roll
Premise: Same as above.

Mechanics of the movement: This is an advanced cross. Basically, the movement is the same as the Forward Roll except here, you initiate the roll by scooping your right (or left) arm under you as you lower yourself to the floor. The first body part to touch the floor is your right (or left) shoulder. Then you continue to roll out from that shoulder. When a cross is complex like this, you will really appreciate your premise. Turn your attention away from fear and tension by focusing on the premise.

• • • • • • • • • • • • • • • • •

Note: Following the premise also destroys the tendency to rush. Rushing is a symptom of self-consciousness. It indicates the habitual desire to "keep up with the Joneses." You will forget the Joneses when you remember your premise.

Monkey Walk

Premise: The attitude of a monkey. You must move from the monkey's nature—not necessarily the *effects* of its nature. You don't want to perform a stereotypical monkey with all the armpit scratching and the other clichéd gestures. You want to get inside the monkey's skin. Let the monkey "get to you" and move from the monkey's point of view. (The study of an animal's nature is discussed in the subchapter entitled "Empathy is the Ability to 'See' Life." See pages 107-110)

Mechanics of the movement: The monkey has a firm and solid center of gravity. Its legs are bent and bowed. Its feet are turned-in. These effects will come naturally, once you find and focus on the monkey's attitude—the monkey's point of view—and the *reasons* the monkey moves the way it does.

Monkey Cartwheel

Premise: Same as above.
Mechanics: Same as a regular cartwheel but in the attitude of a monkey.

Monkey Slide-Glide

Monkey "Slide-Glide"
Premise: Same as above: the attitude of a monkey.
Mechanics: Squat close to the floor and prepare to move sideways. If you are moving left across the floor, your right hand will touch first followed by the left hand, then the right foot, followed by the left foot. Then the right hand begins the same sequence again.

Horse

Premise: Horse-like. The feelings, attitudes, and dynamics of a horse take over your body until you feel and move more like a horse than a person.

Mechanics: Here again, you are not doing a photo-representation of a horse. Rather, you are feeling more and more *horse-like* as you cross the floor. As you "give in" to the premise, you will notice the back of your neck elongate, your shoulders and legs tighten with galvanic strength and agility, etc. These qualities should *happen to you* as you cross the floor; they should not be applied or contrived. Simply empathize with the horse—find the horse within yourself. Let your own equestrian dynamics color your feelings, mood, and manners.

For this exercise you may break with the typical format of the cross. You may want to move together (i.e., the whole class at once) through the room. This way each individual has more time and space to "accumulate" the horse's characteristics. You should feel that you are "collecting the horse" as you move. The horse and its surroundings should become more clear in your mind's eye with every move. Your horse takes on specific characteristics as you move. It evolves into a wild horse, a race horse, a circus pony, a plow horse, etc. Your environment begins "filling in" around you. You may see the racetrack, other horses, or a wide, open field. This is what I mean by *collecting*: You *collect* more and more of your character and scenario as you go along.

(Use this cross for any animal.)

Elephantine

Elephantine

Premise: Slow, heavy, lumbering walk (elephant qualities).

Mechanics: You begin with your hands and feet on the floor, knees and elbows straight and weight evenly distributed between the hands and feet. The body is in an upside down "V" shape. Begin lumbering across the floor keeping the knees straight at all times

Finesse: Immediately after the right foot has stepped toward the right hand, the hand "peels" off the floor and "steps" forward. Repeat this with the left hand and foot. This creates a graceful, smooth chain reaction between the feet and the hands.

Horse and Rider
Premise: The lower body represents a horse while the upper body represents the rider.

Mechanics: The mechanics of this cross are fairly straightforward. Children playing Cowboys and Indians perform this cross quite naturally, without thinking. The legs gallop, canter, trot, or walk in an equestrian manner as the upper body maintains the human characteristics of the rider. The upper body holds the reins and *thinks for* the lower body. Sometimes, the lower body will appear to have a mind of its own, as when the rider pulls back on the reins to slow his horse down. Here, the upper body leans back, pulls against, and resists the forward motion of the lower body.

"OOOOOOO"
Premise: The attitude of a flirtatious but slightly prudish person who has been pinched from behind.

Mechanics: Three steps followed by a little hop (the "OOOOOO!") indicating that the pinch has happened. As you hop, each knee should cross swiftly (one-at-a-time) in front of your body. You are delighted but you feign consternation. Repeat: three steps and an "OOOOOO!" across the floor.

Storybook Dragon
Premise: Ferocious but not too ferocious. You are a fire-spitting dragon, but you are not so terrifying as to frighten children. You want to delight and entertain children, not scare them.

Mechanics: These are up to you. Do whatever you want to do.

"I'm Going To Be Happy Even if it Kills Me"
Premise: "My life is falling apart. I'm the most unfortunate person who ever lived, but I will be strong. I will fight this urge to sob inconsolably. I'll show the world how brave and happy I can be. Yes, I will *SMILE!*"

Mechanics: Without speaking, walk across the floor as if you are thinking the above thoughts. The audience should see the urge-to-cry stifled by the I'm-a-martyr attitude.

"I'm Miserable...."
Premise: "I'm miserable and I'm going to *act* miserable."
Mechanics: Again, without speaking, walk across the floor as if you are thinking the above thoughts.

"OOOO"

• • •

These are just a few of the crosses I use regularly in class. I also watch the students closely to see which type of movement or attitude is missing from their "ready vocabulary." I then design a cross on the spur of the moment to access this attitude.

Sometimes, we'll do crosses in the style of Groucho Marx or Chaplin or a clown. We often do graceful crosses working on the attitude of floating, perching, or balancing.

Through crosses, you touch a variety of dynamics that occur naturally in life. This gradually expands your choreographic vocabulary as it increases your range of movement.

Premise and Real Life

Premise work is a way of becoming conscious of a natural process that before was unconscious.

Premise work makes you aware of the natural cause-and-effect law governing your life. In life, desire always precedes the fulfilling of a desire. A motive (unconscious?) always precedes an act. A premise always precedes a conclusion. A cause always precedes an effect.

If you want to see premise-in-action, watch a baby learning to walk or trying to get something. The baby's body is entirely relaxed, and the only *force* operating on that body is the premise (i.e., the baby's *intent* to walk, get something, eat). You see the principle of premise operating in babies to bring about coordination and strength.

In adult life too, premise dictates our actions and movements. When we want a glass of water, say, we open the cupboard, take a glass, turn on the water, fill the glass, and drink with absolute ease. We don't think about our actions; we're concerned only with the cause of those actions (our thirst).

In life, there is no separation between premise and behavior—intent and action. This is the law which makes the psychological gesture an invaluable tool for the actor/mime (see page 29). *Behaving* like Hamlet can and will generate Hamlet's *character* (his personal premises) if you let that behavior "get to you."

The only difference between life and stage is that in life, the average person is *unaware* of the premise and unaware of the process whereby the premise controls his/her thoughts, words, and actions. The artist, however, is aware of the premise. The artist knows how to control thoughts, words, and gestures and how to make all of them *believable*. Further, the artist knows how to *conceal* his/her knowledge—how to make the skill of acting look like the spontaneity of living. This is possible only through an awareness of premise and a visceral sense of the connection between cause and effect.

The more skilled you become as a technician/artist, the more control you have over the premises governing your behavior (on stage and off) and the more premises you are able to assimilate at one time. The mime is able to maintain a character, perform an accurate, clean illusion, "read" the audience, and adjust his or her timing accordingly. The ballet dancer is able to stretch feet, turn-out from the hips, pirouette, dance to the music, and stay in character. Such control doesn't require super-human strength or talent. It is more a mastery of mind than of body, and an understanding of premise work can supersede years of back-breaking physical labor and a legacy of "good genes."

All class exercises should be designed and assigned in response to the students' need. When exercises are used as occupational therapy (i.e., to fill time and keep the class busy), the teacher has fallen asleep. Some students will rebel against occupational therapy either by becoming disruptive or by refusing to participate emotionally in the exercises. The polite students will simply go through the motions, matching their teacher's rote performance of duty.

Designing Exercises: An Education for the Teacher

A class should be a dynamic event, shifting to the special needs of the students without compromising the art form or subject matter.

Designing and teaching exercises in response to the class' need is always a challenge for the teacher. Sometimes the teacher wakes up to the inherent wisdom of the exercise only after the exercise has been designed and performed for a while.

For example, I designed the exercise called "crosses" to introduce my students to the concept of premise. The *need* for this exercise occurred to me when I found myself in front of the class trying to explain a point. The word "premise" kept coming up in my explanation. I was thoroughly satisfied with the word and the explanation, but the students still didn't seem to understand what I was talking about. They didn't "get it."

I had a problem. But the awareness of a problem precedes the solution to the problem. Soon, I was having the students roll across the floor with a simple premise: the dead-body roll. Gradually the premises became more complex and the word "blending" came up. Our vocabulary was expanding, becoming more to-the-point. The class was a learning experience for me as well as for the students.

Months later, I noticed that this exercise had solved another problem. All of my students up to this point were looking like me! This was a major concern, but I didn't know what to do about it. Then I saw that premise work had solved this problem as well. The students had stopped using *me* as their model. Now, the *premise* was their model; they were following their own minds.

While the students were following a premise, they were also letting go of the physical and emotional tension that interferes with self-expression. I awoke to this added fringe benefit of premise work only after the exercise had been designed.

The learning process didn't stop there. Thinking about these exercises and seeing their results, I eventually understood the pitfall of teaching and learning by rote.

Crosses as Prevention Against Learning by Rote

Teaching technique is, typically, the act of telling students what to do; *learning* technique is, typically, the act of following directions. Blindly following rules and regulations, the student acquires the ability to manipulate the exterior form and lock certain standards into the corpus. Students of this "school," often feel like prisoners of their own standards.

Correcting this potentially dangerous situation is not difficult. First, the teacher should be intensely aware of *why* he/she is telling the students to do certain things. If the motives are not noble, the teacher should re-think his/her approach. Also, the teacher should be on the lookout for students who are blindly following directions. Remind them to go back to their premise—the origin or *cause* of their actions. Encourage them to adopt better and better *reasons* for what they're doing.

Technique must be understood and perfected *consciously* before it becomes a tool of artistry. When technique is perfected out of a sense of obligation, it is empty, cold, and unforgiving. As soon as one appreciates the cause for the technique (the *reason* for it), one is no longer imprisoned by technique, no longer manipulated.

Crosses and premise work do not allow you to manipulate the corpus the way technical drills and calisthenics often do. Most drills and physical exercises are the process of adding new tensions to pre-existing tensions. However, when you cross the floor holding onto a premise, this new idea assumes your full attention. This attention supplants tension and replaces it with mobility.

• • • • • • • • • • • • • • • • •

Interestingly, the word "attention" sounds like a-tension. The letter "a" as a prefix means *without, not,* or the opposite of *to.*

Sometimes I tell students that your premise is your *home—* your comfort zone. Working strictly on technique can often feel like leaving home. You may feel uncomfortable, frustrated, and *foreign* in the strict technique class. This is because technique, by itself, is concerned with only the outward appearances of things. Premise work takes you back to *cause;* back to the voluntary and sometimes involuntary intentions that determine the expression of yourself.

The Future of Premise Work

I think everyone who has learned a skill has experienced the phenomenon of trying to catch up. It doesn't matter what this skill is, the student feels disoriented and rushed, trying to remember a thousand things at once. At such times, the demands of the moment seem to be way ahead of the student's recall and coordination. Feelings of frustration and inadequacy indicate that the student's mind has been neglected, left behind in the mad rush for physical, tangible results.

I know that the educational system will one day catch onto the value of premise work. When students' attention is constantly turned away from effects and back to cause, they discover better and better *reasons* for doing what they're doing. They discover the inspiration to try new things and the courage to become mavericks.

This will *not* result in chaos—every man and woman for him- or herself. Once we stop straining and racing to achieve certain results, and once we attend the mind that produces those results, we will find ourselves riding the currents of inspiration. This will undoubtedly reveal a deeper, more significant, and vital relationship between the individual and the rest of humanity.

4

ISOLATION
EXERCISES AND
ILLUSIONS

The Class:
Isolation
Exercises

Learning mime illusions starts with the mastery of simple isolation exercises. I begin with the head isolation. If possible, watch yourself in the mirror to make sure your isolations are clean and accurate.

Now that you are familiar with premise work, get in the habit of discerning a premise before each exercise. In all of the isolation exercises, your premise is an instruction, a mission or an objective. The premise for the head isolation is: *Your head stays still relative to space.*

Head Isolation 1: Look at your face in the mirror and isolate your head as you rotate the body (from the neck down) to the right and left.

Hint: the head will move relative to the *body* but not relative to *space*.

Head Isolation 2: Your head remains stationary while your body moves forward and backward.

Head Isolation 1

Head Isolation 2

Head Isolation 3: Your head remains stationary while your body moves from side to side. The front of the body faces the mirror while the whole body "sidles" from left to right of the head.

Head Isolation 4: Your head remains stationary while your body walks in a circle under the head.

In the mid-1800s, François Delsarte developed a system of movement sometimes referred to as "Applied Aesthetics" (see pages 125–129). Delsarte's advice for the isolation exercises was: Except for the isolated section of the body, the entire body must remain relaxed, pliant, and supple—*especially* the joint *right next* to the isolated section. In the head isolations, for example, the *neck* should remain especially pliant; in the hand isolations, the *wrist*, etc.

Head Isolation 3

Hand Isolation 1: Keeping your elbows relaxed, hold your hands out in front of you with the palms facing the floor. Keep your hands isolated as you move away from them and toward them. When the elbows straighten, you can still move back farther. The object (the premise) is to get as far away from the

Drawings by Tony Montanaro

Hand Isolation 1

hands as possible and move in as close to the hands as possible without moving the hands. In the beginning, it might be helpful to hold your fingertips a few inches away from a wall and watch to make sure that the distance between your fingertips and the wall doesn't change. Remember to be especially relaxed in the wrist area!

If, while you are moving away from the hands, you find that you are poking your derrière back *before* your elbows have straightened to the maximum, this means you have abandoned your premise in an effort to simulate an effect. The premise is to isolate the hands and move as far back as possible. Your body does whatever it should (and *only* what it should) to serve the premise.

If you are attending the premise, the following chain of events will happen *naturally* (that is, without your having to tamper with the body): First, your elbows will straighten. Next, your chest will extend back, followed by the hips, derrière, and legs. Finally, you are on tiptoe. All of these effects come at the right time if your premise has 100% of your attention.

Hand Isolation 2: Isolate your hands as you jump above them and kneel below them.

"Pointe Fixe": (This is the beginning of the Tug-O-War illusion.)

Make a fist around a fixed point in the air. Now move *away* from this point.

Finesse: Take an antagonistic attitude toward the point. You are trying to pull it away from its spot in the air, but it won't budge. When an attitude (in this case, antagonism) is part of your premise, you are no longer doing an isolation exercise; you are performing a mime illusion. The difference between an isolation *exercise* and a mime *illusion* is that the exercise is strictly a way of perfecting technique. It does not tell us anything about life or about human nature. The mime *illusion*, on the other hand, says something about life. The illusion always reveals plot and character even if those plots and characters are fantastical.

Body Isolations: In body isolations your body remains stationary while the head, an arm, or a leg moves. The mechanics of these isolations are pretty much straightforward. For example, when the arm moves against the stationary body, you must keep the arm rigid and slide it into and away from the body. The *isolated* parts of the body (the trunk and torso) meet the *mobile* part of the body (the arm) at the shoulder joint. Therefore the shoulder joint is the only part of the body moving *within* the body and the arm is the only part moving within physical space.

A famous example of a body isolation becoming a mime illusion occurs in the Chaplin movie *Limelight*. Toward the end of the movie, Charlie Chaplin and Buster Keaton perform a brilliant comedy routine in which Chaplin's leg appears to shrink inside his pant leg. He wears very baggy pants so that he can pull his leg up (he must bend his knee, too) while his body remains motionless in space. The effect is delightful and very funny.

Understanding the Mime Illusion

The difference between the isolation exercises and a mime illusion is that the exercises do not occur in everyday life. For example, you would not see someone jumping above and kneeling below his/her hands in everyday life. The difference, then, between the exercise and the illusion, has to do with your *reasons* for doing both. There is only *one* reason for doing an exercise, and that is to perfect a skill. There are always *several* reasons for performing an illusion: to perfect a skill, create a character, and/or develop a plot. You could, however, change one of the exercises into an illusion by *motivating* it— giving it a purpose in addition to that of perfecting a skill.

Take the Hand-Isolation Exercise 2, for example. If you are a child trying to jump up on a kitchen counter, your premise would be true-to-life: you want a cookie, say. With this premise, you transform the isolation exercise into an illusion. Your isolated hands indicate the kitchen counter that you push against in your effort to reach the cookie.

In all the mime illusions (as in life), a series of forces acts on the body. These forces are tactile as well as emotional and mental. Learning the mime illusions, we are primarily concerned with the tactile forces. But you should not take these skills onto the stage before you understand (and can *show*) the emotional forces. The understanding of emotional forces is requisite to good mime because in life, emotional forces always characterize our encounters with tactile, physical forces. And mime (or any art form) is nonsense unless it relates to life in someway.

For instance, the child in the above example is pushing against the kitchen counter, but she is also responding to emotional forces. The emotional forces determine *why* she

63

wants to jump up on the counter and *how* she'll do it. (She's trying to grab a cookie on the shelf. Is she doing this sneakily or playfully?) These emotional forces are more interesting than the tactile forces, and the audience must see the emotional forces before they'll appreciate the illusion.

Using Premise in the Mime Illusions

As you become adept at premise work, you will experience external forces (as well as internal forces) acting on your body as the need arises. For example, in the tug-o-war, you will actually feel your "opponent's" tug coming at you from the outside! These forces are generated by your premise; you don't need an actual opponent or a rope. That's the "incredible credibility" of mime: you and your audience will see, believe, and experience things that aren't there.

In the tug-o-war, you must feel your "opponent's" tug *before* you move. If you don't feel it, everything you do will look and feel false. Your movements may be technically correct, but they won't look right—they will look like effects without a cause.

• • • • • • • • • • • • • • • • •

Last year, a teacher sent me an essay written by a fourth-grade student who had seen my show. The student wrote, "I liked the part when Tony pretended to be an invisible man who was fighting with him." This boy had "seen" my invisible opponent in the tug-o-war illusion. He also knew that I was my own opponent. This proves the remarkable effectiveness of premise work and believing.

In my classes, I spend a lot of time watching and directing solo mimes and solo performances of all disciplines. (Many of my students are singers or dancers. Many are clowns. Even trapeze artists build makeshift rigs and perform their routines in front of the class.) I direct them, watching closely to discern their intentions and to see whether or not these intentions are carried through.

Very often the students themselves aren't sure what their intentions are! When students are not sure of their own intentions, they appear to move without thinking. There is a randomness about their work.

In the beginning of my teaching career, I'd watch these students and suddenly notice that my attention had drifted. It was difficult to stay interested in what they were doing. I knew this was not my fault—I'm a very good audience. (I taught myself to be a good audience because if you can't *watch*, you can't teach.)

When a performance failed to hold my attention, I knew something was missing from that performance. That elusive "life-quality" just wasn't there. Now when I teach, I use my attention-span as a gauge for criticism, but in the early days, I didn't know about premise work. It hadn't occurred to me that the *motivation* behind the movement actually determines the credibility and vitality of the movement.

The following story beautifully illustrates this point. All of my students have heard this story at least once. It's from the play, *Deburau* by Sacha Guitry. This play is based on the historical careers of two of the great early mimes: Jean-Gaspard Deburau and his son, Charles Deburau. The play takes place in Paris in the early 1800s. It leads up to that poignant moment when a father passes his legacy on to his son.

Deburau's Legacy to His Son

Jean-Gaspard Deburau was one of the most famous Pierrots in history. He was the mime who established the character of Pierrot as Everyman. Before Deburau, Pierrot was a weak, love-sick lackey. He never would have survived history as his former self, but Deburau turned him into a powerful but infinitely sensitive idealist—someone everyone could relate to. Deburau's performances were riveting and the French audience adored him for this.

Jean-Gaspard was getting on in years and his retirement from the stage was imminent. He taught his son, Charles, all of his tricks—but withheld his "secret." The father was still unable to part with the exclusive admiration the audience held for him.

When Charles was ready to perform, Jean-Gaspard refused to let his son use the name of Deburau. "That [name] happens to be mine, you see. Your name is Charles."

His son corrected him, "Charles *Deburau*." At this, the father flew into a rage and told his son to drag his own name into the dust, not the name of Deburau!

The aging father began to lose his prowess on stage. During one performance, the audience started to "boo" him. They continued hissing and booing until he paused in his work. The audience went silent. Deburau then walked down to the footlights. There he performed a pantomime of an apology and bid farewell to the stage. The audience slowly filed out of the theatre; all were silent and deeply moved by the master's final performance.

This left the Theatre Funambules in a tricky situation. Who would replace the great Deburau?! The obvious choice was a Pierrot from a rival family. This thought was anathema to Jean-Gaspard. Jean-Gaspard told the director of the Funambules that his son Charles would be his successor: "Let *him* have my name." Bertrand, the director, was uneasy, "But he's a child!"

The father began to direct and coach his son in earnest. The son worked hard and perfected all of his father's tricks. He looked like his father and moved every bit as well as his father did when his father was young. But still, something was missing. Everything was correct but his performance lacked something essential, something vital. The director, the other performers, and Charles all noticed that something was dreadfully wrong but no one knew what it was (let alone what to do about it). Everyone knew that despite all of Charles's agility and talent, he couldn't replace his father. They were sure the performance would flop.

Opening night arrived. The audience was simmering with anticipation. Charles and Jean-Gaspard were backstage waiting for the curtain to go up. Charles was terrified. He took his place center stage and prepared for humiliation. Seeing his son's courage, Jean-Gaspard's heart broke. His *real* heart broke through the ego-heart, and he took his son into his confidence to share his deeply held secret. He told him:

"An audience isn't difficult
To please; if you find them so, that's your fault.
It's only that they won't stand blundering.
You must never leave them wondering
What on earth it is you're at."

"It's a secret anyone's welcome to,
Theirs for the guessing.
(Come a little closer.)
Now; the ordinary gestures, the 'Yes, sir' and 'No, sir,'
You can't grow wrong over. When you come to expressing
Something elaborate; first think it right.
Nothing hard in that...
(Quite still now, don't move)
If you want to convey 'What a pretty girl'
Think it and do
Whatever comes into your head to do.
If it's madness or love,
That you're frightened, or pleased, that your

head's in a whirl,
Think, think hard, think intensely
That you are in love, or in a fright.
Then, when you can't keep still any longer,
When your feeling grows stronger
Than you are, still hold yourself tensely
And steep yourself in it
For the millionth part of a minute,
Then...let yourself go,
And it'll come right." [6]

This was the legacy—the "secret"—that the master passed
on to his son. The play ends with the promise that Charles *does*
live up to his father's legacy.

• • •

Jean-Gaspard's advice to his son is a more poetic description of premise work than I have given in this book. Poetic or
not, premise work is the "secret" of performing.

There's an expression in theatre, "He waited so long, you
could have driven a truck through." This means that the performer has waited a remarkably long time before he has
spoken or moved. This time-lapse should never be dead space;
the performer should feel the *reason* for moving or speaking
closing in on him. When the performer waits for "cause" to
accumulate and overcome him, the audience also waits with
bated breath for the outcome. These moments aren't necessarily loud and dramatic but they are always captivating—
always convincing.

Believing

Many years ago, I was on stage performing my "Tightrope
Walker" sketch for the 'nth time. I never announced this
sketch. I'd simply begin climbing an illusionary rope. I'd climb
a certain distance before hopping onto an illusionary ladder
to continue my ascent. Then I'd tiptoe gingerly out onto an
illusionary tightrope. By now the audience knew who I was (a
tightrope walker) and what I was doing. I'd do a few gags and
finish the sketch. The audience always laughed a bit and had a
good time. But one day, in the middle of the sketch, I suddenly
became bored with the whole thing. I decided on the spur of
the moment to change the choreography.

[6] Guitry, Sacha, *Deburau*, trans. H. Granville Barker (New York,
London: GP Putnam's Sons, 1921), p. 208-209).

I had started out as usual, climbed the rope, and continued my ascent on the ladder—and then (this was new), I went back to the rope again. The audience tittered. Then suddenly, in the middle of the climb, I stopped and dropped my hands as if to say, "Enough of this." I broke the illusion completely. The audience reaction was tremendous—a jubilant burst of laughter and applause.

The moment I broke the illusion and dropped my hands, the audience realized that their *belief* had strayed very far away from the actual "fact of the matter." They had seen and believed that I was climbing higher and higher. When I dropped my hands, there was a split second in which everyone expected me to plummet several feet to the ground. When I didn't, they realized that they had been fooled. They relished and applauded their own folly.

• • •

As I performed the rope climb, I thoroughly *believed* that I was leaving the earth and ascending higher and higher in physical space. My belief was contagious. The audience suspended their disbelief and willingly accepted the fact that I was going up, up, up. When I suddenly dropped my belief (my premise), the audience *had* to drop with me since *my* belief was the only thing holding all of us up.

A belief is a premise, and the simple act of maintaining a belief is inextricably linked to premise work. Therefore, if this section on believing is enigmatic to you, I urge you to go back to the opening crosses (i.e., the dead-body and crescent rolls, the "ooze," and the forward rolls) until you *sense* that your mind (your *attention* to your premise) initiates and sustains your movements.

As you become more versed in this work, you become aware of a clarity very much like "seeing" although it's not ocular. It's a keen sense of control. This sense of clarity and control comes when your attention fastens to a premise. Keeping your attention on the premise is like keeping your eye on the road.

Premise work and the act of believing are one and the same thing. The clarity of your mime illusions depends on your clarity of mind—your skill at premise work.

Many mimes have mastered the *technique* of the mime illusions and still, their gestures lack a certain razor-sharp quality. This razor-sharpness is the same clarity that you sense during the crosses. It is the clarity of your premise—your belief—reflected on your body.

When I lean on a wall, I honestly *believe* that the wall is there. When I fly through the air as the legendary Icarus, I *see* the Aegean waves surging beneath me.

My ability to believe these things, these images, determines the clarity of my gestures and the integrity of my sketch. My belief ignites my audience's belief, and they join me in my adventures.

I explained this concept to a class of fourth-grade students from Skowhegan, Maine. They were too young to understand the philosophy of premise work so I changed my wording a bit. I talked to them about moving *like* something or someone. I had them moving *like* cats, *like* monkeys, *like* marionettes. I taught them some puppet-*like* movements, and everyone walked around the room carrying the image of a marionette (strings, suspension) in their imagination.

Then, without telling them *how* to do this, I asked them to sit down on the floor in a puppet-like way. All of them did this beautifully. Next, I told them to get up without losing that feeling. This was a bit more difficult for them to do since they were going *against* gravity now—they had to *push* themselves off the floor while still believing that the puppet master was *lifting* them from above.

I explained that the more they *believed* that they were being lifted from above, the more their audience would *believe* their puppets. "The audience won't *notice* that you're using your hands to push against the floor. They won't see your 'getting-up' muscles. What will they see?"

One student piped up, "They see your mind!" He had obviously understood the essence of premise work.

A few years ago (in 1991), I produced a video-book entitled *Mime Spoken Here*. Volume I consists of a thorough, visual description of nineteen mime illusions. I produced this video-book knowing that it's easier to learn the illusions by watching than by reading. But both watching and reading are unnecessary, if you understand premise work. The inventors of the various illusions studied real-life situations until they understood the tactile forces *causing* the physical effects. Once they discerned the cause, the effects (i.e., the technique) came naturally. Ideally, all of us should invent or re-invent the mime illusions.

While you are learning the appropriate effects, glue your attention to the forces (tactile and emotional) *causing* your shape and appearance. Your attention should not, for one second, lose contact with those forces. As long as your mind is

The Class: The Mime Illusions

constantly tuned to the forces *causing* your shapes and behavior, your body will do the right things naturally without your having to force or strain.

For example, when I teach students how to push an illusionary wheelbarrow, most beginning mime students concentrate very hard on putting their body parts in the correct positions. Their attention is totally fixed on effects and the illusion never looks exactly right—no matter how perfectly they reproduce those effects.

To correct this mysterious aberration, I tell them to be constantly aware of forces acting on the body from the outside. When they push the wheelbarrow forward, a sling-shaped force acts to push their hands and arms back behind the torso. This force extends from hand to hand and bows out over the hips. As soon as students attend to this sling-shaped force, their fixation on body parts breaks. Instead of worrying about arm and hip placement, they focus on the line-of-force *causing* the correct placement. Now their body parts automatically do the right thing, and the illusion looks correct.

Remember: In lieu of an actual wheelbarrow, your attention serves as the object. Therefore, if your attention—even for a split second—loses contact with the lines of force acting on your body from the outside, your wheelbarrow "disappears." The illusion breaks when your attention breaks.

This is true for all of the mime illusions. The actual physical objects are unimportant. You want to show what these objects *do to you.* You want to show the external forces moving and sculpting your body into different shapes and postures. These forces act on you from the outside, but your awareness of these forces is, of course, initiated by your attention—the deep inner workings of a sharp and observant mind.

Use the following instructions as you'd use the "Solutions" page to a crossword puzzle. Try to master the illusions without reading the instructions first. If you have to cheat, make sure you understand what you're doing and *why.*

The Wall

Over thirty years ago, I was improvising with my friend (and an excellent mime) Carlo Mazzone. We did the "Mirror" exercise (see page 144) in front of each other to make sure our mimes were clear. At one point, I wanted to indicate a wall. I held my hand up to the wall and touched it. Carlo was amazed—he could *see* the wall. He did the same gesture for me and I saw the wall, too. We were thrilled. He hadn't expected this simple gesture to be so visually convincing. As far as I know, this was the birth of the now (in)famous "wall mime."

In 1960, I performed this illusion on television for CBS, Camera 3 out of New York City. Later, I taught the wall mime to all of my students as a way of teaching the concept of "authority."

Exercising authority is difficult for some people. I ask them to show me a wall and they stammer, "Where should I put it?"

Such a reaction reveals a fear of assertiveness—a reluctance to act authoritatively. This problem is simple to correct. I have found that learning the wall mime gets to this problem quickly and efficiently. I tell students, "The wall is wherever you want it to be!" They reach out tentatively and touch their own imaginary wall. Once they have done this, they aren't afraid to touch it again. And the next touch has more authority than the first.

• • •

The mechanics of the wall mime are as follows:

Each hand is used in two ways: It is a "hand" until it touches the wall. As soon as the hand touches the wall, the palm flattens and the hand freezes and isolates. Now the hand is what I call a "wall-hand." When you pull the "wall-hand" away from the wall, it relaxes into a "hand" again.

Using *both* hands allows you to create a ghost image. The ghost image creates the magic of the illusion, and this image occurs as long as at least *one* hand is on the wall at all times. Both hands can be *on* the wall at the same time, but both hands should never be *off* the wall at the same time. When there is no hand on the wall, the ghost image is lost.

When a hand is a wall-hand, this means that it is perfectly isolated in space. You may *think* that your wall-hand is maintaining the ghost image, but if that hand is moving in space, it is not perfectly isolated. Consequently, the ghost image is lost and the illusion is broken. (Incidentally, there is some leeway in the isolations. If you move with authority, skill, and clarity, the illusion may work even though the isolations are slightly less than perfect. But if you are a beginner to the art of mime, I suggest you become a stickler for the isolations—go for perfection every time.)

The tricky part of the wall mime illusion comes when you walk along the wall. Your body must *travel* while you *isolate* your wall-hands in space. Your wall-hand freezes in space until you walk ahead of it. Once you have moved past your wall-hand, you can remove that wall-hand from the wall. The hand then relaxes slightly (becoming a "hand" again) as you move it to a new section of wall ahead of you.

Leaning on a Table

Give yourself a good solid base by standing with your legs fairly far apart. If your "table" is on your right, bend your right knee slightly as you lean toward it. Raise your right arm (relaxed but straight) to prepare for the lean. The palm of your hand should also be relaxed (i.e., *receptive* to the "table top"). Once your hand has contacted the table, it is no longer the hand; now it's a table-hand and indicates the table's surface. When the hand represents a flat surface, the palm flattens to reveal the perfectly flat surface of the table and the hand isolates to reveal the table's immobility. (Your hand, then shows the *qualities* of the table's surface rather than the table, itself. When these *qualities* are well represented, the table *is* visible in a strange, inexplicable way.)

After your hand has contacted the table, your elbow should be perfectly straight and your arm must not move (your whole arm from the shoulder to the hand remains isolated. But don't shift your body weight totally into the lean yet.) This is the critical moment in the illusion. Your hand has made contact with the table. Your hand and arm are isolated. The body is relaxed—ready to "fall" into the isolated arm. These two motions (the arm isolation and the shift of the body into the lean) intersect in the shoulder. That is, the arm stays in one place while the torso slides forward into the lean.

When all the weight has shifted into the lean, there is a very slight, unpretentious "jerk." This tiny, little "jerk" indicates that inertia (i.e., the steady momentum of leaning) has been overcome. Watch these "jerks" happening in real life. Lean on an actual table or wall and notice the very subtle movement that happens when all of your weight is transferred into the lean.

This and the majority of mime illusions consist of two forces: "trust" and "thrust." In the leaning illusion, you *trust* the table and the table *thrusts* back at you. The trust is depicted by the body as it leans, relaxed and easy, on the table. The thrust is depicted by the hand and arm that remain isolated (i.e., fixed and "supportive") during the lean. Your isolated arm represents the table thrusting against your lean. "Trust" meets "thrust" at your shoulder joint.

Leaning on a Table

Ladder Climb

Hand Action: Start this illusion by defining your ladder. Simply touch your ladder at different points with your hands. Don't move your legs or attempt climbing, yet. Grasp a rung and isolate your fist. With the other hand, grasp the rung above (about a foot above the rung you just defined). Isolate *that* fist. Let go and grasp the rung below. Define the sides of the ladder as well. Practice this. Continue grasping the ladder in different places until you are familiar with the hand isolation and the ladder. When you add the legs to this illusion, the hands may become sloppy. So make sure you have mastered the hand isolation and have a clear sense of the ladder before attempting the climb.

As you practice, remember that one hand must be isolated while the other hand is moving. As in the wall mime illusion, both hands may be *isolated* at one time, but both hands can never be *moving* at the same time. At least one hand must be touching the "ladder" at all times. This guarantees that the ladder is always represented.

Leg and Foot Action: The most important thing to remember as you climb is to move the legs and feet *without* moving the body up and down. Remember, the essence of this illusion is the *suggestion* of climbing and not the actual "going up." You cannot actually ascend above the earth without the aid of a solid, physical ladder, so don't even *attempt* to go up in space during this illusion. In other words, don't rise to your toes during this illusion. What goes up, must come down. If you go *up* on your toes, you'll have to come *down* on your heels eventually. The illusion of climbing is destroyed as soon as the body comes down. Therefore, it's best not to go up at all.

Ascending the Ladder

The leg and foot maneuver is fairly simple. The feet do not *travel* anywhere. The knees bend and straighten as the heels go up and down. Begin by standing with the feet slightly apart and parallel to each other. Raise the heel of the right foot and press the ball of the right foot into the floor. (The right knee is bent.) Now, *without going up or down*, simply lower the right heel and straighten the right knee while you raise the left heel and bend the left knee. This exchange of one bent leg for the other bent leg indicates that you have ascended one rung.

Arms and Legs Together: The trick of this illusion is combining the leg action with the hand action. Every time a bent leg straightens, this indicates that the climber is ascending

73

one rung. Therefore the hand isolation must indicate this ascent also. *Before* the knee straightens, the climber is holding on to two rungs (one rung is above the other and the hands are isolated in space to indicate these rungs). Now, *as the knee straightens*, the hands must remain isolated in reference to each other, but they must *lower* exactly one foot (or one rung-distance) in reference to space. In other words, the two hands remain equidistant as both hands lower the distance of one foot. This hand/arm action indicates the climber's ascent. Instead of the body *going up*, the mime's arms *go down*.

Now, reposition your hands: the lower hand lets go of the lower rung and grabs the upper rung. The other hand remains isolated. Once you have repositioned your hands, you are in the correct position to take the next "step" up the ladder. Remember that the hands remain isolated *in reference to each other*, but they both lower one rung-length as you shift your weight from one leg to another.

• • • • • • • • • • • • • • • • • •

Many of the mime illusions are based on the principle of translation. An upward movement in a real-life situation is translated into a downward movement in a mime situation. For example, in real life, when a person climbs an actual ladder, the body goes *up* while the hands and arms stay still (i.e. isolate in space). In the mime illusion, the body stays still while the hands and arms go *down*. In this illusion, the upward motion of the body is simulated by the downward motion of the arms. This same principle applies to the illusionary walk in which the straight and weight-bearing leg in a real walk becomes the straight and *moveable* leg in the illusionary walk—and the bent and moveable leg in the real walk becomes the bent and *weight-bearing* leg in the illusionary walk (see page 96). In other words, the *appearance* of the body is the same whether you are in a real-life situation or in a mime situation, but the relationship of the body to *space* changes. The real-life situation travels and the mime situation stays in place.

Finesse: You should be aware of the upward focus and intent of the climber. The climber is looking ahead to the next rung and his or her intent is on a destination. Therefore, your chest should be lifted, your gaze should be upward, and you should *believe* that you are rising toward a goal or destination. This belief (premise) should affect everything you do.

Also, once you are familiar with the basic mechanics of the

illusion, you may want to vary your patterns. For example, you may want to isolate your hands and take *two* steps up the ladder instead of just one step. (To do this, lower your arms in two separate increments without repositioning your hands as you exchange your legs two times.) Occasionally, you may hold the *sides* of the ladder instead of the rungs. Any variation on climbing may work as long as your isolations are clear and your arm/leg coordination is correct.

Descending the Ladder

Descending the ladder is a common-sense reversal of climbing the ladder. The arms and hands rise to indicate the descent of the body. The two arms rise in increments of one foot (or the distance between rungs) while remaining equidistant to each other.

The leg action remains the same as for the climb or you may want to learn a more complicated, more impressive leg action. For this leg action, you start with the right knee bent and the left knee straight. Lift the right foot off the floor slightly and extend the right leg behind you, as if you are about to lower that leg to the rung underneath you. In the real-life situation, you would be stepping *down* onto this right leg. However, in the mime illusion you cannot go down—you are already on the floor. Therefore, once you have extended the right leg, you must gradually straighten the right knee as you bring that right leg in underneath you. It should look as if you are scooping your right foot *under* the floor. To create the illusion of the right leg coming under the left, lift the left heel as the right foot slides in next to it. The right foot should appear to displace the left foot (i.e., the left heel *lifts* and the left knee *bends* as the right foot slides in). After the right leg has slid into place, the left leg is bent and the right leg is straight. You are now ready to extend the left leg behind you and repeat the "stepping down" process. Every time you extend a leg, you bring *that* leg in straight causing the other knee to bend and the heel to lift.

As in the climbing illusion, this leg action must be coordinated with the appropriate hand/arm action. While the legs are stationary, the upper hand lets go of the upper rung and grasps the lower rung. (Of course, the other hand remains isolated.) Then, as the legs move to indicate the lowering of the body, the hands and arms rise together in reference to the body. This rising of the arms indicates the lowering of the body. The arms and legs stop moving at the same time to

Descending the Ladder (simple leg action)

75

indicate that your have stepped down precisely one step on the ladder.

• • • • • • • • • • • • • • • • • •

As I said before, the illusions are the depiction of *forces*, not so much the depiction of *objects*. In the ladder climb, you want to show your *grip* on the rung rather than the *shape* of the rung. Therefore, do not try to indicate an invisible rung by holding your fist slightly open. The audience will see the rung as long as your isolation is clean and correct. Close your hands into tight fists and forget about leaving a space for that invisible rung.

Rope Climb

No one taught me this illusion. I analyzed the mechanics of a *real* rope climb and devised this technique for the *illusory* rope climb using common sense and an understanding of the isolation exercises. If I can make up my own illusions, you can too.

The mechanics of the rope climb are similar to the mechanics of a ladder climb. In both illusions, the hands and arms remain equidistant as the body ascends or descends. They remain equidistant because they are (theoretically) holding onto a solid object—a ladder or a rope—and this object does not stretch or contract. The ladder obviously does not stretch or contract. The rope is also a fixed length when it is held taut by the weight of the body.

To introduce students to this illusion, I ask them to grasp (with *one* hand) an imaginary point above their head and to hang from this point. They automatically isolate this point and hang correctly. In other words, their center of gravity naturally falls directly under the imaginary point.

This illusion teaches several principles of physics. When you hang from a point above your head, you are entrusting this point with your full weight. When you stand on the ground, you are entrusting the ground with your full weight. The principle of hanging is no different than the principle of standing; only your point-of-contact with the earth changes. When you hang, your point-of-contact with the earth is *above* your head. When you stand, your point-of-contact is *below* your feet. But whether you are hanging or standing, gravity acts *through* and *on* the body in the same way.

In order to stand upright on the earth, all the heavy sections of your body must be centered directly *above* your balancing point. Likewise, during the rope climb, the heavy sections of your body must be centered directly *below* your

Rope Climb

hanging point. The force of gravity is thereby focused into a straight line (from head to toe), and you stand straight up or hang straight down.

Students grasp this concept automatically when I ask them to hang from one hand. Their chest and hips automatically align themselves directly *under* their hanging-point (the point where the hand contacts the rope). Sometimes, I have to tell students to be more relaxed through the rest of the body. I remind them to let the head and neck fall easily to the side or to let the opposite shoulder droop comfortably.

However, as soon as they have to hang from two hands, they begin defying the laws of physics. Suddenly, they begin holding themselves away from the "rope." The heavy sections of their body no longer align directly *under* their hanging point. Watch out for this when you attempt the rope climb. Make sure that your sternum (the median line through your chest) hangs directly under your hands. The sternum should also be *lifted toward* that point. This happens because the shoulders are pulling down against the rope in order to lever the chest upwards.

Another common mistake in this illusion is the tendency to hold one's elbows out away from the rope. If you were to climb an actual rope, you'd pull the elbows down toward the ground as forcefully as you could. In this position, your arms are stressed the least. To climb the rope efficiently, the direction of your climb should run parallel to your arm bones. When your elbows pull straight *down* away from your wrists, the body is propelled straight *up* the rope. Your bones (from wrist to elbow) align with the downward pull of gravity and the upward thrust of your climb. However, if you try to hold your elbows out to the side as you climb, you will notice that your intent to go straight up acts *against* your bones instead of in line *with* them. When this happens, all you can use is muscle and there's not much leverage in muscles. You'd have to be Hercules to climb a rope with your elbows jutting out to the side.

These are fairly complicated concepts in anatomy and physics. If you are not interested in this analysis, simply follow these simple rules: Keep your elbows down and make sure that your chest bone (your sternum) hangs directly under your hands. Lift your sternum up to your hands as you climb. Now, I'll go into the mechanics of the climb.

Hand/Arm Action: (This is not the actual rope climb, yet. It's a remedial drill to make the mechanics of climbing easier, later.) Reach up with two hands and grab an illusionary rope. Now pull down until both hands are in front of your face. As you pull down, the two hands remain equidistant to each other. Now, let go with the lower hand and place that hand *above* the other hand. (Keep the *other* hand isolated in space as you move the lower hand.) Now you are ready to pull down again. Keep the two hands equidistant and pull both hands down until the upper hand is in the place where the lower hand *used to be*. Let go with the lower hand and reposition that hand above the other and so on.

You must remember two things during this drill: 1) Remember to keep both hands equidistant as you pull down; and 2) Remember to keep one hand *isolated* while the other lets go of the rope. This hand-over-hand exercise teaches you the most basic isolation in the rope climb illusion.

Finesse: You can prepare for the rope climb as you perform the above drill. Simply *believe* that you are climbing that rope. Instead of thinking that you are *lowering* the arms, believe that you are hoisting your body *up* toward your hands. You will notice that the mere act of *believing* will change the shape and attitude of your body.

Lower Body Action: The trick of the rope climb illusion is that you can't actually go up in physical space. You have to create the illusion of climbing. In order to do this, I devised a tricky little leg action which allows me to rise on my toes and lower myself unobtrusively so that I can rise again and create the illusion of climbing. The lowering action is unobtrusive because it is in keeping with the "real thing." An athlete climbing a real rope *does lose ground* ever so slightly whenever he or she lets go of the rope with one hand. And the athlete *must* let go of the rope with one hand in order to put that hand above the other. I noticed this and realized that this brief moment of lowering provided me with an opportunity to cheat: I could lower my heels in order to lift them again.

The mechanics of the rope climb illusion are as follows: Grab the "rope" above your head. (One hand should be placed higher on the rope than the other hand.) Entrust the rope with your full weight. You should experience a tremendous force *above* your head to indicate that you have shifted your weight from the floor to the rope. Of course, all of this shifting of weight and trusting of ropes takes place in your belief. But the more you *believe* what you're doing—the more you *yield* to the belief system that *is* the rope climb—the more you will experience these forces and objects as palpable "things."

Now, pull your two hands down *as* you rise to your toes. This is important. You must *begin* rising to the toes *as* you begin lowering the arms and you must also *finish* both moves at the same time. Now, here's a tricky mathematical concept to explain why this illusion is so effective. Note carefully: You can rise only three or four inches on your toes, but your arms can come down a full sixteen inches or so. If you traverse both distances at the same time, your audience will assume these two distances are equal! In other words, if these two maneuvers both begin together and end together, your audience will *assume* you have risen sixteen inches even though you are only three inches off the floor. The two distances (i.e., the three-inch rise to the toes and the sixteen-inch drop of the arms) are proportional to each other, and the eye *assumes* they are equal as long as they are traversed at the same time.

If both distances are assumed to be equal, why does the audience believe the more fantastic distance? Because that's what you *want* them to believe. The mime, like the magician, knows how to direct the audience's attention to the illusion and away from the strategy. In the rope climb illusion, you direct your audience's attention to the sixteen-inch "rise" and slip your three-inch recovery in there without anyone noticing. The mysterious, "convincing power" of the mime illusions has as much to do with the infectious nature of beliefs, desires and thoughts as it does with mathematics and physics.

Back to the illusion. Keep your knees slightly bent at all times during this illusion—even as you rise to your toes. This makes your illusion true to life. (If you were climbing a real rope, your legs would not be bearing your weight; they would be bent in a relaxed position.)

Once you have risen to full height on your toes, let go of the rope with your under-hand and position this hand above the other hand. *As* this happens, lower your heels back to the floor to indicate the slight loss of height that happens as a natural result of letting go with one hand.

Another very subtle movement takes place as you let go with one hand and lower your heels to the floor. The *other* hand that is still clasping the rope must rise slightly—an inch or two—in physical space. The audience reasons (subconsciously?) that you have lost a *bit* of height because you no longer have the strength of two arms holding you up. The logic of this arm movement distracts the audience's attention

Rope Climb

| Heels flat | On toes | Heels start low- ering to floor | Heels fully on floor |

from the illogic of your leg/heel action (i.e., as you lower your hand slightly, you sneakily lower your heels to the floor and recover your starting position of the legs).

The two movements (the lowering of the heel and the slight lifting of the rope-hand in physical space) happen simultaneously and steadily *until* the moving-hand grabs the rope from above. As soon as you grab the rope from above, there is a slight jerk to indicate that the inertia of the lowering action has been overcome.

Now you are back in your initial position. Your heels are on the floor and your hands are no higher or lower than they were when you started the climb. You are ready to pull yourself up to your hands again. (In fact, you are not *pulling* yourself *up* to your hands; you are *pushing* yourself up and *bringing* your hands *down* to meet you at the same time. The push up and the pull down both translate into the illusion of climbing.)

The "trust and thrust" principle (see the LEANING ON A TABLE illusion page 72) also applies to the rope climb illusion. Actually, the trust and thrust principle figures in *all* of the illusions, since this describes our basic relationship with the physical realm. We trust or depend on physical objects and they "return" that trust in the form of a thrust. In the rope climb, you trust the rope with your full weight and the rope *meets* and *matches* your trust by supporting your full weight. In real life, you "trust" and the rope "thrusts" (i.e., it supports you). As a mime, you have to duplicate this phenomenon by pulling *down* with your elbows (trust) and pushing *up* with your chest (thrust).

Tug-O-War:
Pull, Be Pulled

Tug-O-War (as a solo or a duet)
You can perform this illusion as a soloist or with a partner.
The illusion is the same either way. The only difference
between the solo and the duet tug-o-war is you have more leeway performing solo. When you are performing with a real
partner, you have to coordinate your moves and keep an eye on
your partner's hands to make sure that the distance between
his/her hands and yours remains constant.

Pull, Be Pulled: This is the first drill to acquaint you with the
"identity shift" that characterizes this illusion. During this
illusion you become, alternately, the antagon*ist* and the antagon*ized*. The two "roles" should feel very different.

The Pull: Imagine that you are facing off with a real opponent. Begin by standing slightly in profile to your "opponent"
with your arms extended to one side of your body as if you are
holding on to an invisible rope. In the "pull," you are the antagon*ist*. This is the most simple move in this illusion, simply
pull or lean away from your opponent. As you do this, be
aware of your opponent's resistance.

Finesse: During the tug-o-war illusion, you want to have one
arm extended—elbow straight all the time. (There are some
exceptions to this rule.) When that arm is out straight, it
serves two purposes: it is a part of your body, of course, and it
also represents the actual rope. That arm is a graphic (see page
224 for the definition of "graphic").

**Tug-O-War:
Jump to the
Right**

Spread your legs apart as you lean. If your opponent is to your left, bend your right leg and lean to the right. Extend the left leg straight and strong between you and your opponent. Lean away as far as you can. Now isolate your hands in space and jump to the right swinging your lower body from the left side of your torso to the right side. As soon as you land from this jump, pull the rope into another lean. Do this as quickly as possible because you are vulnerable when you first land— your torso is leaning precariously *toward* your opponent. You want to pull your torso back to the right and *away* from your opponent.

When students first learn this illusion, it usually looks as if they are doing everything. It looks as if all of the tugs and jerks come from them. In this illusion, some of the tugs and jerks have to come from your opponent and you have to look like the victim. You have to be caught off-guard sometimes, you have to be surprised—buffeted about into some undignified and unseemly positions. This can happen only if your body remains loose, lanky, responsive, ready for anything.

If you have ever played tug-o-war for real, or if you've ever wrestled with someone, you notice that you instinctively assume an "emergency mode." Your muscles are relaxed, but not lethargic. They are ready to contract instantly when you need them for offense or defense. Otherwise, they are relaxed, suggesting potential rather than kinetic energy.

This same attitude must come into your illusion. The audience must see the muscles contract instantly and return to neutral as soon as they aren't needed anymore. To do this, make sure that your attention stays glued to that external force coming at you from your opponent (via the rope).

Be Pulled: Now your opponent tugs against you. You are the antagonized. Experience your "opponent's" tug before you do anything. You then respond by tightening your fists and letting the pull reverberate through your body. Your hands are the first part of your body to react. This is logical: your hands are holding the rope. The next part of your body to react is your elbows—then your chest. Finally, if the force is strong enough, your legs may get into the act. You may have to take a frantic step or two toward your opponent. But for now, take the frantic part out of the exercise and simply observe the various shapes that the body assumes during the illusion.

Allow your opponent's pull to force your arms and torso away from your legs until your balance is jeopardized. You are now in what I call a "negative shape." This means that your opponent's tug is forcing you to hover precariously over empty space. You are not strong in this position—if you were to give in to gravity now, your opponent would win.

Instinctively, you try to regain a positive shape. In the positive shape, you have a strong, straight leg extended between you and your opponent. I call this the "strong leg." This leg provides you with the strength of a pyramid to resist sliding toward your opponent. Another advantage of this shape is gravity is on *your* side. You can use it against your opponent. You *try* to have a strong leg out there at all times.

While you are recovering your positive shape, there is a certain moment when you isolate your hands. This indicates that you have met and matched your opponent's force and the rope is locked in physical space. You have matched your opponent's force, but you still want to *exceed* that force. To do this, you must bring more of your body between you and your opponent. The more of your body you wedge underneath the rope and the more forcefully you tilt away from your opponent, the more of an advantage you have.

But *how* are you going to wedge your lower half in between you and your opponent when every time you take one foot off the earth, you lose strength? You must position yourself as quickly as possible. I teach a little side-hop action in which you hop from a negative shape to a positive shape as quickly as possible while staying as low to the ground as possible. Remember: Your hands must remain isolated in physical space as you hop into your positive shape.

The Skud

The Skud: The skud happens when your opponent's tug is stronger than yours, but you are holding yourself so taut that he drags your entire body over to him. You do not change your shape at all. The logic of this is: You are already in a strong position—a positive shape. If you maintain this shape as you are being dragged, your feet might eventually dig into the earth and if your feet *stop*, your body stops (provided you hold your position tightly enough). During the skud you appear to be sliding or stuttering in one shape across the earth.

The following is the sequence of events that make up the skud: Your opponent suddenly pulls you off balance and toward him. You then—as quickly as possible—lean away and plant your strong, straight leg between you and your opponent. From this position, you begin a series of quick, short hops from both feet (both feet leave the earth and return to the earth at the same time). These hops stay close to the ground and they travel sideways.

Only a few hops are justified (less than ten, I'd say). The last few hops are shorter and quicker than the first hops. This indicates that your skud has been successful. You have managed to lodge yourself against the earth and arrest your opponent's advantage.

Over the Shoulder: As long as you are standing in profile to your opponent, you aren't as strong as you could be. You're relying heavily on your arm muscles, and you're only as strong as your weakest muscle. You'd be better off with your back toward your opponent, and if you could lever the rope to your shoulder, you would relieve the tension on your arms.

I often ask my class to analyze this situation: You are challenged to the utmost extent of your strength. You can no longer maintain your strength in a profile position. How are you going to put the rope over your shoulder? What do you have to do? Most of the time, they answer this question by simply bringing their hands in and up over their shoulder. This is the wrong answer. If you could bring the rope up and over your shoulder that easily, then your opponent must be a real weakling. You can't actually bring the rope up at all because the sideways pull from your opponent is too strong. The right answer is: If you can't bring the rope to you, you have to go to the rope. Isolate your hands in physical space and bring your shoulder *back* and *down* under the hand that is closest to your opponent. Now, with your back to your opponent, lean into your shoulder and try to walk away.

The Shoulder Jolt: This maneuver adds a comic touch to your illusion. The shoulder jolt happens when you have your back to your opponent and the rope is anchored over your shoulder. In this position, your hands are pressed very firmly into one side of your chest. (If the rope is over the left shoulder, your hands will press into the left side of your chest.) The comedy of the jolt makes use of the fact that you are using the chest as a foundation for your hands. Therefore, if your opponent yanks at you hard enough, this will upset your chest as well your hands. (Your chest and hands move in one piece.) As your shoulder lurches backwards, your head bobs forward in a reverse-whiplash. When two or three of these jolts happen in rapid succession, you look ridiculous, your head bobbing back and forth uncontrollably. Then finally, in one last jolt, your hands break loose from your chest and shoot straight back toward your opponent. In response to this violent action, your body flips around to face your opponent. Your opponent has a clear advantage now.

The shoulder jolt is a good move to learn for several reasons. It is very funny when it is done correctly. Also, because these moves happen so quickly, they add a tempo change to your sketch.

The Winch: I invented this complicated maneuver shortly before I studied with Marceau. I remember Marceau was impressed when I showed it to him.

My winch is a replica of the real machine. The dictionary defines winch as a "...hoisting machine having a drum around which a rope or chain winds as the load is lifted." In the tug-of-war, my mid-section acts as the drum and the "load" I am lifting (pulling, actually) is my opponent. All during this illusion, you must make sure that you have a strong leg between

Over the Shoulder   you and your opponent. (Reminder: The strong leg is the straight leg that slants down from you to your opponent, providing you with pyramid-like stability and leverage against your opponent's force.)

For the sake of simplicity, let's say that your opponent is to your left. Begin by standing profile to your opponent with your arms extended straight out to the left. You will be leaning to the right—*away* from your opponent—and your left leg will act as your strong leg.

Now you want to bring your hands to your waist to establish your waist as the barrel of your winch. Of your two hands, your right hand is the closest to your waist. Position yourself so that you can press that hand to your belly and begin the winch. The left arm is still extended toward your opponent. Lock the right hand to your stomach (this provides you with some valuable friction) and begin winding that rope around your waist by rotating your body to the right. As you turn, you "eat up" the rope, which means that the left hand that is holding the rope out in space now closes in toward you.

As soon as you sense that your waist has turned sufficiently to secure the rope, you can let go of the rope with your left hand and bring that hand to your waist as well. By now, your back is turned to your opponent, both hands are on your waist. Your left leg is still strong. Now, quickly reach back with your right hand and blindly grab the rope behind you. This will become your leverage for the next part of your turn.

By this point, you notice that your legs are beginning to feel twisted and weak. You want to situate them in such a way as to acquire maximum leverage and stability. Your left leg had

Shoulder Jolt

been the strong leg. Now you want your right leg out there. But your opponent is still tugging at you. You'll have to hop as quickly as possible into an optimum position. Don't move your hands as you do this. You're too busy stabilizing your legs to do anything with the rope.

Now you have your back to your opponent. Your right arm is extended behind you and your right hand is gripping the rope. Your right leg is strong and your left leg is slightly bent so you can pivot toward the right leg. It should appear as if your mid-section is rotating with tremendous effort as you continue turning to the right. Turn until you face your opponent. Your right arm is now extended straight in front of you toward your opponent. Your right leg is still the strong leg, but as you continue the rotation, you will have to switch legs again. Now your left leg is strong and you are back in your original position. Repeat the whole process until you have completed three or four rotations.

This has been a step-by-step description of the illusion, but these steps are not "written in stone"; they may be changed somewhat. For example, you may want to switch your legs and *then* adjust your arms. Or you may want to adjust your arms first and then switch your legs. You will instinctively choose the right order of events as long as you are constantly tuned in to that almost overwhelming force coming at you from your opponent's direction.

You are also supposed to *try* to keep a strong leg between you and your opponent at all times. You will do this naturally too, as long as your mind is intent on the pull of that "rope."

The Winch

· · · · · · · · · · · · · · · · · · ·

Please understand this most difficult and crucial concept described in the preceeding paragraph! You may encounter a certain resistance to this new way of working and thinking. You may
not *want* to let something so nebulous as a *force* hold the center
of your attention; you'd feel much more comfortable focusing
exclusively on *real* things like arms and legs, right? But you will
never achieve a convincing illusion if you continue working this
way. You may manage to put the corpus into all the correct
shapes and postures, but your illusion will not come to life. It will
not titillate your audience, and you'll soon tire of the illusions.

After I have rotated my winch three or four times, I finish
with one last comic maneuver. I pretend that my opponent
pulls the rope with enough force to totally unwind my winch.

6

7

8

He yanks the rope and forces me into a tailspin. The force begins at my opponent and goes (via the rope) directly to my waist. At this point, I spin very fast in the opposite direction of my winch and finish the spin by grabbing the rope again in one last desperate attempt to regain my composure.

Suitcase

The suitcase is a fairly simple illusion, but it teaches a fundamental skill: How to make something out of nothing and how to make that "nothing" look heavy. It teaches the concept of weight and counterweight.

Let's say the suitcase is on the floor to the right of you. Reach down with your right hand and grasp the handle. Keep your right elbow slightly bent as you reach down, to indicate that your arm is not yet stressed. Also, bend your right knee

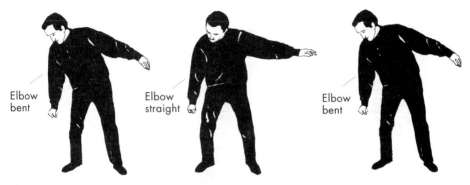

Elbow
bent

Elbow
straight

Elbow
bent

Suitcase

slightly as you stoop down to grab the handle. Your right hand is open gently to allow for the handle.

Once your hand is low enough to reach the suitcase, close your fingers tightly (but without tension) into a fist to indicate you have grasped the handle. Now isolate your right fist and pull the rest of your body up. In other words, start straightening your right knee and bringing your shoulders back to an upright position. Your elbow *must* straighten now, because you are straightening up and isolating your hand at the same time. (All this happens *before* your suitcase actually comes off the floor.)

Rather than focus exclusively on the isolation, be aware of the weight of the suitcase pulling down on your fist. This downward force is the *reason* for the isolation.

In this illusion you want your audience to "see" a heavy object being hoisted off the floor. When you don't have an actual object—an actual weight—to lift, you must create the illusion of weight by showing the counterweight. Show what the suitcase *does to you* and your audience will "see" an actual suitcase.

As a beginning exercise, I have students pretend that their suitcases are far heavier than they expected. They approach the suitcases expecting them to weigh a certain number of pounds, but they weigh twice as much. The resistance is therefore a surprise, and the impact of that surprise is enough to send their bodies lurching over their suitcases.

The mechanics of this move are exactly the same as I described earlier: Stoop down to the right and bend the right knee. Clasp the handle of the suitcase, isolate the hand and extend the elbow as you straighten up. All of this happens *before* the suitcase leaves the floor.

If you want to show that the weight of the suitcase takes you by surprise and sends you flying, you must perform the straightening-up moves fairly quickly. The momentum of your lift determines the impetus of your lurch. The mechanics of the lurch are as follows: Your fist (the suitcase handle) remains isolated in space. No matter what you do, this fist remains locked in space, apparently "resisting" your effort to stand up. The quicker you try to straighten, the quicker your elbow pops straight and the more forcefully you lurch toward your suit-case. No matter how violent your lurch is, the most salient impression you (and your audience) should have is that of the hand isolated in space.

Performing this maneuver convincingly is a subtle issue. Your lurch should not appear deliberate or premeditated. It must take you by surprise. Therefore, it must appear as if something *outside* of your body caused you to lurch. To do this, fix your attention on the hand isolation and the sense-of-weight (the suitcase) holding that fist in place. When your attention is focused *primarily* on this sense-of-weight, the body is an afterthought. This way, the weight of the suitcase can and will take your body by surprise.

The next part of this illusion is *lifting* the suitcase. The suitcase comes off the floor right after your elbow straightens. Therefore, after your elbow straightens, the weight of that suit-case must read into your subsequent gestures. Immediately after your elbow has straightened, all of your next moves must be slower—they should (appear to!) require more effort.

After your right elbow has straightened, the suitcase lifts off the floor. Lean to the left (away from the suitcase) and extend your *left* arm out into space. Your lean and your extended *left* arm act as a counterweight. Plaster your right arm to the right side of your body.

In real life, the weight of your suitcase determines how far you have to lean *away* from your suitcase. In mime, the extent of your lean determines the weight of your suitcase. Whether you are working with a real object or an illusion, the heavier your suitcase, the more you have to lean away from it in order to lift it. The more weight you have to lift, the greater your counterweight has to be.

Some beginning mime students think they should indicate both the *shape* and the weight of the suitcase as they lift it. No matter how heavy their suitcase is, they always leave a space between their arm and the body to indicate the shape of the suitcase. As I said before, most of the mime illusions are more concerned with *forces* than they are with *objects*. In the suitcase illusion, the weight of the suitcase is more important than its shape. Therefore keep the suitcase-arm plastered to the side of the body. The insistence on showing its shape may actually interfere with the clarity of your illusion. For example, when you hold your working arm *away* from the body to indicate shape, you might be telling your audience that your suitcase isn't very heavy.

Putting a suitcase down is the reverse of lifting it up. Of course, the way you lower and/or lift a suitcase depends on the weight of that object. If it's heavy, you have to use your knees more than you would for a light suitcase. Let's suppose you are carrying a fairly heavy suitcase with your right arm and you want to lower the suitcase to the floor. Your right fist is clenched and your right arm is almost painfully straight. (The weight of your suitcase is constantly pulling your fist, arm, and shoulder down to the floor.)

Before you attempt to lower the suitcase, first make sure your right leg is directly under your right shoulder for balance. Then, tilt away from your suitcase as you lower the case to the floor. More specifically, lean your upper torso to the left. The more you lean to the left, the farther out to the side your left arm extends.

As you lean, lower your body by bending the right knee until your fist reaches an appropriate height. (The "appropriate height" is where your hand or suitcase handle should be when the *bottom* of your suitcase makes contact with the floor.) As soon as your hand reaches this height, the earth receives the weight of the suitcase and all the strain on your body disappears, instantly. The density of your previous moves suddenly disappears to indicate that the downward force of gravity no longer affects you. All of your joints return to a relaxed position. Your right arm, hand, and shoulder slacken. The upper torso, which had been leaning very far to the left, now bends comfortably to the right. (The torso bends to the right only during that brief moment *after* the earth receives the weight and *before* you let go of the handle.)

Now open your fist and straighten up.

Shift of Suitcase from One Hand to the Other: Begin with your suitcase lifted off the floor. In this starting position, plaster your right arm to the right side of your body. Lean your upper body to the left and extend your left arm out to the left side. No matter where your suitcase is in relation to your body,

**Shift of Suitcase
from One Hand
to the Other**

your torso must lean *away* from it. The suitcase is the weight;
your torso is the counterweight. As you bring the suitcase in
front of you, grasp the handle with both hands and lean back.
As you transfer the suitcase to your left, let go with your right
hand and lean to the right. Your final position should be the
reverse of your opening position: left arm plastered to the left
side of your body (left hand, arm, and shoulder pulling down
to the floor), upper body leaning to the right, and right arm
extending straight out from the shoulder.

Robot

   *This illusion was made famous by the mime team Shields
and Yarnell in the 1970s when these performers appeared regularly on television.*

   Your robot can be as crude or as sophisticated as you want
it to be. It may be a cheap import from Hong Kong or a techno-
logical breakthrough from a futuristic society. In either case,
the distinguishing characteristics of the robot are mindless-

ness, lifelessness, and a certain predictability of movement. The robot has no life or intelligence of its own. Its movements are mechanical, dry, and limited. The robot cannot stretch or overextend itself. It is never excited. There is no glint in its eye, no strain on its face, no feeling in its expression. As a matter of fact, you (as a robot) should feel that something is controlling you. An external and *distant* source of intelligence makes all of your decisions—initiates and terminates your every move.

Let's analyze a cheap toy robot. This robot moves by way of simple gear structures. It can move only one or two joints at a time and these joints move either up and down *or* sideways; they cannot move up, down, *and* sideways. They cannot move obliquely. The oblique movement requires much more sophisticated joint structures and engineering.

The quality of movement is characterized by a series of jolts or jerks whenever a movement starts or finishes. Mimes sometimes refer to each of these little jolts as a "tak" (pronounced "tahk"). If you picture a simple gear structure, you can understand why these little jolts or "taks" happen. It is the same principle described in many of the illusions: Whenever inertia is overcome, there is a slight, almost imperceptible little "bump."

To set a gear in motion, a moveable part must bump into that gear to overcome the gear's inertia and to set the gear in motion. Then once the gear is turning, its inertia must be overcome again to stop this action. At this point, there is another bump indicating that an equal and opposite force has overcome inertia and stopped the gear from turning.

Before you begin a series of movements (characteristic of the cheap robot), check all of your possibilities out separately. You decide what your robot can and cannot do based on the above stipulations. For example, maybe your robot's head can move in and out of three basic positions: straight forward, facing slightly left, and facing slightly right. Practice moving the head through these three basic positions. Feel the little jolt or "tak" initiating and terminating your movements. The jolt that initiates the movement will feel like a tightening or a build up of potential energy. Then the movement begins. The head turns slowly and deliberately from one position into the next. When it reaches its next position, it jolts into place as if it has reached a limit. An equal and opposite force has blocked its progress and caused the head to bump to a stop.

As you practice this, you will develop a *feel* for the robot. You will begin to understand the robot's dynamics. With this newly acquired affinity with the robot's dynamics comes empathy for the robot. You will suddenly know how it feels to be controlled or manipulated by a foreign, remote intelligence and to have no feelings, no interest, and no say in the matter.

After you have practiced the head movements, you should practice the arm and leg movements separately as well. Like the head, the arms and legs move by virtue of simple gear structures, but the gears for the limbs are larger and heavier than the gear for the head. Therefore, the little "taks" that happen at the beginning and end of a movement are a bit more pronounced for the limbs than they are for the head. In other words, the bigger the part, the bigger the "tak." The "head-tak" is soft, the "arm-tak" is ever-so-slightly more pronounced, and the "hip-tak" is the most pronounced.

When it's time to practice the robot-walk, you may simply "robotize" your normal walk by starting and finishing each step with a tak and by making each step slow and mechanical. Or you can try the following move for finesse: The ankle and knee joints of a cheap robot do not bend. Therefore, the robot slides its feet across the floor as it walks. An interesting effect is created when you plant your front foot into the floor and use the friction (of the foot against the floor) to *pull* the back foot forward. You are therefore *isolating* your front leg and using that leg as a lever to *drag* the back leg forward.

The first "tak" is created when the friction between the front foot and the floor overcomes the weight of the back leg, and the back leg begins dragging forward. The second "tak" comes when the friction (i.e., the *cause* of your drag) is removed. When this happens, the inertia of the drag is overcome and the foot stops moving forward.

The nature, character, and capabilities of your robot are a matter of personal choice. If your robot is more sophisticated than the version I just described, the jolts and jerks before and after a movement are softer, less pronounced. The sophisticated robot has more movement possibilities. This robot may even be able to move its hand in an arc to wash a window, say. The sophisticated robot may be able to move several parts of its body at once. Just remember that whether you move forward/back, side-to-side, or obliquely, every movement must have a definite beginning and a definite ending. You should not slur a straightforward movement into an arc-shaped gesture. There should be a deliberate stop and start between the two gestures—the two directions. Also, each part of the robot should appear to move independently of the other parts. Each

Illusionary Walk

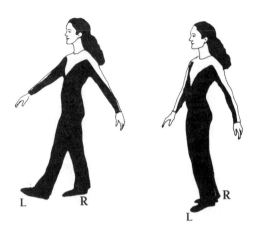

part moves in its own direction and at its own speed. The legs may walk quickly and steadily forward while the head turns slowly to the right and left, say. The head movement should not alter or interfere with the leg action in any way nor should the legs interfere with the head. Each part of the robot's body has a "mind" (a gear) of its own.

Illusionary Walk

In French, this illusion is called *marche en place* or, literally translated, walk in place. The illusionary walk allows the mime to walk without traveling. Using this invaluable choreographic tool, your character can walk to the store or walk to the ends of the earth without "eating up" all of your stage space. In many mime sketches, the illusion of traveling is enhanced by a moveable backdrop: the mime walks in place while the scenery changes behind him/her.

In my estimation, this is one of the most beautiful and ingenious mime illusions. I believe it was invented by my teacher, Etienne Decroux, but some people think the illusionary walk was invented by Jean-Louis Barrault, the actor/mime who perfected the illusion for the film *Children of Paradise*. It's difficult, if not impossible, to credit one person with the invention of a mime illusion. It seems that all of our minds operate on the same track, and all of us discover the same things, eventually.

In life, the object of walking is to move forward. In mime, the object of the illusionary walk is to stay in one place and *appear* to walk forward. Therefore, in the illusionary walk, the leg action must look the same as in the real walk, but somehow the traveling must be eliminated. Both of these require-

ments are fulfilled by the principle of translation. In the *real* walk, the straight leg is the leg you stand on and the bent leg moves through the air. In the *illusionary* walk, the straight leg is the leg that moves through the air and the bent leg is the leg you stand on. The principle is simple, but performing the illusion correctly requires strength, balance, coordination, and finesse.

Begin the illusionary walk as you would begin a real walk. Stand on the right leg, say, and extend the left leg in front of you as if you are about to step out on that left leg. At this point, both knees are straight.

Now the translation starts. Instead of stepping *out* to that straight left leg, bring that left leg back to you. (Keep the left knee absolutely straight as you bring it back.) The sole of your left foot should skim the floor as your left leg slides back. *While* (and I emphasize the word "*while*") the left foot is coming back, lift the heel of the right foot off the floor and bend the right knee. All three movements must happen *at the same time*: the right heel should lift, the right knee should bend, and the left leg should slide in—simultaneously.

Because the right heel continues to lift as your left leg slides back, that heel rises pretty far off the floor before the left leg is in place under you. You will discover that you need a tremendous amount of strength in your right leg as well as a good sense of balance. For this maneuver, all of your weight must be supported by the right leg even as you lift the right heel and bend the right knee.

Once the left leg is directly under you (straight up and down under the hip), you can now shift your weight onto that left leg and extend or unfold the right leg out in front of you.

Repeat the whole process balancing on the bent left leg as you pull the straight right leg back.

Finesse: After these basic movements are comfortable, you can add the appropriate arm gesture. Whenever you extend a leg forward, the opposite arm should extend forward too. This should be a very slight and comfortable extension. As the bent leg receives your weight and the straight leg slides back, your body should list very slightly over the straight leg. The fact that your torso is inclined toward the straight leg indicates that you are entrusting that straight leg with your weight. (Of course this is an illusion since your straight leg is lifted slightly *off* the floor.)

It is a challenge to make this arm movement look natural and relaxed. You must *believe* you are walking somewhere. Focus on a "destination"—notice the landscape change around you. Do anything, but don't let your audience see that you are concentrating very hard on your arms and legs.

The illusionary walk is a beautiful illusion, but it's rarely used on stage. When this illusion is performed well, the movements are too stylized and too classical to fit most characters. (Pierrot would walk this way, but a typical pedestrian, never.) In performance, most mimes use a scaled-down version of the illusionary walk. (See definition of "composite illusion" on page 103.) The scaled-down version consists of a simple shift of weight from one foot to the other, combined with an upper-torso indication of walking. The torso action for this illusion is exactly the same as the torso action during a real walk. Therefore to teach the illusion, I have students walk normally. Then I tell them to continue the movement, but stop traveling. This way, the correct torso action continues as they shift their weight from one foot to the other.

Climbing Stairs

Climbing stairs is a fairly straightforward illusion. It consists of a simple foot action combined with a simple hand action.

Whether you are ascending or descending stairs, the foot and knee action is the same. It is a simple shifting of weight from one foot to another. (The knees simply pass each other, similar to the action described in the ladder illusion.) The knee is bent and the heel of one foot is slightly lifted off the floor. Now press your weight through the ball of the foot and lower the heel to the floor. (Straighten the knee as the heel lowers.) While you are doing this, the other heel lifts and knee

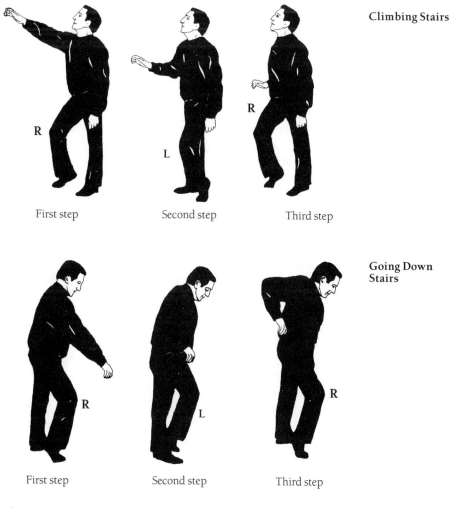

Climbing Stairs

First step   Second step   Third step

Going Down Stairs

First step   Second step   Third step

bends. Repeat these moves in succession to show that you are stepping up or down stairs.

Do not travel forward as you move your feet and do not bob up and down. There is only a small, barely perceptible shifting of weight from one foot to the other. Lean slightly over the working foot.

The precise hand action depends on whether you are going up or down the stairs. If you are traveling up, extend one arm up and out in front of you to grab a part of the banister. As you step with your feet, the hand holding onto the bannister travels down and toward you in a straight line (tracing the line and angle of the bannister). The speed with which you lower that hand depends, of course, on the speed with which you step. Remember that the hand-movement and the knee-movement begin and end together.

To go down stairs, extend your arm *down* from your shoulder. As you step, the hand holding the bannister travels *up* toward you in a straight line (in line with the bannister).

To create the illusion of running, full speed, up or down stairs, use the "blurring" technique (see page 102). During the blur, you don't have to emphasize each step and you don't have to worry about the hand/knee coordination. Simply grab the bannister and run in place—top speed—as the hand travels up or down the bannister (depending on whether you are going up or down the stairs). As you reach the end of your stairway, break the illusion by removing your hand from the bannister and walking or running naturally.

Eagle

The eagle is a beautiful, classic illusion. The sense of flight and empathy for the eagle are essential parts of the technique.

Begin this illusion with your arms extended out to the side and with your body curved forward so that your head and upper torso indicate the horizontal position of the flying eagle's body. Your arms are your wings, and you should believe that they are the most substantial part of your body. They extend far, far out into space.

When I first performed this illusion in the studio, something was wrong. My wings looked insubstantial and weak. They certainly did not look strong enough to support the weight of my body in flight. Then I realized that if an eagle were *my* size, its wings would be at least thirty feet long. This, then, became my premise. As I moved my wings, I believed that they were thirty feet long. This gave my arm-movements the power, the tempo, and the majestic quality of the eagle's wings.

It is also helpful to think of the air as a dense substance around you. Think of pushing against the air or floating on top of it. Sometimes an air current surges up under one arm and pushes you sideways. No matter what you do, the air is your medium and your wings are your leverage.

Try this exercise in "believing" before moving on to the actual illusion: Assume the opening position with your upper torso inclined forward and your arms extended sideways. Now, simply lift your heels off the floor and rise to your toes. When you do this, you are pushing up from the floor. Now try something else: Let your *premise* (i.e., the air and the sense-of-flight)

Eagle

do the work. Assume the opening position and feel the *air* surge up and under your arms to lift you to your toes. Notice and appreciate the difference between *pushing* off the earth (from your feet) and *being lifted* off the earth by your belief. At no time during the flight-illusion, should you feel that your movements are initiated by your feet; everything begins with your wings and the air currents.

The first move is a simple up-and-down movement of the wings. This should be majestic and slow. As you push your wings *down*, press against the air and lift yourself up—that is, rise to your toes, but maintain the original crouched position. As your arms *lift*, lower your body and replace your heels on the floor.

After you have mastered this move, you can begin to experiment with air currents. In this part of the illusion, the air is going to surge under one wing and push you side ways. Let's say the wind surges under your *right* arm. Experience the idea of wind billowing under your right armpit. This billow is strong enough to push you to the left.

Float (walk) sideways to the left as if you are flying, until the billow of air travels past you and lifts the other side of your body. The air empties out from under your right arm pit. Therefore, your sideways momentum to the left decreases as the billow of air empties out from under the right wing to pick up under the left wing. As your left upper arm lifts, you should also experience the force of the air current pushing you to the right.

Imitating the eagle's intense stare is a good lesson for the mime, as well. Most of the beginning mimes I've seen think that the eagle looks angry. They therefore knit their eyebrows and pretend to be mad at someone or something. They don't look like eagles this way.

If you ask yourself *why* the eagle looks the way it does, you discover that its eyes are piercing and intense because the eagle can see very, very far away. The eagle is not angry or mad; it hunts from the sky and it has to focus intensely on tiny rodents way off in the distance. The imperative to survive (capture its food), combined with the phenomenal acuity of its vision, *causes* the eagle's eyes to appear almost mad. The stare resembles anger, but it's very far away from *being* anger.

• • •

When a mime illusion is correctly used, it is *never* the primary focus of the audience's attention. The audience will notice the illusion and admire it, but the primary focus of their attention must be the *relevance* of the illusion or the *theme* of the sketch—the "humanity" or the life-force behind everything you do.

For example, I tell all of my students, "no one goes up stairs." In life, no one goes up stairs; the person is either going somewhere or getting something, and climbing the stairs is an insignificant part of that whole event. (An exception to this might be the small child who sees the staircase as a challenge and climbs it for the adventure and the experience.) Therefore, when you perform an illusion on stage the audience's attention must focus on your character—the mood he's in and his reasons for going up stairs. The illusion by itself is uninteresting. Only the real-life situation can animate the illusion—bring it to life.

Vocabulary Words Pertaining to the Mime Illusions

The Blur: Normally, every mime illusion consists of many details. The opening of a door, for example, is a complicated maneuver. First, the hand reaches for the doorknob. (The curve of the hand must be slightly wider than the curve of the knob.) Next, the hand contracts as it fastens on the doorknob. The hand then turns the knob. The door opens and swings in an arc comparable to the size of the door. The person enters the doorway and lets go of the doorknob at precisely the right moment. Finally, the person either closes the door or lets it stay open. If the person chooses to *close* the door, there is another series of details to learn and master.

In real life you rarely see a person belabor the act of opening a door. Likewise, on stage the mime should rarely belabor the illusion. Therefore, once you have mastered the illusions, you should learn how to minimize your gestures or "throw them away."

The "blur" is what the word implies. It is when all of the details of an illusion—such as those described in the first paragraph—are condensed, minimized, or blurred together.

Blurring is an important technique for the mime. For one thing, it saves time by abridging the generic illusions. Blurring may also enhance the credibility of your sketches, since most of your characters are probably "regular people" who perform mundane maneuvers quickly, nonchalantly, and unconsciously. If your characters act this way, these qualities should read into your illusions.

Priority: It is important to be aware of your character's priorities while you perform a mime sketch. You must know what is first and foremost on your character's mind. From here you can judge how much emphasis to give to the illusions.

Etienne Decroux, one of my early mime teachers, used the analogy of a candlestick to explain the concept of "priorities" to his students. Decroux maintained that intelligence is measured by how long and how intently the character looks at the objects he's handling. If a simpleton, for example, were to pick up a candlestick, that stick would take top priority in his attention. His eyes would remain glued to the object. A more intelligent character wouldn't have to concentrate so intently on the candlestick. He could turn his eyes away from the object sooner. Finally, the most intelligent person would handle the candlestick with extreme dexterity without ever having to focus on it.

A six year old making a scrambled egg for his mother on Mother's Day would not handle an egg with the flare and confidence of a master chef. The way someone handles an object, reveals *who* that person is and what's first and foremost in his/her mind.

Composite Illusion: When you first learn an illusion, you learn the bare-bones, generic version. The illusions still need to be "fleshed out" before they are stageworthy. They have to reflect your character. During the fleshing-out process, the generic illusion goes through many changes until the end product often doesn't look anything like the generic version. I call this end product a "composite illusion."

The illusionary walk is a perfect example of how the generic illusion changes to form a composite illusion. The description of the illusionary walk given on page 96 covers, simply, the mechanics of walking. It does not reveal *who* is walking, where, or why. If you were Pierrot walking in the moonlight, you wouldn't have to change the basic illusion very much. But, a 98-year-old woman would not walk this way. Perfectly straight legs, supple feet, and a carefree swing of the arms do not *say* "old woman."

In this case, the generic illusion would have to be modified to fit your character. You would probably want to keep the knees slightly bent, the ankle bones and feet immobile, the back and shoulders slouched. The end product, then, is the composite illusion—a feeble shifting of weight back and forth with a bare minimum of movement.

Composite illusion: The synthesis of a generic illusion, a character's personality, and the specific needs of your sketch forming a whole new illusion.

Poetic License: There are very few rules in mime technique that *can't* be broken. Since you are not dealing with actual, solid objects, you can concern yourself more with the *appearance* of reality than reality itself. The literary poet is not bound to rigid rules about grammar and syntax. Likewise, kinetic poets (mimes) are not bound to any rigid rules about how the physical world behaves.

For example, if you were a burglar sneaking into a house, you might have to open a door at some point. There's nothing wrong with opening a door and sneaking into the room *at the same time*. You might walk ten feet into the room and still have the doorknob in your hand. No one will mind that you can't do this with a "real" door. If it serves the theme of your sketch, you can do anything you want with your technique. As a mime, your poetic license is one of the most valuable tools you have. Practice using it and enjoy how compelling and malleable the physical world can be.

5

CHARACTER
WORK

Tony in his
"Baseball" sketch,
1993.
(Photo by C.C.
Church)

L ife is synonymous with self-expression. "Being alive"
means "being expressed." This is the character's dilemma. The character has no life of its own; it can't express
itself. It needs your life in order to express itself. A character
needs your mind in order to think, your lungs in order to
breathe, and your body in order to move. Likewise, if you don't
give the character your mind, breath, and body, *you* won't
know how to express yourself as this character.

Paradoxically, when you do not loan *all* of yourself to your
character, you have to treat your character as a separate entity
and *speculate* on his/her feelings, thoughts, and behavior.
While you're busy speculating on your character's behavior,
you can never move and speak spontaneously. But if you "*give
in*" to your character, if you let the character "get to you," then
the correct thoughts, words, and actions will *occur* to you, as if
by magic.

**Bringing a
Character
to Life**

These are the terms of the actor/character alliance. If they are met, everyone is happy. The character comes to life and reveals new things to you *about you*. You, in turn, are shown off to your advantage. The audience is happy because they thoroughly believe you, your performance, and your character.

Character work is not the simple imitation of effects (i.e., facial expressions, mannerisms, and affectations). It's not a matter of memorizing a few mug-shots and gestures and then reproducing these on stage. If it were this, then every mimic and every impersonator would be a brilliant artist. In order to play a character convincingly, you must get to know your character so well and so intimately that the audience can't tell where your life ends and your character's life begins. Character work is an exercise in empathy.

> **empathy** - 1. The attribution of feelings aroused by an object in nature or art to the object itself, as when one speaks of a painting full of love. 2. Understanding so intimate that the feelings, thoughts, and motives of one are readily comprehended by another.
> —*American Heritage Dictionary*

The practice of empathy brings the performer, the audience, and the subject matter together into one life, one moment, one event. When you know what *true* empathy is and how to practice it, you will discover that there is really no separation between you, your character, and the audience.

Perhaps you've heard a fantastic singer on the radio, and his/her performance first incites you to think, "What a wonderful voice!" In my estimation, that performance has not been successful.

Edith Piaf, for example, has a wonderful voice, but this is not the first thing I hear when she sings. I hear Paris, romance, earthiness, the pain and rapture of being in love, and *then*, I think, "What a wonderful voice!" I can think this now because she has touched me personally. I haven't noticed that she is a superior human being or that she's separate from me in any way. A great artist reminds his/her audience that we're all participants in the same life.

Acting is not a split-personality experience. You're not being possessed or manipulated by various characters. When you practice empathy, you find that you can play Adolf Hitler just as convincingly as you can play Albert Schweitzer. Your judgment of your characters and your personal preference of one character over the other can be consciously suspended whenever you want them to be. This ability to empathize with all of humanity at will paradoxically gives you a profound sense of your own identity. You realize that you can *choose* who-you-are.

Empathy is the conscious yielding to a character's belief system and your conscious subjection to the laws of that system. But since this is a *conscious* decision and not some blind emotional impulse, you can never be tricked into doing the unconscionable. Once your sketch is over, the need for your characterization is over and you are no longer subject to your character's point of view.

Two mimes may be on stage performing the exact same illusion. Their bodies and gestures may be identical, yet one mime captures the audience's attention and the other doesn't. One performance enlivens the audience's imagination, and the other doesn't. One performance is believable and lifelike. The other performance is unbelievable and lifeless. The factor missing in the latter's performance is empathy.

The Empathy Factor

Empathy is *essential* to mime technique. In any other art form, technical skill alone is enough to momentarily impress an audience. Not so in mime. If empathy is lacking from the mime's performance, the technique falls flat. It looks static, clichéd, almost ludicrous.

I do not mean to imply that learning mime is a formidable task. All people are fundamentally empathic beings, and all of us would practice empathy if we knew what it could do for us. Empathy is more than just a moral attribute; it's a powerful tool for gaining insight into human nature. Such insight is absolutely essential to success in any field.

Every summer, a few people from New York City come to study with me at The Barn.[7] One summer, one of these students stood up in front of the class and did a mime of a cow. When he was done, I asked him, "Do you know what a cow is?"

Empathy is the Ability to "See" Life

The student shrugged and said, "Yeah" (as if to say, "Of course I know what a cow is"). I took him over to Starbird's farm next door and told him to stand next to one of the cows. He was impressed—and admitted he hadn't known what a cow was before this experience.

---

[7]The Celebration Barn in South Paris, Maine, is an internationally acclaimed theatre and school that I founded in 1971. It is presently owned and operated by Carolyn Brett. I am the artistic director.

Another student, Ledlie Borgerhoff, came to me instinctively knowing the importance of empathy in stage work. Without my telling her to do this, Ledlie spent hours in Starbird's field watching the cows. After a few days of studying her subject, she came back to the barn and performed a cow. The rest of the class was spellbound.

What was remarkable about Ledlie's cow was that she had captured its temperament. Her cow depicted the "long-suffering" complacency characteristic of *all* cows. Later that week, when she performed her cow in front of an audience, it literally stopped the show.

Through empathy, Ledlie discovered the vital connection between herself and the cow. From this fundamental understanding of nature (her own as well as the cow's), she was able to represent the outward form of the cow accurately. For example, a cow typically walks with disjointed hips—the hips appear to slide in and out of place as it walks. When Ledlie's hips moved, they suggested resignation, lethargy. The hips were not a separate, isolated effect; they were an intrinsic part of the cow's character.

> **integrity** - 1. Rigid adherence to a code of behavior; probity. 2. The state of being unimpaired, soundness. 3. Completeness; unity. —See synonyms at **honesty**. [Middle English integrite, from Old French, from Latin *integritas,* completeness, purity, from *integer,* whole. See **integer**.]
> —*The American Heritage Dictionary*

Ledlie didn't need to crawl on her hands and knees as she walked. Often, she stood on two feet and held her arms out in mid air as if she were walking on them. She could have done anything, as by now she had captured the cow's temperament and everything she did in this vein looked "correct."

. . .

Once, many years ago, I was on stage performing a giraffe for children. The first few times I performed the giraffe, I tried to show its height. As I walked around the stage, trying to make myself taller and taller, I knew that the children were not seeing a giraffe. They were seeing some guy walking across the stage on tiptoe. I learned then that height, by itself, doesn't say "giraffe." Height is relative; if I'm the only one on stage, no one notices how *tall* I am.

I knew I'd have to change my approach in order to make my giraffe recognizable—*believable*. I asked myself the same thing I would ask a student: "What *is* a giraffe? What are its

Razzmatazz! in the late 1970s. From left to right: Ledlie Borgerhoff, Carolyn DeNigris, and Gretchen Berg. (Courtesy of Carolyn DeNigris)

essential qualities?" In answer to this question, I recalled a safari program I had seen on TV. Watching the giraffes in this program, I had been struck by the sweet, graceful way these animals "deferred" to the trees. I remembered the giraffe's *character* —its temperament. I didn't remember the outward, physical appearance of the giraffe; I remembered how *I felt* watching him.

The next time I performed, I remembered the qualities of the giraffe and moved from this memory. As I moved, I felt that I was "above it all" by virtue of my sweetness. I wasn't worried about my height anymore; I carried the giraffe's "attitude," its comportment. I dipped and rotated my torso slowly with each step, bowing to the trees. The children watched with rapt attention. I knew they were accepting *this* performance—they *saw* a giraffe. More specifically, they saw *me* as a giraffe and they identified with *my* character.

Another remarkable thing happened as a result of experiencing giraffe-ness. I found myself bending at the hips as I walked. Later, I realized *why* this happened. Since the neck makes up about half the giraffe's height, my animal's neck started at my hips (the *mid-section* of my body). In other words, my empathy for the giraffe and my attention to my own feelings were determining the outward shape of my body without my having to worry about it. (This is another example of premise-at-work. My premise had been empathy for the giraffe, and this premise produced the appropriate "conclusions" as long as I *stayed tuned* to it.)

The Class: Image Work as Inspired by the Writings of Constantin Stanislavski

As I search for a graceful way to broach the subject of image work, my thoughts turn to my predecessors and all that I have learned from their work. Not all of my predecessors called themselves "mimes." As a matter of fact, many of them would have rejected this title if it were given to them. But they all had one thing in common: All of them wanted to know how to make something look *real* on stage. They wanted to know how to *convince* —how to *persuade* an audience.

The "passionate pursuit of the real" inevitably leads to unequivocal conclusions. It makes no difference whether you are a mime, a pianist, a photographer, or a pediatrician; all artists begin to discover the same unequivocal truths about their work. They discover that greatness has more to do with morality and correct thinking than it has to do with technical proficiency or physical attributes.

Some artists won't discuss the deep inner workings of their work, either because they don't understand it or because they're afraid to sound maudlin. Spencer Tracy, for example, when asked to reveal the secret of good acting, said something to the effect: "Remember the lines and don't bump into the furniture." Anyone who has seen Spencer Tracy work knows that he had a profound understanding of acting. (Perhaps he understood its simplicity?) But he obviously didn't want to discuss this understanding—not in public, anyway.

But when great artists *do* talk about "artistry," they invariably allude to such faculties as honesty, awareness, humility, persistence, empathy, vulnerability, spontaneity, courage, the appreciation of beauty. They discover that these moral, mental attributes have practical uses in their work and on the stage. François Delsarte discovered that certain "laws of aesthetics" determine every movement of the body (see pages 123–129). Herbert Whone, a renowned musician, talked about the "power of let." Michael Chekov taught vulnerability to his acting students. Constantin Stanislavski discovered the practical uses of the imagination....

When I first read *An Actor Prepares* (by Stanislavski), I, too, was beginning to suspect that the imagination could be an invaluable tool for mimes—*if* they learned how to use it. Stanislavski discovered some specific and practical guidelines for the uses and abuses of the imagination. I encourage anyone who is interested in this topic to read Stanislavski's work. You may discover aspects of his teachings that speak directly to you. But here, I would like to talk about my interpretation and my specific application of his work.

All of theatre depends upon the imagination. A play, a piece of choreography, a mime sketch, a set design, or a costume first takes shape in the mind. According to Stanislavski, all of theatre begins with the big "*if*."

"You know that our work on a play begins with the use of *if* as a lever to lift us out of everyday life onto the plane of the imagination."[8]

Experience has taught me that the imagination is a two-edged sword. Sometimes, the imagination is an *escape* from reality. It's a make-believe world, precisely fashioned to conform to the person's fears and fancies. This is not the imagination we want to develop in theatre. The correct use of the imagination warrants vulnerability, attentiveness, and courage. In many ways it is a *confrontation* with reality rather than an escape from it.

The correct use of the imagination is like watching an image slowly appear on the screen of consciousness. You pick up a spark of inspiration. At first this spark is very dim, but you grasp it (ever so gently) with your attention. Then, under the nurturing influence of that attention, the image begins to unfold. It begins to take shape, it moves, it escalates and progresses, and you have to watch it closely because you are never quite sure what it will do next. This process requires so much attentiveness, that you actually forget any ego-based fears or distractions as you follow your image—your imagination.

The exercise called "image work" was inspired by Stanislavski's writings. I designed this exercise on the spur of

[8]Stanislavski, Constantin, *An Actor Prepares*, trans. Edith Reynolds Hapgood (New York: Theatre Arts Books, 1983), p. 51.

the moment when I encountered a problem in one of my classes. A student (several students actually) expressed extreme frustration at not being able to write sketches. I immediately understood that the student was not using his imagination. This realization acted like a bugle call, summoning up the information I needed to solve this problem. I remembered Stanislavski's ideas and designed this exercise, then and there.

In this exercise two or three people (maybe more, depending on the size of the class) take center stage. They sit quietly with their eyes closed for two or three minutes. During this time, I ask them to "empty out"—let the mind rest in a neutral position. I sometimes refer to this preliminary stage of the exercise as "I AM" work.

I AM work means that you experience your own *presence* and nothing else. Everything you know or think about yourself falls away and the only impression that holds your attention is the thought: "I am."

Typically, our own sense of being is attached to myriad predications:

I am *a mime.*
I am *too fat.*
I am *hungry.*
I am *in a hurry.*
I am *happy. etc.*

But during I AM work, you want to let go of predications. You want to experience the I AM all by itself. You are like an idling motor, disengaged from the world, your history, your dreams, desires, and opinions. You're in a neutral position, ready to shift into any gear as the moment dictates.

One day I was teaching image work to four or five students. We had progressed through the I AM part. Theoretically, all of them were in a neutral state of being. Then I asked them to imagine a cockroach. When one of the students reacted with disgust, I knew she had not found the pure, unadulterated "I am" part of her being. The other students didn't flinch. The word cockroach had no connotations for them. Their opinions, tastes, and prejudices had fallen away from their sense of self. They were prepared for anything.

After the students have attained neutrality (two or three minutes is ample time for this), I call out the name of an animal or a character, etc. There is still no movement. The students remain seated with their eyes closed as they watch the animal or character slowly appear in front of their mind's eye.

Let's suppose we are working with the word "gorilla." After you (the student) have heard the word, you take another two or three minutes to simply *watch* the gorilla come into focus. You picture its weight, its smell, its size, coloring, breathing, etc. Then, when I say "go," you must do *exactly* what your gorilla is doing. Don't do more or less than that. Don't get ahead of your gorilla and start doing stereotypical movements. Simply *imitate* your imagination. This should be an absolute, non-theatrical, non-original, *rank* imitation of the picture in your mind.

I usually let this process continue for five to ten minutes. Sometimes I add another "ingredient" to the imagined scenario (i.e., "A kid is throwing pebbles at you" or "Something has frightened you."). Now you must *watch* and *imitate* your own personal gorilla as it reacts to the situation I have just suggested. Do not try to imagine how a generic gorilla would behave. In the first place, there is no such thing as a *generic* gorilla. And in the second place, you shouldn't *try* to do anything. There should be no trying—no effort. You don't want to *force* or manipulate anything. You want only to observe and follow the images as they occur on the screen of your own consciousness.

The beauty of this exercise (and many of the exercises I teach) is that you don't have to repeat it every day. Even after one session, you will have learned the *process*, and this understanding will stay with you. These exercises are not like calisthenics that require constant repetition and ritual. These exercises are events. They change your approach to your work.

Once you know what it *feels* like to pay scrupulous attention to your own mind and to follow the images that appear there, you will have an easier time writing sketches, creating characters, choreographing, etc.

One of the most common mistakes in image work is to lose touch with one's image—to let that image lapse in and out of focus. When a distracting thought (i.e., self-consciousness or doubt) interferes with your clear view of that image, this creates a stuttering effect—that is, you look dumbfounded or "vacant" until you can refocus on your image.

This mistake is easy to correct. Simply don't allow anything to take your attention away from your image. And don't allow anything to stop you from *following* that image. This should be one, continuous, uninterrupted process—watching and following.

Image Work: Breaking Through the Ego Barrier

When your attention remains fixed and focused, a wonderful thing happens. You eventually "break through the ego barrier." (This is how many of my students describe the phenomenon after they have experienced it.)

The unbroken stream of attention is extremely powerful. When it remains fixed and focused on a premise, a task, an ideal, an image, it chips away at obstacles even if you are not consciously aware of any progress. Then suddenly you break through. In image work, the obstacle is the ego and this yields readily to the constancy of your attention.

The "view" from the other side of the ego-barrier will surprise you. You will suddenly know what to do and how to think. And everything you do and think will be correct, convincing. You won't have to ask anyone, "Was that good?" You (and your audience) will *know* it was good.

Usually a success in image work is so obvious that no one discusses it. It happens, everyone *sees* it happen, and that's that. But when I told one of my students, Sherry Lee Hunter, about writing this section, she told me what "breaking-through-the-ego-barrier" felt like for her.

I remembered the event she described. We were doing image work in class and I asked Sherry to imagine a rabbit. Her initial reaction was typical—she doubted herself. She had never studied a rabbit; how would she know what to do? But she sat quietly for a few minutes as a rabbit appeared in her imagination. Then she started copying the rabbit as it moved in her mind's eye. All of us watching noticed that she was not staying tuned to her image. She would stop moving and we'd see Sherry again, wondering what to do next.

We talked about making sure that the process of watching-and-following remains unbroken. She started again and after a few seconds, she "broke through." This was as obvious to us as it was to Sherry. Suddenly, all of her movements looked authentic, convincing. She was no longer trying to *look like* a rabbit; Sherry and the rabbit were a single entity.

This was the event as we, the audience, experienced it. But Sherry told me now that the ego barrier became something palpable when she broke through it. It was like crossing a threshold: on one side was distraction and doubt, on the other side was clarity and ease. When she was on the other side, she had "rabbit thoughts." She experienced fear and timidity. She knew what it felt like to be stalked.

Whenever I do image work, I become very fond of my creature. I always discover something *new* about the animal I am playing, something I never thought about before. At one point in my career, I had to play a fly on stage. Before I choreographed my moves, I did image work on the fly. As the fly came into focus and as I followed this image, I suddenly felt very, very tidy. My fly was always cleaning himself, preening his wings and scrubbing his little legs. I saw his tiny, little neck no bigger than a hair, his blue-bottle eyes reflecting a whole spectrum of colors, and I *liked* this character. He was proper, tidy, and earnest.

Incidentally, my fly was a big hit on stage. He did nothing spectacular or impressive, but all of the movements *originated* in image work. They came from my honest empathy for the fly and my willingness to let the *image* (my imagination) lead and dictate my moves. The audience adored that fly and I liked him a lot, too.

After you've broken through the ego barrier, you realize your oneness with the character, creature, or thing you're playing. And your audience enjoys this affinity with you.

Image Work and Freedom

Stanislavski's ideas and techniques made the task of *persuading* an audience much less mysterious and elusive. But the beneficial effects of this work extend beyond theatre. Everyone would do well to study his/her own imagination, to learn more about what it is and how to use it. The imagination plays a crucial role in deciding our thoughts and actions, but often this imagination takes us for a ride. It *uses* us. We become almost hypnotized by its charms and devices until our thoughts flow incessantly along old familiar ruts and patterns, likes and dislikes, fantasies and nightmares. Then we wonder why nothing exceptional, memorable, or thought-provoking ever happens to us.

In the arts, in theatre, you learn how to confront and *use* the imagination. Watching the imagination is like watching a thief—under surveillance, a thief can't steal anything. Likewise, under surveillance, your imagination can't lull you into a stupor and waste your time.

Once you begin watching your own mind, you also discover that those old "karmic tracks" that you used to run on unconsciously are not law. You don't have to submit to any fatalistic or limited view of your own potential.

And finally, I think one of the most valuable aspects of image work is that it frees you from the character you are playing. I have a saying: "Whatever you can *do*, you're *not*." If you can *perform* a murderer convincingly, you are *not* a murderer. I know this is a very bold assertion; I often exaggerate when I'm teaching in order to make a point. But there is some truth to this. Let me explain:

The murderer is created by the thoughts he/she entertains. More specifically, a heinous act is created by the *blind submission* to certain thoughts. The unchallenged, unscrupulous imagination eventually "robs" the person of his/her innate ability to reason correctly and act morally.

As you develop the empathy and skill necessary to play a wide variety of characters, you gain a certain objectivity. You appreciate the fact that you always have options. You realize that your thoughts and feelings are malleable and governed by choice. Despicable characters have forgotten this important fact. They automatically assume that their thoughts and feelings are valid, so they *believe* them and submit to their designs. The longer negative thoughts go unchallenged and unscrutinized, the more they usurp their "host" and rob the individual of his/her natural and peaceful problem-solving abilities.

The *blind submission* to the imagination—*not* the imagination itself—*creates* the murderer. As a matter of fact, the blind submission to the imagination is the creator of all despicable personalities. Therefore, if you become wise to the imagination, you will not be its pawn. The *conscious* exercise of the imagination means freedom from its mindless, fraudulent designs. And when the imagination is used correctly it is a joy, a revelation, and an indispensable tool for all artists.

Character Work

Character work is the process of "trying on" a new personality, a new attitude about life, a new way of thinking, and moving. You have to suspend your own opinions and inclinations as you *let* this new personality borrow your feelings, thoughts, and behavior.

But character work is not the process of *becoming* someone else. It's not a disappearing act in which *you* vanish into thin air and "The Character" moves in to take your place. Remember: The character, as a separate entity, does not exist. It has no life of its own, no history, no feelings, no thoughts. It needs your history, feelings, and thoughts in order to come to life. When your character appears to move, think, and feel things, it is actually *you* moving, thinking, and feeling things.

Empathy in reference to character work means that everything you do on stage must come from you and your natural affinity with the role you're playing. Every time you perform, every time you step into another character's shoes or another animal's skin, you discover an aspect of yourself you never knew existed. Empathy brings more of you out into the open. It awakens dormant thoughts and feelings, and reminds you of your natural affinity with everyone and everything around you.

preconception - 1. An opinion or conception formed in advance of actual knowledge.
—*American Heritage Dictionary*

The Pre-Conception: The Stillbirth

Beginning mimes often try to reproduce a static photograph of their subjects. They play "show and tell" by getting up in front of the class and "aping" their subjects. This is not mime.

It is important to remember that mime is a reflection of life, and that life is much more than the *outward* appearance of a living thing. For example, suppose you want to do a mime of a tiger. The way a tiger looks to the eyes and sounds to the ears, the way it behaves are all *effects* of the tiger; they are not the cause of the tiger. An effect without a cause is a corpse.

You cannot presume to know what a tiger is if your information is based solely on how it appears from the outside—that is, how it appears to the physical senses. You must know how the tiger *feels* on the inside. You have to know its point of view.

This ability to see life from another's point of view is not only essential to a convincing performance, it also launched my teaching career back in the early 1960s.

When I was just starting out in the mime profession, I realized I needed to *teach* in order to improve my own understanding of what I was doing. I applied at several acting schools, but was turned down; no one could imagine what mime had to do with acting.

Then I approached Lonny Chapman at the Curt Conway School of Acting in New York City. He was very nice but said, "I don't see how mime could benefit the actor. We use our voice on stage and props; mimes don't use either." I asked him if I could show him my work to demonstrate its value to the actor. He agreed and let me come back the following night to perform for his acting students.

The next night, in front of about twenty students, I demonstrated a few illusions. Everyone enjoyed the work but Lonny said, "That's all very well and good, Tony. You're a talented mime, but we don't need that. We need *acting* skills."

I said, "Well, I think there's a common ground here. For one thing, I can perform animals, and I think that an understanding of the animal's feelings can be used in character work—the anger of a tiger, the treachery of a hyena, the deceitfulness of a snake ...."

This interested Lonny. "Yes, that's good. We do that in acting. We often take on animal qualities. What can you show us in this area?"

I had performed the tiger on stage before this, and had already been using the techniques of "premise" and "believing" without realizing it. Whenever I perform an animal, I take on the animal's point of view. I did this even then. I learned later that they call this "method acting," but I didn't know at the time that there was a name for this technique.

In front of the class, I got down on my hands and knees and began pacing back and forth. On hindsight, I realize I was also using Michael Chekov's technique of the "psychological gesture" (see page 29). In front of the class, I assumed the shape of the tiger and one of its actions (pacing) and then I let this "get to me." I felt my relaxation deepen. My chest sagged down between my shoulder blades. My face darkened. I felt the tiger come over me.

I paced back and forth as if I were a tiger in a cage. I looked at the students and within a few seconds, I didn't like any of them. As a *tiger*, I didn't like them. In other words this hate was not my *personality* hating the students; it was the tiger's nature. There was nothing pathological or personal about it.

I felt the tiger's resentment of people; he was afraid of them, but he could devour them in seconds if he ever got out of that cage. He glowered at them, not with human hatred, but with simple, constant, and natural imperative.

I was pacing back and forth (still on all fours) and I knew that I had their attention. Then I remembered my purpose for being there. I knew I should make the transition from "mime" to "acting."

This is the unique power of premise work: ideas come to you at precisely the right time. These thoughts are not distractions; they are *insights* into what you're doing. They're always appropriate, unpredictable, and timely.

I slowly stood up on two feet, menacingly—still carrying the tiger's point of view even as my body assumed a human posture. I moved right up to the students, stopped, and glowered at them. There wasn't a sound in the room. I stood stock-still for about ten seconds and then with a hiss, I lurched at them, leaping forward about three feet.

The reaction was tremendous. All the students—every one of them—literally jumped out of their chairs. Then all of us cracked up laughing.

"That's it!" Lonny said. "That's acting."

"That's what *you* call it," I said. "I call it mime...." Twelve students enrolled in my first mime class that night and this was the beginning of my teaching career.

Empathy is not Vicariousness

Vicarious acting is not good. (Vicarious acting is when the actor tries to literally *become* the character.) I've seen vicarious acting on stage and it was a disturbing spectacle.

A friend of mine and I went to see a production of the play *Zoo Story*. We were sitting in the front row. The actor playing the psychopath was *lost* in his work, and the audience feared for its own safety. We weren't afraid of his *character*, because we couldn't see his character. We were afraid of the *actor*; he looked as if he might "snap" any minute. My friend and I got up and moved to the back of the theatre. Later, we heard in the news that this actor did hurt a couple of his fellow actors on stage.

On another occasion, I saw an *artist* in the same role. Never once did I doubt the sincerity of his character, and never once did I fear for my own safety.

When a performer is lost in his/her work, this may be convincing (i.e., it may look "real"), but it's strangely unnatural. You, in the audience, want to turn your head. It's as if we're being forced to witness something we're not supposed to see.

In vicarious acting, the person is lost. He has lost himself in the work. There is no longer an artist up there. Personally, I don't think that getting lost is ever useful, not even for therapeutic reasons. In truth, the Artist is never lost and never *pretends* to be. In every one of us there is an inner eye, an Artist, watching over the various states and stages of our experience, making sure that everything is all right.

The Earned Gesture

I have coined this phrase to indicate the difference between an imitation and the real thing. Imitations are borrowed or plagiarized. The real thing is earned—you've made it your own.

When I see mimes copy or imitate Marceau (or each other), I often have the impression that they are simply duplicating a series of effects. They have not *earned* Marceau's gestures, they have copied them. Sometimes the imitation looks exactly like

Robert Post in per-
formance.
(Photo by Doug
Martin)

the real thing on the surface, but there is a subtle *quality* missing from the imitation.

In the first few rehearsals of a sketch, it is often *necessary* to
copy another person's gestures before you earn them. But once
you have copied and learned the outward effects, you must
motivate them—find the feelings that *produce* those effects,
naturally. You must develop a personal *relationship* with your
gestures until they feel natural and instinctive.

One of my protégés, Robert Post, once asked me if he could
perform my Baseball sketch. It took him a lot of courage to do
this. The Baseball sketch is one of my trademarks. He was
uneasy about performing a sketch that I had perfected over
thirty years, but he was mostly afraid of stepping on my territory. I admit, I did have a few reservations about teaching him
the role. But he said he'd give me credit for writing the sketch,
and I knew that Robert would do a good job with it. He's a ter-
rific performer.

We had a few sessions together. I taught him all of my
moves and he instinctively set out to "earn them," make them
his own. Pretty soon the sketch had changed quite a bit.
Things that felt natural to me did not feel natural to Robert.
(He's a tall guy and we are two very different types of people.)
He repeated some of my gags—the ones that came naturally to

him—and made up a few of his own. He added his own finesse points.

The sketch began to look more and more like *Robert's* sketch and I felt a little strange watching this transformation of "my" moves. I felt as if I were losing my sketch. This was exactly what was happening. If Robert had tried to copy me, he would have looked like me and I would still have been the *owner* of the sketch. But Robert hadn't copied me. Even the gags that were play-by-play duplicates of mine, looked like Robert's. *My* sketch had disappeared; now it belonged to Robert. He had earned it.

When you motivate your gestures, you tailor them to fit *you*. They accommodate your body type and reflect your temperament, your personality, and disposition. These gestures appear to come *from* you instead of *at* you. This is what I mean by the "earned" gesture.

Problem: How to Look Drunk

So many of my students have asked about the "correct characterization of a drunk" that I thought I'd include this little study just for them. Of course, there is no such thing as a "correct" technique for achieving the look of drunkenness. Whatever looks right, *is* right. So, if you're satisfied with your characterization of a drunk person, you probably don't need my analysis of drunkenness. But, if you're not satisfied, the following might help.

My analysis of drunkenness involves four stages or varying degrees of inebriation. The first stage (A) is absolutely sober and perfectly balanced. The B stage is slightly tipsy. The C stage is staggering drunk and, finally, the D stage is falling-down drunk.

To teach drunkenness, I have students notice the feeling of control they experience in the A state—perfectly sober. Then, I ask them to shift their weight slightly to experience the mild vertigo of the B state. (The B state also serves to illustrate puppy love—that blissful state of emotional intoxication.) In this state, students are flirting with gravity. They are playing with their weight, but this play is more voluntary than involuntary. The B state is characterized by precarious little tilts from which you can always return, at the last minute, to A.

Next, I ask students to experience the C state. This means shifting the weight very far away from the A center until you *genuinely* experience a loss of balance and a lack of control. The body actually staggers of its own accord. The progression from B to C is critical. This is the progression from control to lack of control. You do not want your staggering to look planned, deliberate, or controlled. The drunk person *intends* to stand upright, but the body does not conform to the drunk's wishes. This discrepancy between the body and the intentions creates the illusion of drunkenness.

The staggering-drunk person vacillates in between the A, B, and C states of balance. If you have to play a drunk person on stage, there will be moments when you actually lose and recover your balance. This effect will be deliberate, but the loss of balance must, for a moment, take you by surprise. This surprise element is absolutely essential to the believability of your character.

The D state is an exaggeration of the C state. This time you lose your balance to such an extent that a wall, a piece of furniture, or the floor is necessary to break your momentum. In the D state of drunkenness, your character careens uncontrollably through all four stages: A - D.

Depending on your character, you may or may not express resignation while you fall. Most of the time, the drunk's mind is in the state of A. Drunk people *think* they are balanced and cogent, but the body says otherwise. Therefore, when your drunk character is *trying to do something* (when he/she is trying to get somewhere or say something), you must show that your character's mind is in A, but the body is in C or D. Your eyes express the gallant effort to focus and perceive, your lips strain to form words correctly, you move with utmost concentration and care, but in spite of your earnestness nothing comes out right.

The look of earnestness is lacking from the clichéd, unbelievable performances of drunk people. In the cliché performance, the audience sees that the actor is trying to look drunk. Instead, the audience should see a drunk person trying to look sober.

• • • • • • • • • • • • • • • •

My son Adam studied acting for many years. When he was studying the dialects, his teacher told him that one of the secrets to performing dialects convincingly is that the character should not *intend* to have a dialect. The character should be trying *very hard* to sound like a native. And yet the dialect comes through in spite of his effort. The actor, then, must be aware of his character's effort to *eliminate* the dialect from his speaking. Likewise, in the characterization of drunkenness, the actor must be aware of the character's earnest effort to appear sober.

Introducing François Delsarte is like opening King Tut's tomb. There is so much mystery and controversy surrounding Delsarte's life and work that I considered leaving the subject alone. But his contribution to the field of mime cannot be overestimated, and I would rather run the risk of misrepresenting his work than be accused of neglecting it.

When I returned to the United States from Europe in the late '50s, after having studied with Marcel Marceau and Etienne Decroux, the mime field was wide open. There were only five or six mimes doing any serious work, and information about the art form was scarce. I couldn't wait to dig into the archives at the New York Public Library to find out more about my chosen field.

One of the first books to capture my attention was entitled *Harmonic Gymnastics and Pantomimic Expression.* The title intrigued me and I began reading the book from the beginning. After a few pages, I recognized that much of what I was reading was material I had learned from Decroux.

This book was edited and published by Marion Lowell in Boston in 1895. The author and source of its information was not clear. But according to book dealers' catalogs, the author of the book was Steele Mackaye. The material comprising the book was simply notes taken from one of Delsarte's classes. Here, I found a detailed description of the Decomposing Exercises (an exercise I had learned from Decroux). I also found a more detailed and scrupulous analysis of gesture than I had ever come across. I wanted to learn more about this Delsarte.

• • •

François Delsarte was born in Solesmes, France in 1811. By the time he was ten years old, his father, mother, and brother had all died of separate and unrelated causes. When his last surviving relative—his brother—died of cold and starvation, François was not far from this fate himself. But just when death seemed imminent, François experienced a revelation. (He was ten years old at the time.) One biographer describes this vision:

"Exquisite forms and colors floated before his eyes; a wondrous ecstasy filled his mind; celestial music cried into his ears and flooded his soul with harmonies which he afterward said haunted him all through life.... The mystic experience of that strange hour penetrated the inmost recesses of his soul, to

François Delsarte (1811–1871)

fill him with a frantic but a divine passion for beauty and harmony of expression."[9]

A man by the name of Père Bambini discovered Delsarte's aptitude for music and secured a scholarship for him in the Conservatory in Paris. There he studied acting and singing and prepared for a career on stage. But these plans were short-lived. Due to improper training, his voice was ruined. And with this latest tragedy, Delsarte's real career began to unfold.

Delsarte's injury prompted him to scrutinize the traditional ways of teaching technique. In Delsarte's day (and still in ours to some extent), technique was strictly the rote transference of rules, styles, and idiosyncrasies from teacher to student. Students were forced to adhere to whatever system or style was popular at the time. Delsarte reasoned that this dogmatic and superficial transference of technique from teacher to student had been responsible for his injury.

Delsarte's training had ruined his prospects for a brilliant singing career, but it also launched him on an investigation into the nature and substance of art—an investigation that would lead him to a scientific understanding of artistic expression.

Delsarte firmly believed that art was a divine dispensation. He is quoted as saying that "the sovereign and irresistible dominion which [art] exercises over all hearts" is derived from its "celestial origins."[10] He reasoned that if art was a divine dispensation, then naturally, the teaching of art should be governed by divine principles. Delsarte's teachers at the Conservatory had been ignorant of such *principles*.

During a lecture to the Philotechnic Society of Paris, Delsarte defined those divine principles as he perceived them:

"And what are the essential principles of art? Are they not, taking them together, the Good, the True, and the Beautiful? And their action, and their end,—are they other than a tendency incessantly directly toward the realization of these three terms? Now the Good, the True, and the Beautiful can be found only in God. Thus, art is divine in the sense that it emanates from His divine perfections; in the sense that it constitutes for us even the idea of those perfections; and,

[9]Mackaye, Steele, *Delsarte Recitation Book*, ed. Elsie M. Wilbur (New York: Edgar S. Werner, 1890), p. xii.
[10]Delsarte, François, "Delsarte's Address before the Philotechnic Society of Paris: as printed in *Delsarte System of Expression*, by Genevieve Stebbins (New York: Dance Horizons, 1977), p.30.

above all, in the sense that it tends to realize in us, about us, and beyond us this triple perfection that it draws from God."[11]

Delsarte believed it was dangerous to consign a divine propensity (for artistic expression) to human interpretation ("...the search for the Beautiful is not an affair of taste ...."[12]). And to avert this danger, he set out to discover the *science* of aesthetics. Eventually this evolved into the science of gesture which he called "Applied Aesthetics" or "*Cours d'Esthetique Applique.*"

"To each spiritual function corresponds a function of the body. To each grand function of the body corresponds a spiritual act."[13] Thus Delsarte defined the premise of his system.

Delsarte discovered that what a person *does* is a direct manifestation of who that person *is*; "doing" is a function of "being." At first, this discovery may seem too obvious, too self-evident to warrant special attention. And yet, Delsarte firmly believed that if this fact had been incorporated into his early training as a singer, he never would have lost his voice.

As a young student, he had been forced to *do* certain things with his voice. He was expected to achieve certain effects. But the *cause* of those effects had been neglected. The *doer* had been excluded from the process of *doing*.

Delsarte believed that technique should be a *natural* and effortless demonstration of one's *self*, one's soul. Likewise, the perfection of technique should go hand-in-hand with the perfection of being. When this is the case, technique does not exert unnecessary stress on the body.

Delsarte became fascinated with the process of *doing*. He watched all types of people in all types of situations and discovered that certain laws or rules governed their movements and determined the authenticity of their gestures. For example, he saw a nurse picking up a newborn child and noticed that her thumb was fairly close to the rest of her hand. Whereas the mother approached her child with the thumbs strongly extended away from the hand. The mother's hand position indicated her unconditional love for her child, her complete "opening up" to it. Whereas the nurse's hand position indicated that this act of handling children was certainly tender and gentle but nonetheless "all in a day's work."

[11]Ibid.
[12]Ibid. pg. 59
[13]Ibid. pg. 67

In Steele Mackaye's book, *Harmonic Gymnastics*, he lists *four hundred and five* variations on eyebrow and eyelid positions and attempts to give the meaning behind each of these positions! There are many books in print and out of print today that offer detailed descriptions of Delsarte's data on body language. But if you are looking for a sensitive treatment of Delsarte's system (his philosophy and theology, etc.), you may have a difficult time finding it. I highly recommend the book *Every Little Movement,* by Ted Shawn. This book is written for dancers, so it covers only those gestures that apply to dance, but it succeeds in giving the reader a *sense* of Delsarte (i.e., the brilliance of his work and the travesty of most interpretations of it).

Unfortunately, Delsarte never wrote anything about "Applied Aesthetics." He never felt that his work was complete enough to set its tenets and principles down in prose. Consequently, many well-intentioned students tried to immortalize his system for him. The result of these attempts was bedlam. Students tried to capitalize on their knowledge before they understood what Delsarte was trying to say. Their coverage of his science ended up being a dry and uninspired listing of gestures and body positions. These gestures were, inevitably, hackneyed and trite, without any suggestion of truth or authenticity. Delsarte's system soon became the butt of jokes and ridicule. And the students of Delsarte who *did* possess a modicum of understanding for his work were afraid to say so. Soon the brilliance of Delsarte's system was almost entirely eclipsed by the insipid translations of it. I experienced, firsthand, some of the controversy surrounding the Delsarte system.

As I've mentioned, my introduction to Delsarte occurred in the library where I came across *Harmonic Gymnastics.* Reading this book in the seclusion of the book stall, I felt that I was being initiated into a private club. It was exciting to discover the *origin* of everything I had learned about mime in the past few years. Since no one had mentioned the name "Delsarte" in all those years, I reasoned that all mime teachers must be bound by a tacit agreement to keep the source of their teachings a secret (the same way all magicians agree to keep their tricks a secret).

But I had a few questions about this vow of secrecy, too. I can understand a magician keeping his tricks secret; the whole fun of magic is that no one knows how it's done. But I could *not* understand why Delsarte was never given the credit he deserved. Why keep someone's good name a secret? I decided to confront my teachers, directly, on the subject of Delsarte. Their responses to my query surprised me.

I first confronted Decroux while he was touring the United States with his mime troupe. I met him backstage after a show and asked if he had ever heard of Delsarte. My question seemed to agitate him. "Who?" he replied.

"Delsarte. François Delsarte." I persisted.

"Yes, I have his book. Why do you ask?" He answered with suspicion and resentment.

"Why didn't you tell us about this wonderful book?" I asked.

He shrugged his shoulders and walked away. I was beginning to suspect that the subject of Delsarte was a bit more complicated than I had imagined. Later, I learned that the Delsarte system was being trivialized and ridiculed at the time. Perhaps Decroux was afraid to be associated with it. Or maybe he felt that his dominion in the mime field was threatened. Etienne Decroux has always been recognized as the *father* of modern mime. I didn't (and still don't) challenge this distinction, but if Decroux is the father of mime then Delsarte must be the grandfather. (And Delsarte never even called himself a mime!)

I also approached Louise Gifford, my mime teacher from Columbia University. Ms. Gifford's reaction to my question about Delsarte was not at all like Decroux's reaction. When I told her I had discovered the works of Delsarte, her whole countenance changed toward me. I think she had always thought of me as an arrogant, over-zealous hambone. Now she saw me in a new light. My appreciation for Delsarte made me a kindred spirit.

"*You* discovered Delsarte?!" she asked incredulously. "My dear Tony, I owe you an apology."

She invited me to her apartment and there on her library shelves were many books about Delsarte and Steele Mackaye. I specifically remember seeing the book entitled *Delsarte System of Oratory*, a compilation of students' notes including those of l'Abbe Delaumosne. (I later read this book cover to cover with great enthusiasm.) When I asked her why she hadn't told us about Delsarte, she replied that most people resented having the lofty and hallowed phenomenon of *stage presence* reduced to a science or system. I appreciated her explanation and since then, have noticed repeatedly that many so-called "creative" artists detest the idea of conforming to a system. They prefer to believe that their talent is exclusive to themselves—a birthright or a personal hotbed of inspiration.

Learning how to appreciate systems is one of the secrets of true artistry, I think. The most valid part of learning a system is the communion that takes place between the student and the originator of that system. The student goes into a field that is already partly cultivated and proceeds to make his or her own mark in that field. This is the essence of progress and evolution. Delsarte's system represents over thirty-five years of scrupulous and painstaking observation. His system is a legacy for all movement artists.

It is unfortunate that so many mimes working today are unfamiliar with the heritage of this art form. Some mimes are not only *unfamiliar* with their heritage, they reject it altogether. Recently, I saw an advertisement for a mime troupe that prided itself on the fact that it didn't "do walls," for example. It's OK (and often advisable) to leave the wall-mime out of a mime performance, but why make this the selling point of your act? (Is your show so devoid of content that you have to sell it on the basis of what it's *not*?) It's OK to leave the mime illusions out of a show, but the mime should, at least, have learned and *mastered* those illusions.

The mastery of a mime illusion teaches much more than the illusion itself; it teaches sensitivity, attentiveness, coordination, and yes, *humility*. A knowledge of mime history is another valuable lesson in humility, respect, and wonder. It shouldn't be an odious chore to learn everything you can about mime—its history, its philosophy, its technique, etc. The more you learn, the more awe-inspiring this art form becomes.

• • •

While Delsarte was alive he was deeply respected and admired. Artists from all disciplines attended his lectures and returned to the stage (to the canvas or whatever) with a sensitivity and authority that defied explanation. Delsarte understood that he was imparting a knowledge of Spirit to his students. But most of his students who later wrote about his system missed this crucial point. Many of them mistook the *spirit* of the law for the *letter* of the law.

Immediately following Delsarte's death in 1871, many of his students were carrying on his work with impeccable sensitivity and understanding, but these students went "underground" for fear of being ridiculed. A similar thing is happening today in the mime field. *Good* mimes are often afraid to call themselves "mimes" because too many beginning mimes have given this profession a bad name. This happens when mime students start performing too early, before they really understand what mime is all about and before they appreciate the subtle difference between an authentic gesture and a contrived gesture.

This was Delsarte's domain. He studied the outward shapes of the body but always connected these outward shapes to some internal cause, to some state of mind. This marriage between cause and effect guaranteed that all of the "Delsartian gestures" looked *real*. Great tomes were written about the Delsartian gestures, but very little was written about the *cause* of those gestures (i.e., the *source* of their authenticity). I think this is why Delsarte's work was consigned to obscurity. If this chapter inspires anyone to investigate the subject of Delsarte and search for the lost element of his teaching, I will be deeply gratified.

All of Delsarte's admirers extrapolated from his work. We discovered little gems among his treasure troves of ideas and used them to adorn our own understanding of movement. Naturally, all of us had our own ideas as to what constituted a "gem." Ted Shawn, the great modern dancer, used those ideas that pertained to dance. I was interested in ideas pertaining to character development. Whatever your artistic needs were, Delsarte had something to offer. Here is one of the gems that I culled from his treasury.

Delsarte: Eccentric, Concentric, and Normal

Delsarte noticed that every position and every gesture could be analyzed and characterized in terms of three basic qualities: "eccentric," "concentric," and "normal." Each of these qualities represents a specific "personality."

Eccentric: Open, extended, outward, extroverted, big, loud.
Concentric: Closed, contracted, inward, introverted, small, quiet.
Normal: Neutral, a point between eccentric and concentric.

Every aspect of a pose or a gesture (i.e., every arm position, every hand position, etc.) may be qualified as either eccentric, concentric, or normal. Consequently, the specific placement of *each* body part reveals something about the personality.

Consider this comic version of an army drill sergeant:

Eccentric stance: Legs spread and feet planted far apart.
Concentric hands on hips: Hands folded into fists.
Eccentric elbows: Elbows flared out and forward.
Eccentric chest: Puffed out chest.

Concentric chin: Chin tucked into neck.
Eccentric eyes: Eyes bulging.
Concentric eyebrows: Eyebrows knitted and pulled down.
Concentric mouth: Corners of mouth pulled down.

This sergeant doesn't have to describe himself or his work ethic to his men; his body position says it all. The physical eloquence inherent in this stance is due to the specific blend of eccentric and concentric positions of the body.

This drill sergeant *flaunts* brute strength and *conceals* any potential for tenderness. If you look at the eccentric positions, you notice first that he has a solid base: his legs are spread and his feet are planted far apart. This eccentric leg position says, "I am fixed, immoveable, and nothing gets past me!"

Next, you notice that all of the eccentric and concentric positions serve to emphasize the "hard" parts of the body and conceal the "soft" parts. For example, by thrusting the elbows out to the side (i.e., eccentric elbows), the sergeant is keeping the tender underskin of his arms *away* from his audience (his men). This may seem like an insignificant point, but a careful scrutiny of character types and body positions proves that, in life, the very tender skin on the underside of the arm is expressive of emotional vulnerability and physical weakness. It is usually *not* exposed to the world. There are, however, certain types of people who *do* expose the underside of their arms to the world. These characters are the ingénue types. They appear vulnerable, innocent, and very feminine.

With the concentric hands, again, the soft part of the body (the palm) is concealed and the hard part (the knuckle) is exposed. The concentric chin means that certain vulnerable areas on the neck are concealed, protected by the protruding chin bone.

The eccentric eyes (eyes bulging) "say" that nothing passes this sergeant's attention. While the concentric eyebrows (eyebrows closing in or knitted) indicate that although the eyes are wide open, his mind is shut tight. (Lowering the eyebrows has the effect of lengthening the forehead as if a shade were being drawn over the mind.) This sergeant is looking for and expecting certain things and he is *not* willing to discuss those things.

I appreciate this system of analyzing the body because it allows for the many contradictions inherent in the human personality. Delsarte understood that the human personality is never a coherent whole; it is always a mixture of the reserved and the out-going, the shy and the brash, the closed and the open. This drill sergeant, for example, is open in terms of animal strength and closed in terms of emotional receptivity. The cliché version of the intellectual depicts him/her as secure in mind and frail in physique. These personality traits are revealed through a specific mixture of eccentric, concentric, and normal positions of the body.

A story from my early mime training serves to illustrate how a seemingly random mixture of eccentric and concentric body positions always translates into a precise, coherent, and convincing personality.

My first mime teacher, Louise Gifford, was a well-educated, cultured, and refined woman. She dressed impeccably and often wore cameos and white gloves. Whether standing or sitting, her knees were always together and she never raised her voice or made a crass comment about anyone or anything. Almost everything about her was concentric except her back which was perfectly eccentric—always erect and befitting a stately, refined lady.

One day, to prove how convincing this work could be, Ms. Gifford did a little demonstration of the eccentric, concentric, and normal body positions. She "reversed herself"—all of her typically concentric positions became eccentric and vice versa. Her typically concentric legs now spread into an eccentric position. Her typically eccentric back slouched forward. None of us could believe our eyes. Our prim and proper teacher suddenly looked exactly like a fishwife from one of Grimm's Fairy Tales!

Our reaction must have been pretty shrill because when she heard us, she suddenly snapped back to her former, formal self and blushed profusely. "You see, these body positions can be very persuasive," she said innocently.

The Class: An Exercise Inspired by Delsarte

The following exercise was inspired by Delsarte's theory about the eccentric, concentric, and normal positions of the body. It's a fun exercise with a huge pay-off: students gain a working knowledge of Delsarte's theory and learn what it means to *buy* a gesture or a position (see pages 203-204).

During this exercise, I simply call out a random combination of eccentric and concentric positions and the students assume these positions. I may say something like: "Eccentric chin." (Chin pokes out.) "Concentric lips." (Lips purse.) "Eccentric chest." (Chest thrusts forward.) "Concentric knees." (Knees turn in.) With every instruction, the person in front of me changes. With every change of the body, there is a corresponding change in the character's personality.

The first part of this exercise is, simply, understanding what the terms eccentric and concentric mean in terms of body positions. The second part of the exercise is being able to *buy* these positions. Once you assume a position, you have to let this position *get to you.* (Become the person for whom this position is natural.) Then add another position to the already existing body-shape until you are twisted up in a series of seemingly unrelated positions. If the student succeeds in *buying it*, all of these diverse positions will relate to each other. They will combine to form one entity, one homogeneous (albeit unusual) character.

At this point during the exercise, I often ask questions and the students have to answer in the "voice" of their characters. I might ask, "What are you thinking about right now?" or "Do you have anything to say?" Inevitably, each student responds in a voice befitting his/her new identity. The student's thoughts also change accordingly.

When I talk to these characters they often come back with a whacky remark that no one (not even the person in the position) expects. I remember one of my best friends, Bernie Kramer, performing this exercise in class. He ended up in an absurd position—a cross between Quasi Modo and a cowboy. When I asked him what he had to say, he chewed for a while and then drawled, "Ooooh.... It's a great day for a wallow."

It is always amusing to see what kind of character evolves out of a random combination of eccentric and concentric positions. No matter how dissimilar or incongruent the positions, they always spawn very specific, believable, and colorful characters. After all, the typical person *is* a bundle of contradictions.

Delsarte: The Mental, Emotional, and Physical Centers

After years of painstaking observation and study, Delsarte reasoned that the human body could be divided into three basic centers: the mental, the emotional, and the physical centers. The mental center is the head itself. The emotional center (also known as the *aesthetic* center) corresponds to the torso—the chest and belly. The physical center corresponds to the limbs—the arms and legs. (The arms and legs are those parts of the body that relate most directly with one's physical or external environment.)

Each of these centers can, in turn, be subdivided again into mental, emotional/aesthetic, and physical regions.

One of the many faces of Bernie Kramer.
(Photo by Thomas Bloom)

Subdivisions of the Mental Center:

The top of the head (the forehead) is the *mental* region of the mental center.

The eyes, nose, and upper lip comprise the *emotional/aesthetic* region of the mental center.

The lower jaw and mouth correspond to the *physical* region of the mental center.

Subdivisions of the Emotional/Aesthetic Center:

The lungs typify the *mental* region of the emotional/aesthetic center.

The heart corresponds to the *emotional/aesthetic* region of the emotional/aesthetic center.

The belly corresponds to the *physical* region of the emotional/aesthetic center.

Subdivisions of the Physical Center:

The hands and feet correspond to the *mental* region of the physical center.

The lower arm and lower leg correspond to the *emotional/aesthetic* region of the physical center.

The upper arm and thigh correspond to the *physical* region of the physical center.

• • •

At first, this explanation may seem belabored and impractical, but don't be fooled: it is truly a profound and ingenious analysis of the body with practical applications for the movement artist. I can think of at least three ways in which movement artists may avail themselves of this information:

1)   Making sure your *body language* accurately reflects your character's personality.

2)   Designing specific *gestures* to suit specific situations in your sketch.

3)   Knowing which parts of the body to *touch* in order to relay a particular message.

• • •

1) Designing a Body Language To Fit Your Character's Personality

The way someone moves is a reflection of his/her personality. This is why mimes and actors often refer to movement as "body language." Every movement *says* something about your character. Therefore, if your character's body language doesn't agree 100% with your character's personality, you work against yourself. Your body language and your intentions contradict each other, and your audience is confused as to *who* you are and *what* you're doing.

A story from my career serves as an example here. Several years ago, before I had discovered the practical uses of Delsarte's ideas, I wrote a sketch called "The Glutton." It's a simple sketch. I sit or stand center stage and do a mime of a man eating. This man eats grapes, peaches, drumsticks, anything he can get his hands on. The more he eats, the more he wants. Finally, there is no more food and the glutton, by sheer force of habit, eats his own fingers.

When I first started performing this sketch, the audience enjoyed the individual illusions. They giggled when the peach juice ran down my arm, they giggled again when I spat the grape seeds out of my mouth, etc. But they reacted to the *illusions*; not to my *character*, the glutton. Consequently, I felt that the sketch didn't hold together—it didn't "succeed."

I was reading Delsarte at the time and when I came to the section about the three centers of the body, I realized that this had practical applications for my sketch. Reviewing my moves, I realized that my body language was working at cross purposes with my character's personality. My posture, gestures, and mood did not always "*say*" glutton. Sometimes, I became a gourmand. Other times, I was an epicurean or simply a fastidious eater. The audience did not see the glutton; they saw a series of disparate personalities eating an assortment of foods. No wonder my sketch didn't go anywhere!

When I read about the mental, emotional, and physical centers of the body, I understood where and how my body language had been misleading. If I picked up the peach with too much dexterity, I suddenly became an epicure. According to Delsarte, the fingers are essentially *mental* instruments. Therefore, the epicure (someone who *knows* and *appreciates* fine food) would eat with dexterity. The glutton doesn't know anything about food. He has no respect for it; he eats indiscriminately, obsessively. Therefore, if any of my fingers or any of my gestures suggested fastidiousness, the glutton disappeared and an epicure took his place.

There were at least a dozen occasions during my sketch where the glutton character was violated by a conflicting body signal. Sometimes I showed too much joy while I ate. A sparkle of pleasure might appear in my eye. The eyes are the *emotional/aesthetic* instruments of the mental center. When they light up, this indicates joy, appreciation, awareness, gratitude. The gourmand enjoys food; the glutton lusts after it. The gourmand enjoys the *subtlety* of food; the glutton lusts after its weight and volume. The gourmand appreciates the texture, appearance, and flavor of food; the glutton can't tell the difference between ground beef and filet mignon. His eating is mindless, habitual, compulsive.

Once I understood the problem with my sketch, I went back to the drawing board. I reasoned that the glutton's interests are purely physical. Therefore the mouth (the *physical* region of the mental center), the belly (the *physical* region of the emotional/aesthetic center), and the upper arms and legs (the *physical* regions of the physical center) should be the emphatic origins of every gesture and every pose. When the physical regions became the focus of my attention, they also dominated my audience's attention.

For an accurate portrayal of a glutton, I reasoned that the physical centers of the body must lead, dictate, and *color* every gesture. I also understood that the mental and emotional centers should remain blatantly *inactive*, no matter what I was doing. Therefore, even while I sat still, I needed to experience the *dominance* of the physical centers and the *deficiency* of the mental and emotional centers of my character.

The next time I rehearsed my sketch, I focused on those physical centers: the mouth and lower jaw, the belly and the beefy upper parts of my limbs. I also underplayed the eyes; the world around me grew dim and uninteresting. Bearing in mind that the mental centers should also be inactive, I felt my thoughts become profoundly simple. I thought about food and belly, only. I felt an incessant flow of food passing from mouth to belly and finally depositing itself in the massive upper regions of my arms and legs.

The next time I performed, the audience reaction to this sketch was exactly as I had intended. The audience *saw* the glutton and actually groaned while I ate.

In this particular application of Delsarte's system, you don't have to *do* anything specific with the body. You only have to focus on or think about the appropriate body parts. This changes the quality of your movement until your character's personality and your body language are in complete agreement.

• • • • • • • • • • • • • • • • • •

WARNING: One time, during a performance, I thought about the mental, emotional, physical centers of my body and became disoriented—confused.

Actors and mimes should acquaint themselves with this and other techniques in rehearsal, not on stage. This way you identify with your character's *personality* before you go on stage, and won't have to fiddle with his/her outward appearance as you perform.

When mimes and actors are first becoming acquainted with this work, I tell them to stand still and simply *think* about the appropriate body parts. If you were working on the glutton character, for example, I would tell you to stand center stage and *feel* the qualities of "glutton" permeate the physical regions of the body. Soon your mouth would suggest gluttony. The lips and tongue would soften in anticipation of food. Your belly would crave your undivided attention and your upper arms and legs would suggest weight, the allure of flesh. From here, you would move, talk, or do whatever you had to do. As long as those physical regions *primed* your actions, your audience would see the glutton.

This work is subtle and extremely accurate. Once, during class, I asked a student to do a character improvisation on "bad seed." But as the improvisation unfolded, I saw that the student's character was not accurate. His character was a *naughty boy* rather than a *bad seed*. I stopped the improvisation, and we discussed the difference between the bad seed and the naughty child.

We came to the conclusion that the bad seed is "rotten to the core," while the naughty child simply lapses into rotten behavior every so often. It was easy to analyze the difference between these two characters, but correcting the student's body language was not so easy. Here, again, Delsarte's ideas proved to be invaluable.

We reasoned that the naughty child is still pure in mind and heart. This child might do naughty things—he might stamp his foot or fold his arms angrily across his chest or scowl, but none of these superficial signs of anger would come from or affect the mental or the emotional centers of his being. The eyes and the heart would still express brightness and purity. The naughty child is bad only when he *does* something naughty. The bad seed, on the other hand, does not have to *do* anything bad. He may be behaving beautifully, but the quality of badness permeates his being.

When the student attempted the improvisation again, he stood still for a few minutes and we, the audience, saw his heart and mind darken. He no longer felt the need to *do* anything in particular. His "badness" was more deep-seated; it had infected his thoughts and his feelings, his core. We saw anger and resentment behind his eyes. The mental centers (the hands in particular) became much more calculated and precise whereas a minute ago (as a naughty child) his mental centers had moved a bit clumsily—indicating that his naughtiness was not premeditated or deliberate. All of us watching this transformation saw the bad seed. The student's body language was now consonant with his character's personality.

I remember using Delsarte's ideas again while directing a love scene in one of my classes. A very shy college student had to play the role of an enamored suitor. No one in the class believed he could do it. At first, it did appear hopeless. The student's performance was absolutely unconvincing. He didn't seem to have any feelings for this woman at all. He had trouble even *acknowledging* her; how could he ever look longingly into her eyes and tell her he loved her. The more we talked about what he *should* feel and do, the more disheartened he became. Sensing failure, the student became more and more withdrawn and shy.

Then an insight came to me. I remembered Delsarte and his assertion that the heart is the emotional center of the body. I took the student aside and told him, in private, that the next time he did the scene he could forget about feeling anything. "All you have to do," I told him, "is focus on your heart. Forget about love. Simply, focus on this particular region of your body, the heart. Every time you say something, think that your heart says it. Every time you move, think that it's your heart moving. When you have to touch [the woman student], think that your heart is touching her." He was relieved. Focusing on the heart region of his body was a lot simpler than trying to feign love for someone.

The next time he did the scene in front of the class, everyone's jaw fell to the floor. He performed with such sincerity and tenderness that no one (not even I) could believe that this was the same person. In a matter of a few minutes, this stone-faced, dejected student had turned into a heart throb.

I see Delsarte's system as a way of *grounding* the performer. It brings him back to the comfort zone where he can work from tangible, scientific concepts. The shy student in the above example at first seemed extremely uncomfortable. He was self-conscious in front of his buddies, shy in front of girls, insecure with the whole elusive art of "acting." All of these distractions led him far outside of his comfort zone. Advising this student to feel certain emotions only confused the issue. But Delsarte's system gave him something concrete to do and think about. He no longer had to flounder in the abstract realm of emotions. He didn't have to compete with all the great lovers from Hollywood mythology. He had a job to do— he had to focus on the heart region of his body. The candid execution of this job relieved stress and yielded a believable and convincing performance.

2) Designing Specific Gestures To Suit Specific Situations In Your Sketch

The scientific sense behind Delsarte's system makes it a practical tool for the movement artist. Take the lungs for example. The lungs, according to this system, are the mental aspect of the emotional center. This makes sense when you think of breathing (lung action) as a metaphor for inspiration. An insight or a revelation is a mental phenomenon that affects the mental portion of the emotional center, lifting the chest and inflating the lungs. (The inspiration of air corresponds with the inspiration of "emotional" ideas.)

This information becomes useful if you're playing a character who has just solved a problem. Consider the character of Tevya in *Fiddler on the Roof*. Remember the moment when he can't sleep because he doesn't know how to convince his wife to let their daughter marry the tailor? Tevya is sitting up in bed, but his chest is sunken (no inspiration) and his head is working very hard. Suddenly he thinks of a way to reason with his wife. He will tell her that their deceased relative has just appeared to him in a dream insisting that they break with "Tradition" and let their daughter marry the tailor. When he thinks of this, his chest suddenly inflates. He has solved the problem!

Granted, Zero Mostel (the actor who played Tevya on Broadway) did the right thing automatically. His chest inflated at the moment of insight. But Delsarte found the reason *why* this happens. The chest inflates because a mental event (the birth of an idea) affects the corresponding mental regions of the body. This science comes in handy when the appropriate gestures are not so obvious as that for Tevya's brainstorm.

There are different types of revelations that affect the body in different ways. Some revelations are strictly mental; others are emotional. The mental revelation may not affect the emotional center of the body (the torso or lungs) quite so dramatically as the emotional revelation does. For example, the mathematician who solves a difficult problem will probably not inspire with the same rapture as someone who has just learned that a beloved relative is returning home from the war unharmed. However, the mathematician may inspire rapturously if the solution to his problem has *emotional* repercussions—if his solution makes him a candidate for a Nobel prize, for example.

3) Knowing Which Parts of the Body To Touch In Order To Relay A Particular Message
The more you observe people in action, the more you appreciate the logic or the science that underlies gesture. This logic is clearly apparent when a person touches another person. It is fascinating to realize that even a rash, compulsive gesture (such as a squeeze, a spank, or a hit) is a specific and strategic maneuver, accurately reflecting the person's personality and intentions.

If a friend is buckling under psychological stress, you might deliver a hearty squeeze to his upper arms. The message relayed here depends on which part of the body *touches* and which part of the body *is touched.* In this case, you are using your hands to squeeze your friend's upper arms. The hands are the *mental* region of the physical center. The upper arms are the *physical* region of the physical center. Squeezing your friend's upper arms with your hands indicates that your mind is strong. You wish that your friend understood things as you do but if he can't, you hope *your* mental strength can bolster and support his declining physical strength.

Very specific messages are relayed through touch even though the precise meaning is often not discussed or even known, intellectually. Patting someone on the head is a condescending gesture, but often the person doing the patting is unaware of this. The top of the head is the apex of mental activity, and patting it with a physical appendage (the hands belong to the *physical* center of the body) is one way of slighting someone's intellectual accomplishments. I've seen many young and not-so-young children interpret this gesture as an insult.

A priest also touches the top of the head. But he gives this gesture the thought and tenderness befitting a blessing. Here the top of the head (the apex of mental activity) is treated with the respect and love it deserves.

I could go into great detail about the various ways of touching another person and what each way means, but the meaning becomes self explanatory the more familiar you are with the Delsarte system.

• • •

The sex organs were not included in Delsarte's study of gesture. This omission was deliberate and, surprisingly, did not compromise the integrity of the system. Delsarte probably realized that in the body, the sex organs are strictly instruments for procreation. Only the human personality credits these organs with their own psychological and emotional significance. What is thought to be a sexual problem is, in fact, a mental or emotional need mistaken for a sexual one. Therefore, if your character is supposed to have a sexual problem, you can find the correct body language by working with the physical, emotional, or mental centers of the body appropriately.

For example, if your character is lecherous, you want to show the deficiency of mind and emotion and an excess of physique. If your character is prudish and judgmental, you want to show a deficiency of physique and an excess of mind. If your character is without sexual aberrations, you want to show an harmonic balance between the mental, emotional, and physical centers of the body.

Except for the transcript of Delsarte's address before the Philotechnic Society of Paris, we have no written account of this man's philosophy or ideology. Delsarte hoped the science of his system would speak for itself. But the science, by itself, gradually solidified into a rigid code of poses and gestures. Now we can only speculate on the exact ideology that inspired his work. This section on the "elliptical gesture" is part speculation.

I believe Delsarte had a notion as to *who* the ideal person was and *what* that person represented. This ideal was the starting point of his system. From there, he reasoned that no mortal human being achieved this ideal. Once he had a sense of the ideal, he could then distort this sense to achieve an accurate illustration of the average human being.

According to Delsarte's system, the ideal person is devoid of hypocrisy and contradictions. The mental, emotional, and physical centers are perfectly balanced and operate in harmony with each other. Consequently, everything the ideal person does is appropriate, direct, and correct.

The average human being deviates from this model of excellence. His/her actions almost always belie some modicum of hypocrisy. This is where the elliptical gesture comes in. The gestures of the average human being are often hypocritical, unconscious, indirect, or *elliptical.*

Examples of the elliptical gesture may be found everywhere you look. People smile when they don't feel like smiling. Parents put on stern countenances when they'd rather giggle at their child's antics. I saw a picture in the newspaper the other day of two dignitaries from opposing nations shaking hands. The position of their bodies, alone, told the reader that this display of decency was far from genuine. Neither man faced the other directly; their bodies were at oblique angles to each other and they deliberately avoided looking into each other's eyes.

Many of Delsarte's students believed that the Delsarte system was a study of the external person—the shapes and attitudes of the body. They learned all of Delsarte's poses and gestures as if these were inviolable renditions of character types. Suddenly, Delsarte's gestures and poses were being presented to audiences as *ideal* depictions of human nature.

But I doubt Delsarte intended for his postures to be associated with the ideal in any way. He studied the incongruencies of human nature and discovered that the body reflects these incongruencies. His system was about accuracy, not perfection. He discovered that there was an absolute correlation between cause and effect, premise and conclusion, mind and body, "being" and "doing." But his was a study of the *imperfections* in human nature and how these imperfections are perfectly revealed by the person's posture, stance, and gestures.

When Delsarte taught, his emphasis was on the alliance between "being" and "doing." Everything a person *did* on stage—every gesture, every pose, every technical feat—had to issue from the person's *being*, otherwise the actions were *sense*-less. Superimposing a technique on a student (before the causality behind the technique was understood) produced mechanical, lifeless, and sometimes dangerous results.

Many of Delsarte's students (who later *taught* the Delsarte system) broke this fundamental principle of his teaching. They neglected the causality behind movement. Delsarte's system became just another technique with inviolable rules, gestures, and postures. When students idolized Delsarte and his system, they ironically trivialized both. Eventually, the public equated Delsarte with the cliché. And his system has not yet recovered from this defamation.

René Houtrides, Peter Ford, and Tony in "The Blind Leading the Blind." (Courtesy of the authors.)

6

PREPARATORY EXERCISES
For Improvisation and Creating Sketches

Tony, in performance with Craig Babcock, early 1970s. (Courtesy of the authors)

Introduction

Both improvisation and writing sketches depend on your ability to use and know your own mind.

—Improvisation brings out the speed and spontaneity of your thought process.

—Writing sketches unveils your *own* perspective on reality and what you, personally, find interesting about it.

As you develop these skills, you discover a problem-solving ability in yourself that exceeds your expectations. You find that you can react instantly, appropriately, and intelligently to what's happening around you.

The ability to think and act this way is innate, but living in the world doesn't necessarily bring this out in us. As a matter of fact, living in the world often means doing the same thing day after day. There is very little risk involved in the typical, contemporary lifestyle—very few chances to exercise our natural and immediate problem-solving abilities.

There is a saying, "What you don't use, you lose." If you are not regularly confronting high-risk situations, you lose your ability to act correctly and spontaneously in the moment. Actually, you never *lose* this ability, but it does atrophy, considerably. The exercises in this chapter resemble "high-risk" situations. They are not like calisthenics that are basically safe and straightforward. These exercises will slightly unnerve you, and they *should*. Only by confronting fear and doubt will you recapture your innate ability to receive inspiration and deal with contingencies.

When you learn to sky-dive, you start by jumping without the aid of a parachute. You start with small heights and progress to bigger ones. The object is to seek out those heights that slightly unnerve you and jump from them. Before each jump, you *should* feel slightly unnerved; otherwise you're not learning anything. After each jump, you're ready for the next unnerving situation. Inevitably, after each jump, a greater height is required to provoke the same level of unease that the smaller height provoked earlier. This is progress.

Likewise, here, each exercise is a little jump, a gentle confrontation with your "unnerves." By the time you have conquered one unnerving situation, you're ready for the next. With each conquering of fear, you recover a bit more of your innate ability to think clearly, correctly, and spontaneously. After the exercises in this chapter, you are ready for the next hurdles: improvisation and writing sketches. Finally you face the moment of truth, the big jump, your first entrance on stage as writer, choreographer, and performer of your own show.

The Class: Mirror Exercise (Another Lesson in Empathy)

My first mime teacher, Louise Gifford of Columbia University, often asked us to perform solo mimes in front of the class. We were not supposed to tell anyone beforehand what our mime was all about; the object being that the clarity of gesture should speak for itself. If the rest of the class couldn't guess what the mime was about, something was wrong. We'd then discuss the problem and decide how the choreography (gestures and facial expressions, etc.) could be improved to make the sketch easier to understand.

I couldn't wait for my turn in front of the class. In those days (early '50s) I was a pretty intense and impetuous guy. I had a tremendous amount of self-confidence and was *certain* that if my gestures were clear to *me*, they were clear to the audience, too.

One time, when it was (finally!) my turn, I performed what I thought was a clever story line. I began the scene as a young man walking down the street going nowhere in particular. Suddenly, I spotted a wallet on the street in front of me. Excitement! I picked up the wallet, opened it, and found *lots* of money and an address. I decided to return the wallet and receive a reward. I followed the address card to my destination, knocked on the door. The owner of the wallet was thrilled to see me. I anticipated a huge reward, but he gave me a small coin, closed the door, and left me in a state of befuddlement.

When I finished the scene, I expected some applause (I had performed so clearly, I thought) but, instead, I heard an awkward silence. The rest of the class looked bewildered. Ms. Gifford thanked me politely and told me to sit down. When I had taken my seat, she asked the class what they had seen.

"Well," someone began hesitantly, "I wasn't really sure. It looked like you found a lollypop on the ground and it got stuck to your jacket. So you went to get it cleaned and then I couldn't understand *what* you did after that."

Someone else thought I had lost a toothpick or some dumb thing. I was devastated. This was certainly a humbling experience. I learned how precise and articulate gestures have to be in order to *develop* rather than *confuse* your story. The audience sees *everything*. If you do too much or too little, they will be confused because they are reading and interpreting your *every* move.

Perhaps after I found the wallet on the street, I brought my hands too close to my face. Hence my audience saw lollipops and toothpicks instead of a wallet. It's not difficult to learn to be clear in mime as long as you empathize with your audience. You must be able to *sense* your audience and *know* what they are seeing. In turn, you must design your sketch according to what the audience *is* seeing, not according to what you *think* they're seeing. Empathy is, I think, *the* most useful choreographic tool you have.

Ms. Gifford didn't have a name for this exercise. We called them "critiques" or "scene studies." When I teach, I call them "mirror exercises." The audience (the rest of the class) is your

145

mirror. If they don't see exactly what you *want* them to see, then *you* have to make the adjustment. If your audience doesn't react the way you want them to, it's not *their* fault.

Even if you've performed a sketch several times and you're confident that the choreography is clear, this doesn't mean that you can stop empathizing with each new audience. One of the solo mimes I perform today is very complicated. It's a sketch about a puppet and a puppeteer in which the puppet becomes conscious of his captivity and rebels against his puppet master. At the end of the sketch, the puppet kills the puppeteer, but just when he believes he's autonomous, one elbow is suddenly yanked up in the air—then the other elbow as if his arms are still attached to strings. The puppet master is dead, but someone or something is still controlling the puppet, dictating his every move.

The sketch is full of details and intrigue. I performed it a few times until I was satisfied with the choreography. The audience reaction and comments I heard after the show convinced me that the choreography was clear. But even though I was confident about the choreography itself, I never stopped empathizing with my audience as I performed. On evenings when my attentiveness to my audience flagged a little, inevitably someone would approach me afterwards to ask what my puppet sketch was about.

It is wonderful to sense your audience. You can feel their attention. You can tell when they've gotten the point or when they need more information. You can tell when to speed up or when to slow down to emphasize a particular point. These subtle cues from your audience come over a "wave-length" that often escapes our attention. Consequently, beginning mime students don't "pick them up" at first. But the more experience you have, the more pronounced these cues become and the easier it is to "read" your audience.

The Class: Open Rounds

The following exercise is an introduction to improvisation. It probes beneath superficial fears and tensions and gives new meaning to the words *spontaneity* and *impulse*.

For this exercise, everyone sits in a semicircle on the floor. Starting at one end of the semicircle, each person, one at a time, gets up in front of the class and moves for about five seconds only. That person then sits down as the next person in the semicircle gets up and takes his/her turn. After everyone has gotten up once, the whole process begins again. I usually continue Rounds until everyone has been "up" four or five times.

The object of this exercise is to move totally from impulse (as opposed to caution). You, the student, should not think about or plan your move. Suspend all judgment and simply move instinctively and spontaneously.

Follow your impulses. The first little twinge of an urge, a desire, a feeling, a fear—let it spill over into movement before it snags in the sieve of self-consciousness.

You don't want to study your feelings or censure them. There are no discussions during this exercise. There's only impulse and raw reaction. The object of the exercise is to find a direct correlation between feeling and movement. No deliberations should come between you, your feeling, and the physical manifestation of that feeling.

I use the expression "half-baked" to describe the movement I want. Your movements should not *mean* anything! They should be as much of a surprise (an enigma?) to *you* as they are to the people watching you.

I start the Rounds by demonstrating what I mean. I do the first movement that occurs to me. I may run in a circle waving my hands over my head. I may jump up and down holding my ears. Seeing me make a fool out of myself assures the students that I mean what I say: talent, skill, and intelligence have nothing to do with this exercise.

After I have told students what to do and before they have actually done anything, each student privately experiences a brief moment of panic. I think *everyone* —without exception— is suddenly face to face with the "I can't" syndrome. A blight of insecurity breaks out. The thought, "What am I going to do? I can't go up there unprepared. I'll look like a jerk!" is like a virus infecting everyone's complacency. Students experience a profusion of threats. They're afraid of being caught short, of being unprepared, of failing. They're afraid of not being original and clever. They're afraid of censure.

Before these fears are *confronted*, they are *subliminal*. Before a fear is active, it is latent. In other words, this exercise did not *create* the fear; that fear was part of the individual's emotional repertoire even before this exercise *exposed* it.

The vast majority of people in the world carry latent fears around with them all day, every day. They are simply *unaware* of these ubiquitous haunts until a situation arises in life (or in the imagination) that brings these "demons" out into the open. Before a fear is exposed, it is an invisible and pervasive restriction, interfering with thought, movement, and expression. For this reason, I believe that every confrontation with fear is an invaluable step toward personal freedom and physical eloquence.

In spite of my instructions, many (if not *all*) of the students silently *plan* their moves. I can see this happening but I'm not concerned or surprised. I actually expect this to happen, but I also know that the best time to move is precisely when you feel the most paralyzed. (And that's why I keep this exercise moving at a fairly rapid pace.) When you feel the most stagnant, the most unimaginative, the most vulnerable and self-conscious—*that's* the best time to make your move. It's as if all of your enemies have lined up in front of you and you send that first brazen impulse right down the midst of them. That first shot is all it takes to destroy many of your "haunts" and clear the air.

By the second or third time through the Rounds, everyone is planning less and trusting more. Students begin to discover a natural and direct correlation between themselves, their impulses, and their movements. Many of the "topical" concerns that previously blocked self-expression, have been knocked down, eliminated.

Once the Rounds start, the exercise itself does the teaching. The only thing I have to do is act as a referee. I have to make sure the pace keeps up. If given the chance, some people may balk when it's their turn to go up, and some people may take *too much* time up there. Therefore, as soon as someone completes his or her move, I say, "Next" to hurry the next person along. There should be a relaxed but fairly rapid succession of turns. (Of course, this pace should never take attention away from the person moving. Every movement should have 100% of the class's attention.)

No one should have longer than a few seconds in which to move. *Developing* movements will come later. For now, we are just breaking through the "ego-barrier." We're letting little bursts of impulse break through the shell that typically protects the ego from injury and embarrassment.

In the first few Rounds, I often have to stop students from completing or editing their moves. In spite of my instructions about "half-baked," many students *still* get up in front of the class and try to show us a pantomime or a complete idea. They'll peel a banana, open a door, hold an umbrella in the rain, etc. Other students may go for photo representations of particular animals or characters. Photos and pantomimes are unacceptable in this exercise. When they occur in Rounds, this means that the student is paying more attention to external effects than to internal impulses.

When someone *does* get up and begin a pantomime, I usually let that person complete his or her performance before delivering my *No pantomime/No photos* lecture to the whole group. This way, no one feels as if I am criticizing or rebuking anyone in particular, and that's important.

As Rounds progresses, students begin trusting and expressing their impulses more and more. The wonderful thing about expressing a feeling through movement is that you can be completely honest and expressive and still not reveal any personal secrets. You are not revealing any information that pertains to *you*, alone; rather, you are expressing feelings and dynamics that are common to all people. Each individual watching you recognizes him- or herself in your impulsive, spontaneous, and honest gestures.

As the entire class is moving from the common ground of honesty and spontaneity, our movement vocabulary begins to expand. Another person's movement may remind you (subliminally) of something from your own life. "That's how I felt the other day at the unemployment office" or "That feels like rain" or "What a majestic creature" or "That reminds me of a parade!" The class begins to associate thoughts, feelings, and memories with gestures, rhythms, and dynamics.

Rounds inspires a non-judgmental, visceral communication between people. Gestures speak for themselves and movement breeds movement. The middleman is out; spontaneity is in.

This exercise is also a safe and gentle way of nudging students through the "I can't" barrier. After their first spontaneous movements in front of a group, students understand that spontaneity is never "dried up" and that the "I can't" barrier is an illusion. This is a vital, indispensable step toward improvisation.

"The Cat's Out of the Bag"

The Rounds exercise is a vehicle for teaching another principle of improvisation—the art of "Buying It."

I describe this principle in more detail on pages 203-206, but for now all you need to know is that "buying" something means that you take full responsibility for that thing. Once you've bought something, there's no time to doubt yourself or wish you had bought something else. In Rounds, in improvisation, and on stage you must buy your gestures *as soon* as they happen! Don't hedge. Don't wait for a "better gesture" to come along. As soon as something happens, justify it. Take full responsibility for the very first movement that bursts into physical space. In other words, once the cat's out of the bag, you have to follow it—wherever it takes you.

Most beginning mime students wait for the right gesture to come along. They make a few tentative movements, and it's obvious they aren't "buying" any of them. They throw them away or ignore them until something "better" comes along. This is not in keeping with Rounds or the spirit of improvisation.

During Rounds, you may find yourself doing something and you won't know why. You may even feel stupid doing it. But don't back out; find a good *reason* for being where you are. Stay where you are until you don't feel stupid any more. Find an internal cause to *justify* that external effect. When you can go from effect to cause and from cause back to effect, then you have mastered one of the most important skills in improvisation *and* performing.

What if you were on stage playing some delicate, graceful creature and suddenly you stumbled like a klutz. If you are skilled at the art of "buying it," you will instantly turn that "mistake" into a part of your act. And your audience will love you for it.

One of my friends went to see a local theatre group put on a play about Native Americans. During a climactic confrontation between the Indian Chief and the White Man, the Indian Chief lost his pants. They just fell down. The actor didn't try to pretend it *didn't* happen. He reached down, pulled his pants back up and said, "Big Chief need new tailor!" This is the split-second thinking that can be developed through improvisation and through disciplining yourself to "buy" or use *everything* you do and everything that happens to you.

Watch your thoughts as you improvise and exercise. Sometimes you will hear yourself think, "Don't do that!" or "That was stupid" or "What did you do *that* for?" That's the personality talking, interposing doubts and fears between you and your expression of yourself.

Go past this psychic chaos, past this cross-purposing of intentions. Remember, the personality is afraid of change and the unknown. It wants everything to proceed according to its rules and expectations. *You*, however, want to be free of such controls. In fact, the thought of being able to predict and control your own life is pretty terrible. You want surprise, adventure, revelation, and the constant unfoldment of potential.

I'm convinced that we know and see everything, but we never *know* how much we know and see because the personality is always selecting our thoughts and visions for us. The exercises in this chapter teach you to instantly veto the censorship of the personality and yield to a higher conscience, a higher wisdom that is constantly revealing the right things to you *at the right time.*

Closed Rounds is a type of brainstorming exercise that may be used as a tool for writing and designing stage pieces.

The Class: Closed Rounds

This exercise is a variation on the Open Rounds, but it's a bit more controlled. In Closed Rounds you move from a *theme.* The theme may be anything ranging from the literal (i.e., carousel, Crusades, prison) to the abstract (i.e., doorway, the color yellow, jealousy).

The same rules apply as in the Open Rounds: Don't think about or plan your moves. Simply hold the theme in mind and watch what happens to you. The movements are still half-baked (i.e., they still don't *mean* anything), only now they are inspired by—colored by—a particular theme or subject. You still don't know how that inspiration will take shape until you actually move from it.

In this exercise, watching is as important as moving. As you watch the other people get up and move, you remember the images and gestures that appeal to you. Without any conscious effort, each individual remembers the moves that speak to him/her personally and forgets the moves that don't. This means that certain images survive the "Rounds process" and other images don't. As the exercise progresses, these lasting impressions evolve into workable choreography and no *one* person is responsible for this evolution. The group mind is the choreographer in this case.

This exercise follows the same procedure as the other Rounds but now, the person whose turn it is becomes the "director." If you are the director, you ask other people (one or more) to join you "on stage." As quickly as possible, tell the other people what to do. These instructions must be simple enough so that you don't need to *discuss* them too much or argue with anyone. Strictly mechanical instructions are best. Tell them what to do with their bodies, but don't worry about "why."

The Class: Group Rounds

As the director, your partners are there to serve *your* idea and follow *your* instructions and do *exactly* what they are told to do—no more and no less. The directors use the people they choose as "foils" for their creativity. The same spontaneity that you exercised in the solo Rounds must propel the Group Rounds. The final product can be half-baked and meaningless, but everyone in your "moving design" should relate to each other in some way.

Each "turn" is still brief: a few minutes to give instructions and a few minutes to carry them out. If you spend too much time constructing a "masterpiece," the value of the exercise is lost.

Talking is often an obstacle to creativity. In Closed Rounds, there is some talking, but no exchange of ideas. One person (the "director") tells the other people what to do. The communication between people is propelled by spontaneity and impulse, and the messages being relayed are private, unspoken. Everyone is collecting and processing impressions. Construction is taking place without deliberation and without anyone's conscious effort.

A discussion of how this exercise is used as a choreographic tool begins on page 226.

The Deeper Implication of Rounds

In everyday existence, we often suppress natural feelings because we think they'll get us in trouble. We prejudge everything we do. This is OK in life situations where certain displays of impulse and emotion are inappropriate. But in rehearsal and on stage (also when you have to play certain characters), you want these feelings and impulses to be free and available again. They must be part of your ready vocabulary.

On stage, you also want to be sure that suppression is a conscious *choice* rather than an unconscious restriction. If your character needs and wants to move a certain way, you must be able to do this. Nothing should block your natural range of movement. Nothing should keep you from meeting your character's demands.

Rounds encourages freedom of movement. You're in a class situation. You're safe. People are deliberately suspending commentary and judgments. Everyone is experimenting with impulses—half-baked or quarter-baked ideas. We are consciously avoiding the "pass/fail" considerations that always interfere with spontaneity and impulse. In other words, this is an ideal environment in which to explore the frontiers of thought and self-expression.

Tony, with his partners Doug Berky and Shelley Wallace in the early 1980s. (Courtesy of the authors)

When people meet for the purpose of exploring impulses, the class stops being a mismatched collection of rigid, separate personalities. The illusive walls (the ego barriers) that typically separate and divide people gradually dissolve and each movement becomes an expression of the group mind. The movements that "speak" to people survive the Rounds process; the movements that don't are forgotten.

During Rounds, the feeling of being among strangers totally disappears. Every movement—every personal statement—is evolving toward a cooperative expression of the group's sensibilities. Everyone discovers (subconsciously?) that the feelings that generate spontaneous and impulsive movements are *shared* feelings.

Many (if not all) of my exercises are designed simply to reinstate a person's natural ease of expression, to make people comfortable in the world (and on stage) again. The key to being comfortable is not to *shun* discomfort, but to *exploit* it— use it—put it to work for you.

I remember being among meditating people who became incensed if anyone interrupted them or made noise. To me, this meant they had missed the point of meditation. The inter-

Expanding the Comfort Zone Through Rounds

ruption or the noise in the next room is not the obstacle to inner peace. The obstacle to inner peace is the *capacity* to become irritated. This capacity for irritation is actually the *cause* of irritating situations. And the key to enlightenment (or to any noble accomplishment) is the ability to "turn lemons into lemonade."

As I said before, the potential to be afraid or irritated is *latent* until a certain situation activates these emotions. Therefore, when people are suddenly face to face with the fear of embarrassment (as they are in Rounds), they are preparing to defuse a previously latent fear. This confrontation is an important step toward repossessing the comfort zone. The next step is learning how to stay in your comfort zone no matter where you are or what you're up against.

So much of life tends to make us uncomfortable. Most of our actions and decisions are *primed* or *caused* by discomfort. This shouldn't be. We should be able to move from comfort at all times, not by denying or resisting anything (resistance and denial are also primed by discomfort); but by learning to *include* every feeling—every circumstance—within the comfort zone. Even external irritations should be included within that internal and indomitable sense of comfort.

You should also know that you don't have to create or simulate the comfort zone; it's already there. All you have to do is bring everything (every thought, every irritation, every hope, desire, and expectation) into it.

The Class: Statuary

This exercise, like the Rounds, is a gentle introduction into the art of improvisation. It helps destroy the latent fear of body contact and teaches students:

— To think fast and impulsively and to translate these impulses *immediately* into physical space.
— To be *gentle* (as opposed to bombastic) in this rapid transaction between impulse and action.
— To cooperate with other people even while acting impulsively.
— To be comfortable with abstract gestures.

In Statuary, two or more people get up in front of the class. (I have done this exercise with as many as seven or eight people at a time. But in the beginning, when students are a little shy and uneasy, I keep the groups small: three or four people at a time.) They stand slightly apart and face each other.

Someone, preferably the teacher, calls out a word or a noun

phrase. After the word is said aloud, everyone stands still for four or five seconds to let the word "sink in." That is, they *think* about the word and notice how that word makes them *feel*. Then the teacher says, "Go." With this, the students (still holding the word in mind) come together to form a solid mass of "clay"—a statue. In a matter of a few seconds, each separate body must be entirely swallowed up in a group pose.

It is important that all of the people come together to form *one* statue. They should look like *one* solid mass of clay. This means, of course, that each individual must conform his or her own shape to the contours of the group shape.

Here's an example. A group of four people stands center stage and I shout out the word (the noun phrase, actually): "Cocktail Party!" Everyone stands still for four seconds and then everyone surges together to form one solid body. In the final pose, the audience may see a few people holding cocktail glasses or smoking cigarettes, but they might also see someone hanging upside down, tilting sideways, or "draped" over other people. Some people may be doing recognizable things (i.e., drinking or smoking), but the overall impression from the statue is abstract as opposed to literal.

The concrete (i.e., literal) translations of the word will not conform easily to the group impression. Abstract translations are more flexible, and students will automatically move (and think) abstractly when they have to conform to a solid mass of bodies.

For example, if the word is "prison" and someone equates prison with the feeling of loneliness and isolation and suddenly four or five people pile on top of each other, then that impression (isolation) will have to be expressed in an abstract way. It certainly can't be expressed literally when four or five people are so intimately connected.

Interestingly, as the individual disappears within the statue, his/her personal feelings *will* find an abstract outlet if the literal outlet is unavailable. The person who equated "prison" with feelings of isolation may cover his face with his hands or simply ignore the fact that the "objects" in front of him are other people. That person may shrink to the floor and peer through legs as if they were prison bars. There are many abstract ways to depict isolation, despite the fact that four or five people are fused together. And each person will discover those abstract expressions when this exercise forces him or her to do so.

In the four or five seconds *after* hearing the word and *before* the statue happens, each individual lets the word (prison, cocktail party, or whatever) *get* to him or her. The word inspires each individual differently. If the word is "cocktail party," one person may think of martini glasses and high heel shoes. Someone else may think of stiff smiles and boredom. Each person comes up with his/her own personal impression of "cocktail party." These personal impressions *prime* the individual's actions, but nothing is conclusive or set in stone, yet.

As each person moves into the group pose, his or her personal impressions assume specific shapes, forms, and dynamics. The end result is very much like a cocktail party. This one solid mass of clay contains literal as well as abstract interpretations of the theme.

After a few trial runs, each individual becomes more skilled at imbibing the word and approaching the group with awareness and receptivity. When four or five people are equally aware and receptive and when everyone is thinking along the same lines, magnificent shapes (statues) begin to evolve. One person may end up horizontal to the floor, supported by the rest of the group. Someone else may be upside down. Anything can happen in these few seconds of cooperation as long as each member of the group moves sensitively and in keeping with the theme.

The beauty of this exercise is that students learn to express more and more of themselves in the statue. The individual's impression of a cocktail party, for example, not only includes things such as martini glasses and high heels, but also memories, opinions, judgments, attitudes. With practice, students learn to bring their multi-faceted impressions of every theme out into the open. Therefore, the final pose is a multidimensional rendition of the real thing. Three individuals in a statue may reveal fifteen, twenty, or more facets of the theme.

This exercise illustrates another approach to premise work. In Statuary, the theme (in this case, "cocktail party") becomes everyone's premise—the *center* of everyone's attention. This common center of attention brings many minds together to form one mind. When several minds are centered around *one* theme, *one* purpose, those minds merge to form one cooperative consciousness. Individuals, therefore, do their own thing within the group parameters.

Even though everyone's body must bend and adjust to the group contours, the *theme* of the statue does not change. The effects change, but the cause of those effects does not change.

Therefore, every movement, every gesture, and pose resonates with the individual's impression of that theme.

Other words or noun phrases to use in statuary could be:
Bronx Zoo
Cathedral of Notre Dame
Playground
Birthday Party
Graduation
The list is endless.

The Loop: A Variation on the Statuary Exercise

The loop is simply a continuation of the Statuary exercise. After the group has taken a pose and frozen in a position, I may tell them to *evolve* this position. When this happens, the statue gently assumes new shapes and positions, all in keeping with the original theme.

At any time during the "evolution," the teacher or director may shout, "freeze." When this happens, the movement stops and everyone holds his/her position. The audience can now appreciate one particular moment in the evolution.

In Volume II of my video book *Mime Spoken Here,* we perform Statuary. (On the tape, I call this exercise "Statues.") For one group I chose the word, "nightmare." In the initial pose Benny Reehl and Jackie Reifer both ended up lying on the floor. Benny was on his side, facing the audience and Jackie was directly behind him.

In this first pose, Benny had his head on his own hand (as if he were sleeping) and Jackie was pushing him from behind— as if he were a part of her nightmare and she was trying to get away from him. I then told them to evolve the pose. Slowly Benny got up and propped himself on one elbow. Jackie's arm then came out from behind Benny and stretched out in front of his face. Benny looked down and saw his own two hands and a third hand in front of him. He picked up the third hand in disbelief and horror. At this point, I told them to resolve the nightmare, to come out of it. Benny took the strange hand and turned it slowly so that the palm faced upward. He then used the hand as a pillow and rested his head on Jackie's palm.

It is important to note that Jackie was sensitive enough to know that her hand was being *used.* She, therefore, did not pull it away but left it there. Her hand and Benny's *use* of the hand became the focal point of the statue. The other person in the group, Christian Murray, became tangled in Benny's and Jackie's legs. He "used" these legs to show confinement, imprisonment. His "predicament" evolved and resolved on cue and contributed to the whole nightmarish impression.

A *loop,* or the evolution of the initial pose, may last a few seconds (and finish with another pose) or it can go on for several minutes. When the evolution goes on for a few minutes, individuals may separate from the group and return to it. But the liberty to physically detach oneself from the group should not be taken until the Statuary exercise has been mastered and everyone understands what it means to *conform* to the group impression.

The Class: Atmosphere Work

In the late 1960s, I taught a mime course for one semester at Towson State University in Towson, Maryland. An exercise I call atmosphere work came out of this experience.

This exercise (and all of my exercises, actually) was designed to solve a problem. During our scene study sessions and solo-mime sessions, I noticed that some of the students did beautiful work. Their movements were timed correctly, their gestures were clear, their sketches were convincing. Other students floundered and struggled, never coming up with a convincing portrayal of anything.

In most learning institutions, the former group would have been labeled "talented" and the latter group "untalented." But I never consign my students to chance. Talent or lack-of-talent is not a genetic fluke. If there's one reason why I have been successful as a teacher it is because I teach from the premise that all students are innately talented. If their work doesn't reflect this, then it's up to me to find the problem and do whatever I can to correct it.

I noticed that some of my students at Towson University were *involved* in their work; they *believed* what they were doing. This work was convincing and captivating to the "audience." But the majority of the students were not so convincing. On closer scrutiny, I noticed that these students moved *ahead* of their motivation. Their words and gestures were not supported by any conviction or necessity. There were too many effects and not enough cause—too much happening on the outside and not enough happening on the inside.

I designed atmosphere work to prove to students how much could be relayed without doing or saying anything. In one session I took one student aside and discreetly gave him a character and a location: Adam in the Garden of Eden. (The rest of the class did not hear these instructions.) The student then stood in front of the class and, without moving or talking, simply *believed* that he was Adam standing in the middle of the garden.

In atmosphere work, you must allow your character and your environment to *occur* to you. If you were this student in the above example, you would "see" the garden appear in the space around you. Trees, birds, and animals may "fill in" first, then the heat of the air and the sound of the wind. Your character also occurs to you gradually. You begin to feel more at home, more natural in your environment.

The people watching atmosphere work witness a transformation. The audience gathers an impression of the character and the situation until finally, it is absolutely clear to everyone that the person is in another world. Now, I ask the audience a few questions: Is this person outdoors or indoors? What's he feeling? Thinking?

I remember that during the "Adam in the Garden of Eden" exercise at Towson, someone in the audience noticed that the character was in a state of awe—on the brink of discovery and adventure. Some of the impressions were surprisingly accurate. One person in the audience saw the beginning of time. Someone else saw a new planet. The answers to these questions proved to everyone in the class, that the audience can learn a great deal about your character even without your *doing* anything.

Atmosphere work was a revelation for my students at Towson University. They began to believe more and *do* less and with this, everyone's work became more convincing.

Jean-Louis Barrault in *Children of Paradise*. (Courtesy of the authors)

159

Surprising Ramifications of Atmosphere Work

One day, I was in front of the Towson University class doing atmosphere work. I told the class that I would go one step further. Not only would I take on a character, I would also sing a song to myself. I wanted to see how much could be relayed without moving or speaking. Privately, I decided to be a child singing "Three Blind Mice." I took my place and let my character, my environment, and my song occur to me.

The class began zeroing in on my character. Everyone saw innocence—a childlike sense of fun. Then someone piped out, "You're singing 'Three Blind Mice!'" I was absolutely dumbfounded. How could *anyone* have guessed "Three Blind Mice?" The class couldn't believe it either; they thought we were teasing them.

The person who supposedly "read my mind" was Bob deFrank. I had been impressed with his work all along; he was an exceptionally sensitive and empathic performer. Now he was displaying a skill that I knew nothing about. "Aw, come on, Bob!" I said. "How did you guess 'Three Blind Mice?'"

Bob just shrugged his shoulders and said, "I dunno. That song just came to my mind and I couldn't think of anything else."

Later we were doing the Mirror exercise (see pages 144–146), and I had the chance to get back at Bob. We were performing famous characters from history or legend, and the rest of the class had to guess who the characters were. It was Bob's turn. He stood up and slowly directed his gaze to the floor. As he stooped to the floor, I *saw* Narcissus. "You're Narcissus!" I said.

Bob was disconcerted. "Sheesh, Tony! You could at least let me finish the sketch!" By now the class was convinced that Bob and I were in cahoots, but I was beginning to understand that the phenomenon of telepathy is probably nothing more than an advanced stage of empathy. I had never displayed telepathic abilities before this. And now that I had, I realized there was nothing miraculous or superhuman about it.

If you pare away all of the words, gestures, and facial expressions from the human forms of communication, you can still understand a person if that person wants to be understood and if you're sensitive enough to tune into that person's desire. I'm quite sure that if the vocal chords, postal services, telephones, and fax machines suddenly disappeared, communication would still continue. The most basic lines of communication are simply the channels of empathy that connect us to all living things.

This exercise is designed to deliver a strong, devastating blow to the ego barrier.

The rules are simple. One person at a time gets up in front of the class and, for three to five minutes, that person moves and talks as quickly as possible without stopping or slowing down. The only rule in this exercise is to move and speak *quickly*. This means that many (most!) of your statements and gestures will *not* make sense. Words tumble out of your mouth in no particular order. Movements, too, are speedy, bold, and senseless. If, by chance, your movements and words start making sense, *let* them, but don't be distracted by this. The intellect will want to analyze what you're doing. It will try to tell you what you should or should not do, but in this exercise, there are no "should nots." There are only speed, impulse, and excitatory responses.

By maintaining a steady tempo, the person is forced to charge through those "roadblocks" that the personality (the ego) usually sets up. Everyone is aware of such roadblocks—those ubiquitous little voices inside of us saying, "No, don't do that, you'll look stupid," or "Now you're trapped, try something else." Self-doubt, self-consciousness, and shyness are the ego barriers that stand in the way of our most organic, promising, and exuberant impulses.

Sometimes the only way to overcome such obstacles is by using speed. You simply don't give yourself the time to heed inhibitory responses. Usually, only one session of Harangue is enough to introduce the students to "life beyond the ego barrier." Once they have been introduced to this phenomenon, they have an easier time following impulses and taking chances when it comes to self-expression. It is a scary but an exhilarating exercise.

(There is a variation on this exercise in which the tempo can slow down, but I allow this variation only after the students have gotten through the first exercise, only after they know what it feels like to be on the other side of that formidable ego barrier.)

During the early years of teaching, I noticed that students tended to favor certain movements and neglect other movements. Some would use their legs, but not their arms. Others (the dancers, usually) would jump and turn but neglect character attitudes. Some would demonstrate flexibility in certain parts of their bodies but not in others. This tendency to favor certain movements and neglect others interfered with their mime studies and sketches. Their range of movement was obstructed by old habits. Consequently, their movement vocabulary was not expansive enough to cover a full range of ideas and emotions.

When a speaker unconsciously repeats a phrase over and over again, or if the tone of his/her voice never varies, the message doesn't get very far. Habitual speech patterns interfere with eloquence. Likewise, habitual movement patterns interfere with the mime's ability to *speak* with the body.

To address this problem, I invented the exercise called the Eclectic (for want of a better word). The purpose of this exercise is to encourage students to be more experimental with their movements, to indulge in a wide variety of uncharacteristic moves. Expanding someone's movement vocabulary is not a matter of teaching that person new *moves*; it's a matter of persuading him or her to move in novel, uncharacteristic ways.

It took me a number of months to discover the best working format for this exercise. After many experiments, I settled on this one. The class sits in a semicircle on the floor. For the sake of simplicity, let's say there are eighteen people in the class. I now choose three people to be "performers." (The number of performers depends, of course, on the size of the class.) The rest of the class acts as an "audience" for the performers. Each member of the audience is assigned to watch only *one* performer. This means that each of the three performers has *five* audience members watching his/her "performance."

During the first stage of the exercise, the performers are instructed to move freely in front of the class. All three performers take "center stage" at the same time and move around each other in front of the class.

The performers do not try to *entertain* their audience! As a matter of fact, they should ignore the fact that they are being watched as they move in every possible style and speed they can think of. They must show as much *variety* of movement as possible. The performers are advised not to repeat moves but rather to show a wide range of movement.

Before the performers start moving, I may suggest a few movements just to give the students an idea of how many movements and styles there are to choose from: movements depicting sports, feelings, moods, memories, literature, occupations, colors, etc.—anything that brings out the full range of their movement. Those are the instructions for the *performers*.

Each *audience* member watches his/her assigned performer carefully. The audience's job is to discern what is blatantly missing from that performer's movement vocabulary.

This exercise can be fun for the performers, but the audience has to be diligent, discerning, and sensitive. The audience must watch the performers with the discerning eye of a director or a choreographer. Each member of the audience must think, "If this performer were coming to me for an audition, what would I like him/her to be able to do?" The audience must be critical and helpful at the same time.

The teacher, of course, has to keep an eye on everyone in the class to make sure that performers and audience are doing their work properly.

After the performers have moved for two or three minutes, they sit down for the sharing of critiques. Each performer is discussed individually and in front of the class. (One performer at a time now has the class's undivided attention.) The five audience members tell their performer what was missing from his/her movement vocabulary, and the rest of the class listens to each critique.

After the audience members have given their critiques, the three performers have a second chance. They take center stage again and move for another two or three minutes. This time, the performers must incorporate all the critiques into their performance—they must include all of those movements that the audience had observed were missing from their first performance.

After this "second-chance performance," the teacher selects three other students to act as performers and assigns five audience members to each performer. The whole process is repeated until everyone in the class has had the chance to perform.

The performers' job is pretty straightforward. They simply have to move in as many ways as possible. The audience's job is not so clear-cut. Audience members have to be open-minded and acute as they watch the performers. Sometimes, the impressions they receive from the performance will not be easy to describe. Audience members may have to talk abstractly or poetically when giving their critiques. They may notice that a performer lacks lyricism or that all of the performer's movements are "jagged." They may have to tell a performer that he/she has an abundance of stylistic movements, but neglects the "regular people" moves. Maybe a performer never straightens his/her knees. Maybe someone is missing bright, sprightly movements. The audience members must notice all of these things and report their observations to the performer and the rest of the class.

I once told a student that all of his movements were grotesque and exaggerated. After I said this, I realized that even before we started this exercise, his whole countenance had suggested cynicism and hostility. He was not an unpleasant person to talk with, but I knew he intimidated people. Several people in the class were going out of their way to be friendly to this apparently volatile, temperamental person. And here I was, telling this man to incorporate beauty and sweetness into his movements! This exercise was precisely the right vehicle for such a comment. It was an impersonal way to make a personal comment.

The man listened to my critique and got up to move a second time. He looked like a different person. It was as if all of the poison had drained out of his system. Some of the students even giggled with relief to see this soft, fun-loving man emerge from beneath that severe façade. I don't know if this experience changed the man at all, but it certainly changed our perception of him. We all felt more comfortable with each other after that.

The Class: Kirtan

This exercise was inspired by a form of musical worship practiced in India. As a student of yoga many years ago, I often participated in kirtans. Even then, I was impressed by the improvisational nature of these rituals.

During the kirtan, one member of the group begins a melodious prayer or a chant. The other worshippers join in, contributing their own unique voice to the chorus. The overall effect is absolute harmony—many disparate voices and sounds uniting to create *one* rapturous expression of praise and thanksgiving.

The object of group improvisations is to find a unique and cohesive blend of many individual instincts. Ideally, each individual harmonizes with the group while maintaining his or her individual "voice." Finding the perfect balance between giving and taking, leading and following, assenting and dissenting is a delicate task. It's the skill of being awake, sensitive, and straightforward. It's the skill of reading and responding to "signals" that only the spirit can receive. As with any other skill, this requires practice, and the kirtan is an ideal exercise for this.

When I teach kirtans in class, I ask one person to start with a sound and to keep this sound fairly constant and rhythmic.

The rest of the class joins in, each person chiming in as they are inspired to do so. Each individual adds a unique sound and rhythm to the group voice. Rhythms and sounds change as the participants' feelings and impressions change. In many ways these basic, sound-making kirtans are reminiscent of improv jazz sessions.

The above is an example of an open (i.e., themeless) kirtan. You can "close" your kirtan by specifying a theme beforehand. You may do a kirtan on marsh sounds, city sounds, circus sounds, etc. Later, once you have understood the basic kirtan of sound-making, you can "expand your vocabulary." You can move, sing, recite poetry, etc.

There are two obstacles in the way of performing the kirtan successfully. As I said earlier, the object of the kirtan is to contribute to the group dynamic without losing one's individual voice. The obstacles, then, have to do with either over-assertion or under-assertion of the individual voices. Either participants try too hard to stand out or they try too hard to conform. Either participants cower on the periphery of the action (afraid of making "mistakes") or they dive in blindly with little or no consideration for what's going on around them. Let's discuss each obstacle separately starting with the tendency to *over*-assert oneself.

The kirtan performed with a bunch of over-assertive individuals sounds like a cacophony rather than a euphonic blend of solo voices. The cacophonous effect happens when the individuals fail to *pay attention* to their surroundings. A tenor may have a strong and beautiful voice, but if he fails to blend with the other voices in his section (and in the choir), he'll destroy the overall effect of the concert. Likewise in the kirtan, the individuals must pay attention and listen to everything going on around them. They need to relax into their environment and open their senses. In this state of ease, attentiveness, and receptivity, the correct impulses rise up and blend with the whole.

The other obstacle in the way of a successful kirtan is the tendency to *under*-assert oneself. Overly conscientious people often have this tendency. These are the people who, when I tell them to notice everything, start taking a deliberate and ambitious inventory of everyone and everything around them. These people simply need to settle down and trust their instincts. They need to *let* themselves be inspired.

The basic sound-making kirtan teaches the under-assertive individuals how to trust and follow their own *feelings* and impulses. It takes them away from an obsession with the physical realm and the physical senses. I often tell these people to pay more attention to their feelings than to the actual sounds they hear with their ears. If you pay exclusive attention to the physical senses, you will be self-conscious. You'll wonder, "Does this sound go with those sounds?" or "Maybe I should make *this* noise, now." Then by the time you make the "right" noise, it won't be right any more.

This reminds me of a time when I was helping Karen with a dance improvisation. She was moving to the music, but something about her spontaneity was choked. It seemed to me as if she was trying to *catch up* to something. She was, in fact, *following* the music. I told her to stop following the music and simply move according to how she *felt*. Suddenly, everything came together. The movement and the music became a single, simultaneous event, and I "saw" Karen for the first time. The music and the movement actually *met* in Karen's feelings.

She understood, then, that her *feeling* was inherently correct. Music and movement *originate* in the private and personal realm of feelings. Therefore, moving from the sentiments means going back to the source. Here, music, dance, and person intersect. Karen didn't have to *listen to* the music; she had already heard it. The music had already affected her. She had only to express *herself* as she danced. When she moved spontaneously and effortlessly, she was automatically musical.

We absorb a lot of information subconsciously. No matter where we are, we imbibe what is going on around us and this *automatically* affects our feelings and impulses. In the kirtan, you don't have to make a special effort to hear and respond appropriately. Whatever you feel like doing, do. Your feelings are informed by the situation. Simply relax, pay attention, and express those feelings.

7

IMPROVISATION

Tony and Jewel Walker (standing), holding up "Happy Patches," late 1950s. (Courtesy of the authors)

T his chapter is divided into three sections: an *introduction* to improvisation, the *practice* of improvisation, and a discussion of improv *theory*.

The "introduction section" consists of a brief description of what improvisation *is*, what it *isn't*, and *why* we improvise. The most basic rules of improvisation are also outlined in this section.

The "practice section" is a play-by-play description of an actual improvisation session. Here, I describe several improvisation exercises and briefly explain how other improvisers

Structure of this Chapter

handled these exercises. I encourage you to practice these exercises before you try to grasp the theory of improvisation discussed in the last section.

The best time to *discuss* improvisation, is *after* you've improvised, not *before*. A premature discussion of improvisation theory may only stifle your natural and spontaneous approach to this art form.

What you know is measured by what you do *spontaneously*— what you do the *very instant* that action is called for. Therefore, it's not possible to determine how much you *know* or *don't know* about improvisation until you've actually tried to improvise. Only after your own (spontaneous) knowledge has proven or disproven itself will you be able to appreciate and grasp a higher understanding.

Introduction

What Improvisation Is and What It Isn't

My definition of improvisation differs from the popular definitions. Let's settle those differences right away and establish a common language between us.

> **improvise** - 1. To invent, compose, or recite without preparation.
> —*The American Heritage Dictionary*

There is a semantic pitfall in this definition having to do with the issue of preparation. The dictionary uses the phrase "without preparation" to mean that your future has not been choreographed or mapped out for you. But whether you can predict the future or not, you're always prepared for it. Each moment is informed by the moment that precedes it. Everything that happens has been set up; it is *prepared* to happen.

No one goes into an improvisation "cold." Everyone is equipped with personal, ethnic, and racial memories, a history, an education, and skills. Everyone has acquired likes and dislikes. All of life is a preparation for improvisation.

• • •

I disagree with the notion that improvisation is an exercise in free association. Free-associative improvs are random, haphazard. They stay on one level. They often don't build, escalate, or resolve. They often don't reveal anything or challenge anyone. Improvisation (as I teach it) is a probing, accumulative, and high-risk expedition into the unknown.

The word "improvisation" has the word "improve" in it.

Improvisations must go somewhere. They must improve. They should never be monotonous or "safe."

•   •   •

Some people believe that improvisations are field days for the uninhibited. This belief attracts some wild and insensitive personalities to improv sessions while it repels the more serene and complacent types. But, the every-man-for-himself attitude is *not* in keeping with the spirit of improvisation. When someone "lets loose" during an improvisation, this usually means that he or she has become oblivious to the present moment. An improvisation should never be out of control or physically dangerous for anyone. Improvisation, approached correctly, teaches acuity, perceptiveness, and *presence*-of-mind. Blind abandon and bald inhibition have nothing to do with improvisation.

•   •   •

Most people think of improvisation as a theatrical exercise. I see it as an exercise in self-revelation that often yields stage-worthy results.

Many "improvisations" I have seen (as an audience) are actually "showcases" for the improvisers. The improvisers come equipped with a certain repertoire of skills and tricks, and they look for opportunities to showcase these skills. Some improvisers bring their own "safety nets" with them—backup plans just in case something goes "wrong."

These improvisers are expecting something from their improvisation; they are planning its future. If the improvisation happens to take them into an area of "weakness," they break the improvisation and follow Plan B—the safe route.

For example, I once saw a dancer/improviser lose her balance at an "inopportune" moment. When she fell, she suddenly broke the improv, recovered her balance, and picked up where she had left off. It was apparent to all of us watching that a chain of events had been interrupted—the improviser hadn't wanted to fall. If I could have communicated with her at that moment, I would have told her to *do something* with that fall. "*Use* it. Put it to work. Follow it. See where it takes you. It has prepared you for the next logical step in your improv. Don't let it slip away!"

Whatever happens in an improvisation is meant to happen. Nothing should be thrown away or ignored simply because it doesn't meet your expectations or accentuate your strengths.

• • •

The improvisations usually shown on TV do not fit my definition of true improvisation. Like the dancer in the above example, most of the TV improvisers aren't tuned into the "here and now." They don't justify and deal with *everything* that happens. (Jonathan Winters is an exception to this. I've seen him do some brilliant television improvisations. He simply refuses to let the camera interfere with his spontaneity.)

Before I go on lambasting these television improvisations, let me say that the improvisers aren't always at fault here. Many of them are skilled, sensitive, and alert individuals. The problem is TV itself. Television is, by nature, anti-improvisation. It places specific demands on its performers that automatically stifle the spirit of improvisation.

The most offensive demand placed on television improvisations is that there must never be any "dead time." That is, there must never be a moment in which "nothing" happens. But an improvisation inevitably goes through many tempo and plot changes, and the improvisers must be willing to follow those changes. They have to listen and wait sometimes, speak and move at other times. The improvisation itself has to tell them what to do and when to do it.

Another demand on television improvisers is that they must be "funny" at all times. If the sketch happens to drift toward darkness, tragedy, or any uncomfortable place, the improvisers must shift gears and force the material into a comic vein. This is not improvisation; this is editing.

The referees on television blow the whistle to *stop* the improvisation precisely when the improvisations are *starting!* That critical moment when there's (apparently) nowhere to go and nothing to do, *that's* when the improvisation starts cooking. And television blows the whistle! I could scream with frustration—but I change the channel instead.

Rules for Improvisation   There are three simple rules to improvisation: read, listen, and follow.

> 1) Read what is coming at you from all directions.
> 2) Listen to what the present moment is "suggesting" to you.
> 3) Follow your impulses dispassionately and faithfully.

An adjunct to these rules is that you should not discount *anything* you're feeling. Your improv needs to have access to *all* of you—every feeling, every frustration and fear, every thought, memory, skill, etc. The moment will decide what's pertinent and what's not. The more vulnerable, dispassionate, and honest you are, the more satisfying your improvisation will be.

During an improvisation, you must translate your thoughts, moods, feelings, and impulses directly into physical space, directly into movement, language, sounds, or some other physical manifestation. If you think of a word, say the word. Then, listen to what you just said to see where *that* takes you. If you feel like crawling or leaping, crawl or leap and watch what *happens* next. If you see a city street in your mind's eye, go there—walk on the sidewalk, through the traffic, and watch what happens to you and around you. Put yourself right in the middle of this stream of inspiration. As soon as you think something or feel something, let that thing "get to you," let it "happen" to you. Rather than *narrate* the events in your improvisation; *live* those events.

The translation of impulse to action takes place so quickly that you often don't have time to discern the *meaning* of what you're doing. You also don't have time to step outside of yourself and edit what you've just done. If you *do* take that time, spontaneity is lost and the improv stalls.

Why Improvise?

Improvisation has a special appeal to an audience. It is uniquely exciting to watch someone venture into "the void"— beyond a repertoire of skills, through a storehouse of personal memories— into the realm of infinite potential.

At such moments, the tension in the air is galvanized. The audience and the improvisers are in the same boat. Everyone feels vulnerable, exposed. We're peering into "the void," waiting for that critical moment when the imperceptible becomes perceptible—when the invisible impulse turns into a gesture, a word, a song, a stillness, or whatever. The possibilities are infinite but what actually happens will depend solely on the improviser. No two people will behave alike in the same improv. This is the unique excitement of improvisation—what it reveals about the performer.

The benefits of improvisation far exceed its unprecedented theatrical value. The act of improvising in front of an understanding audience (fellow improvisers) teaches you more about yourself in two minutes than you sometimes learn in two years! Improvisation is a great accelerator of personal evolution.

171

Practice

A Week of Improvisation

Just as I was preparing to write this chapter on improvisation, four of my protégés from Canada (members of Jest in Time Theatre) came down from Nova Scotia to Portland, Maine, to study improvisation with me for a week.

Jest in Time is a movement theatre ensemble consisting of three women (Sherry Lee Hunter, Mary Ellen MacLean, and Shelley Wallace) and one man (Christian Murray). They are all seasoned performers: actors, mimes, comedians, and just all-around great people. To have the opportunity to improvise for six hours a day with Jest in Time was just what the chapter on improvisation needed. For two of the sessions, we were joined by two other actor/mime/comedians who have studied with me extensively: Jackie Reifer and John Saccone. (Jackie, Johnny, and Shelley were also members of my third mime troupe, The Celebration Theatre Ensemble.) My wife, Karen, also participated in most of these improv sessions and we had a fruitful week.

Jest in Time Theatre, in "Handmade." From left to right: Mary Ellen MacLean, Sherry Lee Hunter, Shelley Wallace, and Christian Murray. (Photo by Cylla Von Tiedmann)

This week was an exercise in improvisation for me, too. Even though I never participated in the exercises, I was constantly reading the moment and watching everybody intently. I had to come up with exercises as the need for them arose. Many of these exercises were brand new to all of us. There was a progression during the week—each exercise was more specific, more challenging, and more complicated than the one that preceded it. Each was chosen based on what I felt the particular needs and capabilities of the group were at the time.

I ended up describing each exercise several times before the improvisation actually started. With each description, the object of the exercise became more palpable until I felt confident that each person had a visceral sense of what the improvisation was all about. I could see people tune into the spirit of improvisation as I described the exercise. They were already "testing the ground," focusing in on the deep inner workings of their own mind where thoughts, feelings, and impulses are mere shadows of things to come. The improvisation started even before anyone stood up to move.

I thought I'd write about this particular week of improv sessions, since the exercises we did and the revelations that surfaced are comprehensive, pertinent, and vital to anyone interested in the art of improvisation.

In one of our early sessions, I asked each person to get up in front of the group and, without doing anything, simply *be there*. Each person was to notice the milieu: the room, the people watching, and most important, his/her own feelings.

First Exercise: "Just Stand There...."

Now, if you're unfamiliar with improvisation, you might not think this a very exciting exercise. But if you had been with us that day, you would have been riveted to this seemingly unimportant event.

One at a time, each person took center stage and experienced what it feels like to be in the spotlight. Each of these performers had been on stage hundreds of times and each had been in front of crowds far bigger than this. But being in front of a crowd is never a routine event.

As each person stood center stage, I'd ask questions like, "How do you feel?" "What are you thinking?" When we talked, our sentences were brief. We sounded like scientists studying a phenomenon. We weren't drawing any conclusions; we were simply noticing things.

At one point, Jackie was in front of the group. After she had been up there for a minute or so, I *saw* Jackie. This was a profoundly moving experience, and I shared my observation with the group, "To really see *Jackie*, it's enough to make you cry." Immediately, four or five of us were actually crying.

Other times, a person would be up there and suddenly, out of nowhere, we'd all start giggling. Faint glimmers of humor would first occur to the person in front of us. That glimmer would brighten into a smile. We'd smile. Then everyone would laugh.

This one session, alone, taught us that humor, comedy, tradgedy, affection (*all* of the emotions) are constantly present and available. Every feeling in the world is right at your fingertips at all times. You are not responsible for the emotional impact of your improvisation or your performance. Your only job is to remain present, alert, and honest at all times.

"Don't Discount Any Feeling"

Early in the week, several people expressed impatience and frustration with their own tension. They knew they should be relaxed but they couldn't seem to get rid of their tension. They'd swing their arms or rub their necks impatiently. I knew they were hoping these maneuvers would dissolve their tension. It never did. One day we talked about this.

When you improvise, you must read what is coming at you from all directions, including *yourself*. You must notice your own tension, your own discomfort. If you take an antagonistic attitude toward anything you feel, you are at a disadvantage. You are also breaking the rules of improvisation by not including *all* of yourself in what you're doing. Preferring one feeling or one impulse over another is the type of prejudice that stifles improvisation.

Everything you feel and think must be *included* in your work. There should be no editing. If tension occurs to you, don't cut it out. You don't yet know *how* it will affect you, but you *need* that tension in order for the improvisation to work.

Also—if, in the middle of your improvisation, you feel you are failing, work with this feeling. If you are angry, work with this anger. Fear and anger are dynamics. Before they have an object or a reason for being, they are simply impulses. If you give these impulses a chance to tell you what you should *not* do, you have waited too long. Remember: Translate every impulse into action the moment it occurs to you. Don't wait for it to become an issue.

After the "Just Stand There" improv, we progressed to the next exercise. This time, I told each person to: "Get up (in front of the group) and express the first thought, feeling, or mood that occurs to you. You won't know what that thought, feeling, or mood *is* until you actually get up there. Once you get up there, simply physicalize 'who you are' at that moment and let the improv evolve. Continue to read what's happening to you and show that."

I also said, "Let the outside look like the inside."

Mary Ellen started her solo improv by commenting on how beautiful she was. She expressed arrogance and self-confidence. She answered a phone, hung it up, and then she hesitated. She seemed to be at a loss for things to do. (There's a big difference between a natural suspension of action during an improvisation, and the cessation of action that happens when the improviser wonders what to do next.)

I began asking Mary Ellen's character questions about her situation. Pretty soon this vain and arrogant woman was surrounded by eight phones. None of the phones was ringing, but this woman was pretty sure that one would ring soon. The audience knew the phones were not going to ring. They realized that the surface appearance of self-confidence was concealing a deep-seated fear of being alone and neglected. The introduction of phones on the scene exposed what had been concealed. Now her "outside looked like her inside."

This is the value of setting up a *situation* during your improvisation. When Mary Ellen's character told us that she had eight phones in front of her, we naturally wondered "why." We wanted to know more about the phones. Were they ringing? Not ringing? We were involved, captivated. The improvisation was successful.

One of the most common obstacles to improvisation is the tendency to idle or repeat the same movements or attitudes over and over again. For example, the improviser may start by strutting across the stage but then this strutting goes on for a minute or two with only minor variations. The improviser may play *within* the strut, trying out new tempos or new arm movements, but otherwise nothing changes, evolves, or escalates.

This happened in the beginning of the week. Many of the improvisations idled. They failed to *escalate* or gather new information. To introduce the improvisers to the concept of escalation, I asked them particular questions about *who* they

Second Exercise: "Let the Outside Look Like the Inside."

The Escalation of Intrigue

were, *what* they were doing, and *why*. These questions were crutches—they facilitated the construction of characters and situations and served to nudge the improvisers out of their ruts.

But, as with any crutch, this practice of asking questions should be thrown away as soon as possible. Once improvisers appreciate the *concept* of escalation, their improvisations should escalate naturally, without the aid of crutches. Rather than answering their *audience's* questions, the improvisers should ask and answer their own questions.

In the beginning of the week, it was necessary for me to ask questions only because the improvisers had failed to become *intrigued* by their own actions. They weren't inquisitive or curious about what they were doing.

When improvisers fail to be intrigued by what they're doing, this means that their attention is in the wrong place. Rather than focus on what *is* happening, they worry about what *should be* happening. Then, they struggle to make their improvisation "work" through cleverness and willpower. In fact, improvising is much easier, simpler, and more fun than that. All you have to do is pay attention to what *is* happening and forget about what's *not* happening (i.e., what *should* happen).

Improvisations should be riveting to watch for the *improviser* as well as the audience. Only when the improviser is intrigued by what's happening, can he/she enlarge upon the audience's interest and involvement. The audience is always intensely interested and involved in what the improviser is doing. Only when their curiosity passes unnoticed and unaddressed do they begin to lose interest.

It is important to remember that the audience sees only what *is* happening; they *cannot* see your intentions or read your mind. Therefore, if you stay tuned to what *is* happening, you and your audience will be starting from the same point. Your audience will then accept anything you do because they know where you're coming from.

Your immediate impulses have their own wisdom and destination. As soon as they take a physical shape, *look* at that shape. (Your audience is looking at that shape, too—wondering what you'll do with it.) Look at it closely and let it intrigue you. Your keen interest in what you're "putting out" will inspire your next impulse.

Following immediate impulses, you also notice that your improvisation "wants" to evolve and escalate. It "wants" to yield a beginning, a middle, and an end—an opening, a complication, and a resolution—but you can never be sure how this will happen until it actually happens. Improvisations never follow a conventional or predictable route. They lead you to places and possibilities you never knew existed. This is why it is crucially important to watch and follow what *is* happening rather than what you think *should* happen.

One of Shelley's solo improvisations illustrates this point. She began the improv by expanding her chest and lowering her chin in the attitude of a tough, manly character. Then this character started pointing his finger and grunting tersely as if he were correcting or reprimanding someone or something. He looked at his watch and resumed the pointing and grunting. Then he walked stage right, pointed to someone, and said, "This is *my* beat so don't give me any lip."

This story illustrates the very subtle difference between "what is" and "what should be." Shelley's improv was evolving correctly, but she became so concerned about *justifying* her behavior that she *overshot* the character that first occurred to her. She silently asked herself, "Who would do this kind of thing?" Instead of being *intrigued* by what was happening, she tried to explain it. She decided that she must be a cop on a beat and then looked for a way to convey this to her audience. (She walked stage right and told someone over there, "This is my beat.")

In the beginning of the improvisation, Shelley followed her own impulses. She assumed a character and let the character do what it wanted. Now, she should have become intensely interested in what her *character* was doing, instead, Shelley took over and told her character what to do. She turned him into a cop, but her first character had not been a cop. He had been a dictatorial, absurd, and comic figure. He was strutting around, pointing here and there and grunting reprimands. When he looked at his watch, I expected him to point at *it* and reprimand it for going too fast.

When I mentioned this to Shelley and the class, everyone understood what I meant. They appreciated the first character that had emerged without Shelley's conscious effort. They also recognized that the improvisation had led to a fork in the road. Shelley had to choose between the predictable or the unpredictable routes. The predictable route is what you think you should do. The unpredictable route is more exciting. It engages your full attention and makes you feel alert and alive.

At first, the distinction between the predictable and unpredictable routes is extremely subtle, almost imperceptible. But with practice, it becomes easier to make the distinction. A couple of "landmarks" help:

Steer clear of the sensation of *working* or *groping*. When you try to make sense out of where you are or what you're doing, you lose the sense of spontaneity and everything becomes cerebral, stilted. The conventional, safe, and predictable route *feels uncomfortable!* Even when you are idling (i.e., repeating the same movements over and over again), you experience the sensation of discomfort. You sense you are working, groping, straining.

It is so much more enjoyable to chose the *unpredictable route*. It's obvious and immediate. It's the path of least resistance. Attentiveness combined with curiosity, spontaneity, and impulsiveness always feels good.

Another landmark is *the character*. Follow your character. Let the character decide what he/she is doing and why. When Shelley decided to be a cop on his beat, she stepped in front of her character. It should be the other way around; the character should lead Shelley into the unknown.

Your very opening move serves to establish a *self*—a being—and this entity determines the whys and wherefores of your situation. The *who* determines the *what*. Therefore, stay with your character. Let the character do what it wants to do. It's no longer *you* deciding what your character should do; it's your character using *you* to come to life.

• • •

Incidentally, we discovered that Shelley's improv had yielded not a cop but a delightful eccentric who went around reprimanding real and imaginary people, telling them (in a very stern but innocuous manner) *not* to do this or that.

That evening, at a local restaurant, Shelley slipped into character again. She pointed at Christian and grunted a reprimand. Christian immediately sat up, wide-eyed and innocent. He automatically assumed he had done something wrong and started to apologize. When he realized the joke was on him, we all cracked up. Shelley's character was comic because his terse reprimands highlighted everyone's guilt. If he pointed and barked at you, you automatically assumed you were guilty of something. This character made a statement about human nature: All of us are carrying little guilts around with us. We're just waiting to be caught.

This next exercise was inspired by a week of working with fourth graders. Teaching mime and improvisation to young people is quite a challenge. Words such as "vulnerability," "honesty," "impulse," and "intrigue" are not yet active in their vocabulary. Also, young people learn by *doing* (not by talking) and they want to *do* things right away.

So I designed the "like" exercise in order to make some complicated ideas immediately accessible to these budding intellects. Now, working with professional performers, this exercise occurred to me again. I will probably use it in all my classes from now on because it's a challenge, no matter *how* easy it is to explain and no matter *how* experienced you are at improvisation.

During this exercise, each person has to move (or behave) *like* someone or something: a sparrow, a child, a tree, a cloud, a king, a street person, etc. The most important rule in this exercise is that you follow your first impression of your character or thing.

Suppose you are moving *like* a tree. You should act on *your* first impression of a tree, not the way you think the world sees a tree. Don't show a stereotypical tree; show what the idea of "tree" *does to you*. Read that sentence over again because it is the whole point of this exercise.

If I had to move *like* a tree, my impression of a tree would affect everything I did. If I were playing a cowboy for example, my character would be stalwart, upright, serene. Since my personal feelings about the tree would prime everything I did, my performance would be a reflection of *me* and not the reflection of the physical tree.

Moving like someone or something, doesn't limit what you can do. Your "like" is simply a starting point that may branch off in an infinite number of directions. For example, if you were asked to move *like* an overweight person, you could sing a song, recite a poem, tap your feet, walk around, react to someone. You can do whatever you want but everything you do must be from the point of view of an overweight person (as *you* experience that point of view).

After we had gotten a feel for this exercise, I asked each person to think of two characters for each of the other improvisers to work with. This was fun because we knew each other and we designed characters that were atypical of each person. We chose introverted characters for extroverted people and vulgar characters for refined people. Jackie had to play an ox-like mogul. John had to play a butterfly-like athlete. Shelley had to play a "bad seed," etc.

This exercise gives you a chance to experiment with your own personality. The personality is a collection of dynamics. The way you move, the tone of your voice, everything you do has a certain texture and quality. You always act *like* yourself. Now you can experiment with your *likes*. You can try on a new set of dynamics and see how they affect your personality—your thoughts, feelings, and behavior. You discover that your personality is actually a very malleable substance. It is not carved in stone. This is an important discovery if you are to perform other characters, other personalities convincingly.

The Use or Abuse of an Impulse

Doubt is the impulse that most often sabotages improvisation. Doubt usually appears as a slight misgiving—that sinking feeling that your improvisation is going nowhere. The typical reaction is to let that sinking feeling take over and seize the center of your attention. In a desperate attempt to *remove* the doubt, you then try to edit, direct, or choreograph your improv. You try to make sense out of your predicament.

The problem here is not the *doubt* so much as it is the *fear* of doubting. You sensed the presence of a threat (i.e., doubt) and tried to protect yourself. But when doubt enters an improv, you should have the opposite reaction. Let doubt intrigue you. Let it intensify your awareness and increase your receptiveness to inspiration. Doubt indicates that you are on the threshold of discovery. You should become *more* vulnerable in the face of doubt rather than less vulnerable and defensive.

Beginning improvisers shy away from this threshold of discovery. They fear the possibility of failure and turn around. They scramble for an escape route through hackneyed but familiar territory. When this happens, the audience is left stranded with a lot of unanswered questions.

When you suspect that the improvisation is going nowhere, *this* is when you need to settle down and pay attention. Say to yourself, "OK I feel trapped but am I? What else is going on?" You will find that this slight fear is a boon, making you perceptive and alert to possibilities. In fact, the person who experiences doubt during an improvisation is better off than the person who doesn't.

When I perform solo, I often close the show with one-word improvisations. Someone in the audience throws me a word and I improvise off of that word. I make it perfectly clear to the audience that they are NOT going to see the *word*, per se; they are going to see what the word *does to me*. When they know that I'm going to do this, their curiosity increases. An individual's interpretation of something is much more interesting than the thing itself.

One day during our week of improvisation, I asked Sherry Lee to improvise on the word "hats." She was caught off guard because I didn't describe the exercise beforehand. I simply said, "OK, Sherry, get up there and do something about hats." We had been working for three or four days now and everyone was in the spirit of improvisation. Sherry didn't focus exclusively on hats; instead, she showed us how *she felt* at that moment, how she felt about being asked to improvise on hats.

The first thing she said was, "Hats? What can I say about *hats*?" She was genuinely at a loss and all of us started laughing. "What are you laughing about?" This was a natural and correct response to our laughter. She had been surprised to hear us laughing and she expressed this surprise. She had not ignored us, but had made quick use of every thought as it *occurred* to her. Even as she noticed our laughter, this did not distract her from the original quandary (what *about* hats?!). By now she was thoroughly confused and the whole thing became more and more comic.

After the improv, she still wanted to know why all of us had laughed at something so "un-funny." I explained, "We laughed because everything you did was *correct*." She had instinctively moved from honesty and impulse. (The next step in Sherry's understanding of improvisation would be for her to *know* that what she had done had been correct.)

This is the miracle of improvisation: If you follow the rules, it works. If you are sensitive to and intrigued by the present moment and if you act on your immediate impulses, then the unique constellation of circumstances (i.e., you, your audience, the theatre, the time of day, etc.) will form the perfect improvisation.

I remember performing one-word improvisations in front of an enthusiastic audience in Hawaii. I felt that everyone in the audience understood and appreciated the art of improvisation and this fact about the audience inspired some of the most remarkable one-word improvs I had ever done.

At one point, someone in the audience shouted out the word "cellophane." The first thought that came to mind was Marilyn Monroe. I didn't know where that idea came from or what to do with it, but that was my present impulse so I acted on it. Other impulses and thoughts came to mind to connect the idea of Marilyn Monroe to the theme of cellophane: under wraps, protected, preserved. (These thoughts that occurred to me were not open for discussion. I couldn't explain them or predict them. They were immediate impulses arising from my rapt-attention to "now" and all I could do was follow them.)

The impulse to sing occurred to me. I began singing a song from Marilyn's point of view and the song *rhymed*! Here again, the personality was doubtful. If you start rhyming a song, you're committed. You have to maintain a meter and rhyming pattern. But the song was coming out in rhyme and I went with it. I can't remember the exact words of the song now, but it told the story of a woman wrapped in cellophane sitting on top of a rum-flavored cake. The cake was presented to a party of beer-drinking men who saw only a sex-symbol on top of a cake and failed to see the human being, wrapped in cellophane. The song worked out perfectly. It developed a theme, it rhymed, the meter was good, and it left everyone (including *me*) spellbound.

• • • • • • • • • • • • • • • • • • •

WARNING: When you watch or hear about a good improvisation, be sure you don't let the puny, little ego make you feel inferior: "Gee! I could never do that!"

You have the potential to be a brilliant improviser, but your improvisations will be unlike anyone else's. No two improvisations will be alike because no two people think or act alike in the same situation, and even the same person cannot repeat an improvisation. (The only way an improvisation could happen twice would be if time moved backwards and the past suddenly repeated itself.)

Comparisons are absolutely irrelevant when it comes to evaluating an improvisation.

Fifth Exercise: Character Improvisations

This is one of the most well-known improvisation exercises. There are many ways to approach character improvs. I've heard of drawing names (of well-known figures from history or Hollywood, etc.) out of hats and then improvising off of those names. But what makes an exercise unique is not so much the format of the exercise but your *reasons* for doing it.

For example, I believe most people do character improvisations to become more clever and versatile. I teach character improvisation to prove that we all have an emotional and psychological affinity with everyone and everything (past, present, and future) around us.

Feelings are expressed through dynamics and qualities of movement. The dynamics and qualities that occur in nature are translated into human experience by way of feelings. Even liquid helium has a quality of movement that inspires us to feel and think certain things. Liquid helium glides along surfaces, clings to whatever it touches and maintains its momentum (*despite* gravity). Watching liquid helium elicits certain feelings. It looks eerie— strange—like something you'd see crawling out of a witch's brew. If you imitated its behavior, if you "took on" its dynamics, you would be reminded of something in your own nature. You'd discover that you have an emotional and psychological affinity with liquid helium! (Chemists should do character improvisations on all the elements. Maybe this would teach them another valid and viable relationship between the basic and complex. Which came first, anyway: the quantum or the quality?)

• • •

We started our character improvisations very simply. I asked each improviser to assume slight modifications on his/her own identity and then perform a simple maneuver. Christian assumed he was fifteen years older and inebriated. Shelley assumed she was a teenager who had to break the news to her father that she had just dented the bumper on his car (after he had expressly told her that she was *not*, under any circumstances, allowed to drive that car!).

Then I asked Christian and Shelley to make their characters relate to a chair. Christian, in his inebriated state, stumbled toward his chair as if it were an oasis in the desert. Shelley, dreading the confrontation with her father, sat on the edge of the chair and kept popping up and pacing around. Both Christian and Shelley *understood* their characters. No one had to tell them how to treat that chair. Once they had stepped inside their character's skin, the appropriate behavior came naturally and effortlessly. They discovered their affinity with their characters and everything they did was believable, correct.

• • •

The acting profession would not exist except for the fact that each and every human being has a natural, instinctive, and visceral connection to every other human being. You don't have to act in order to prove this to yourself; every time you relate to or loathe a character in a movie, you demonstrate a certain emotional alliance with those characters.

The Role of Props in Improvisation

When Shelley and Christian incorporated the chair into their improvisations, we proved that the simplest object or the simplest situation can be an invaluable tool for character development. The "To be or not to be..." soliloquy is not Hamlet's only chance to reveal himself. Everything he does, everything he touches becomes a vehicle for revealing the inner workings of his mind.

Remember, too, that it's not the object, itself, but how the character *treats* the object that is important. I remember hearing about a Hollywood actor who insisted on having a real gun rather than a rubber gun during one of his scenes. This actor had a misplaced sense of his own identity. He believed that his strength and his credibility depended on *mindless*, physical objects. Consequently, he was never really *mindful* of what was going on around him. During one particular scene, he was supposed to knock someone over the head; he ended up knocking the other actor out cold. He had become oblivious to the cameras, his fellow actors, the director. This is not acting. Acting is an exercise in awareness, not a state of delusion or oblivion.

"Become the Person for Whom that Behavior is Natural"

Whenever you are asked to *do* a particular thing during an improvisation, you should ask yourself, "what kind of person (or creature) would do that naturally?" Then *become the person (or creature) for whom that behavior is natural*. Remember, there is only one nature. Your nature and your character's nature both stem from the same nature. Any behavior can feel natural to you if you let it.

During our week of improvisation, we worked with many characters. Everyone discovered an affinity with whomever or whatever they played. During one session, I asked Mary Ellen to play a gorilla in a cage. I told her to feel the gorilla's weight, smell its odors, see the people outside the cage. She discovered a complicated blending of emotions in her character: the sense of confinement, the loneliness of being on display, the predicament of having so much strength and nowhere to put it.

Next time you're in the zoo, empty your mind of "me thoughts" and really *look* at a gorilla. Look at it through dispassionate, discerning eyes, not through the eyes of your personality. Appreciate the fact that without doing anything, the gorilla is telling the story of its life. This story could very well be your own.

During one of our sessions, I asked Sherry Lee to be Joan of Arc walking into a church. "You don't know *why* you're here, yet, but you were compelled to enter—you feel your destiny unfolding."

Incorporating the Historical Fact into Your Improvisation

Sherry did something I didn't expect. She came into the church very boldly and decisively. I had been expecting a more subtle, contemplative entrance but my expectations didn't keep me from appreciating Sherry's approach. The audience will accept anything you do as long as you justify it—make it believable.

When the improv was over, Sherry didn't seem happy with the way things had gone. She explained that she had once read that Joan was a bold and decisive woman. "I think I allowed what I had *read* about Joan to interfere with *my* own possibilities."

She had brought up an important point. It's good to be well-read and to research your characters. But, as you collect the historical facts, make sure that you take them *personally*. Sherry Lee *remembered* that Joan of Arc was a bold and decisive woman. The fact that she remembered this at the precise moment she started to improvise, means that this information was correct to use. Sherry Lee was on the right track. The next step would have been to "buy" her bold and decisive behavior (see pages 203-204) and to follow the impulses that *this* commitment inspired.

A "closed" improvisation means only that you choose a particular starting point for your improvisation. You start with a particular character or a particular situation; you may also have to work with a particular prop. Sherry Lee's improvisation on Joan of Arc was a closed improvisation because she couldn't start just anywhere; she had to be Joan of Arc walking into a church.

A Closed Improvisation is a Challenge, Not a Limitation

It may seem that specifying a situation or working with props *limits* what you can do during an improvisation. The word "closed" usually implies limitation, confinement. But when that word refers to improvisation, its connotations change. There are always an infinite number of things you can do during an improvisation. When you are dealing with infinite possibilities, limiting your choices does not lessen those possibilities. In a closed improvisation, specifications do not confine you; they *define* you. Situations and props become vehicles for defining and developing your character.

The only way a closed improvisation could feel restrictive would be if you had a specific goal in mind and you thought that something prevented you from achieving that goal. If, for example, you wanted to reveal your dancing skill, but your closed improvisation called for you to be staggering-drunk, then you might feel restricted by those demands. In fact, you're not restricted, you're challenged. How can you be a believable drunk and still display impeccable dancing skill? It's not easy but it's certainly possible—and *very interesting*.

Improvisation is an investigation into your own nature—a chance to see how you respond to unusual circumstances and "impossible" demands. Therefore, the more closed your improvisation becomes, the more probing and revealing this opportunity is.

Each specification becomes an opportunity to find your own nature in "foreign territory"—to find out what *you* would do, naturally, in another person's shoes or in a strange situation. Sherry Lee never knew what it felt like to be Joan of Arc until she had yielded to this character and had seen the world from Joan's point of view.

When you are asked to be a certain character or to behave a certain way, these instructions should change your thoughts and feelings and alter your behavior. If your character is supposed to behave a certain way (as when Sherry thought her Joan of Arc should be bold and decisive), you should *become the person for whom this behavior is natural.* Once you have allowed all of the specifications to define your *nature*, you will no longer feel *unnatural* or restricted in the improv.

Sixth Exercise: Two- (or More) Person Improvisations

If you think solo improvisations are challenging, wait until you get into group improvs! The rules for group improvs are the same as those for solo improvisations; the only difference is that the "thinking organism" will be composed of two or more individuals.

Performed correctly, group improvisations are uniquely thrilling. You discover a new level of communication with people, one that challenges the popular definition of the word "cooperation." We tend to think of communication and cooperation as a collection of separate personalities coming to some sort of agreement. Usually, cooperation involves compromise, diplomacy, discretion, tact, and an overall watering down of intentions until each individual consents to the final agreement, often reluctantly.

This is the attitude with which most people approach group improvisations for the first time—as if they will have to concede to or lead the other personalities in the group. After this expectation has botched things up a few times, however, each member of the group begins to relax into the miracle of improvisation. Each begins to understand that real cooperation is *not* the act of backing down and making concessions to other people; it is the act of *yielding* to the group mind. (This *group mind* is much more clever and inventive than the "sum of the parts.")

Most of the time (in everyday life) the personality holds the center of attention. This is why "cooperation" usually entails compromise as the stronger personalities lead and the weaker personalities concede. But the success of improvisation depends on ousting the personality from the central governing position. The personality no longer occupies the *center* of anyone's attention; it yields to the present moment. The present moment now occupies the center of attention and all minds share that same center. Therefore, no *one* mind or *one* personality holds an advantage over another.

If the present moment is the center of everyone's attention, then everyone will be following the same "informant." Many personalities (with their individual backgrounds, skills, strengths, and weaknesses) will now cooperate to meet the demands of the immediate moment. Those demands will employ each individual differently.

"Successful" improvisations are not always stageworthy. Sometimes they are simply valuable learning experiences. We were working on open (themeless) group improvisations. I asked three people to take the floor and to stand apart from each other. "Now begin moving just as you would for a solo improvisation. Let your awareness of the present moment incite you to action. Become aware of the other two people. Include them. Allow everything they do to *get to you*. Pay attention and let your impulses arise naturally from this state of awareness. Do and say whatever comes to mind."

During this particular improvisation, Christian, Mary Ellen, and Karen were "up." Mary Ellen immediately broke into a jig. She started dancing and Christian, in turn, started a mime of a fiddle player. He sang as if his voice were the fiddle music. Karen joined in the jig. Then suddenly, Christian stopped playing. Everything was quiet and the dancing stopped.

Karen then asked, "What happened to the music?" Christian said nothing and Mary Ellen responded, "I dunno." Christian plucked the invisible violin but no sound came out. Everyone was quiet for a few seconds until Karen said, "Let's sing then." Everyone started singing and the original frivolity resumed. As it continued, Christian and Mary Ellen started dancing together and Karen danced away from them. Then suddenly, Karen shouted, "The Indians are coming! Run! Hide! Protect yourselves!" This was such an abrupt turn of events that Mary Ellen and Christian were dumbfounded. Somebody made a wry remark as if to say, "Where the heck did THAT come from?" The improv stopped and we talked about it.

I pointed out that the audience's interest peaked when the music stopped. We wanted to know *why* that happened. For everyone watching, that moment suggested mystery, folklore, a fairy tale possibility. Why did that violin suddenly stop making sound?

The situation itself had introduced the feeling of mysticism into the improvisation. The audience and the improvisers had been led up to this event and *all of us* wanted to know what would happen next. After we had discussed this, everyone realized that this moment was a turning point in the improvisation. It was the departure point where the opening moves suddenly yielded a situation, intrigue, potential. But in this case, that opportunity had been neglected, passed over.

We also discussed the abrupt appearance of Indians on the scene. Most of us (the audience as well as the other improvisers) were not ready for Indians. Karen had equated the jig and fiddle-playing with early America: cowboys, Indians, and hootenannies. The rest of us had subliminally thought of Scotland: a highlander's jig. The Indians therefore caught everyone off-guard. That doesn't mean Indians were a *mistake* (in an improvisation you have to deal with everything that happens); it means only that most of us didn't know where they came from. The discussion on *that* particular improvisation ended there. But Karen's private analysis of it went much deeper.

She felt she had "botched" the improvisation on two occasions: once when the music stopped (and she told everyone to start singing) and again when she told everyone to protect themselves from the onslaught of the Indians.

Now it's important here to say that no one *except Karen* thought that Karen had made any mistakes. In an improvisation no one thinks about someone else's mistakes because everyone's too busy dealing with *anything* and *everything* that happens. This is what makes improvisation a unique learning experience—you learn privately. No one tells you what you *should* or *shouldn't* do. Simply by noticing the interesting moments in an improvisation, you begin to see and appreciate what's possible. You become more and more keen to possibilities and less and less set in your ways.

Back to Karen's analysis of her "mistakes." She thought that by telling everyone to sing, she had, in fact, *vetoed* Christian's impulse. Christian had stopped playing the "fiddle" but Karen hadn't expected this to happen. Rather than *respond* to the unexpected, she had reinstated her own expectations. She got the music going again and ignored that moment of intrigue (when the music suddenly stopped for no apparent reason).

I must add here that even though Karen told everyone to start singing ("Let's sing, then!"), no one had to *follow* her instructions. They could have chosen to *not* sing. They could have said, "Wait a minute, something strange is going on here." There are an infinite number of ways the improvisation could have continued and still have made use of this moment of intrigue.

Maybe the people in the improvisation who followed Karen's instructions realized later that they didn't *have* to do this. Perhaps they now understood that a certain personality tension had caused them to follow directions when they *wanted* to do something else. This is an example of how improvisation exercises may act to upset ego tensions and reinstate the person's natural ability to act appropriately in any given situation. It might have been too late for them to change what they did in *this* particular improv, but there would be other chances for them to exercise choice, freedom, and the sense of propriety in future improvs.

Notice, too, a discrepancy between what the *personality* (it doesn't matter *whose*) wanted to do in this improvisation and what the *present moment* suggested. The present moment opened up a path of possibilities, but the personality asserted itself on several occasions to divert the improvisers from this path. As I have said before, the personality will always avoid the unknown. It's afraid of losing control and consequently, it will always shy away from intrigue, risk, and *true* improvisation. But as soon as the personality is *subject* to the demands of the present moment, it becomes a colorful and useful *tool* of improvisation.

The other mistake Karen thought she made was when she introduced Indians into the improvisation. After privately reviewing the situation, she realized that before the idea of Indians occurred to her, Karen had been *certain* that the whole improvisation was going nowhere and that it was up to her to do something about this. This was, of course, an inaccurate assessment; a *lot* was going on. People were dancing and singing, a violin had mysteriously lost its sound, the story line was *loaded* with possibilities, the stage was set for mystery.

No *one* person is responsible for directing a group improvisation. But Karen was paying more attention to her assessment of the situation than she was to the situation itself. Later, she recalled the thought process that took place before she summoned up the Indians. She remembered going through a list of alternative situations to see which one would be the most interesting. The idea of an Indian raid was not interesting, but at least it was eventful—it would give the others something to do. Hence the war cry, "The Indians are coming! Run! Hide! Protect yourselves!" With that, she had not only given the others a situation to deal with, she had even told them what to do! She made herself the director and stopped being a participant.

One of the most common enemies to improvisation is the fear that the improvisation is going nowhere. This fear is triggered by the mistaken belief that you are solely and personally responsible for the success of the improvisation. The fear, in turn, triggers an inner dialogue that takes your attention far away from the present moment.

This is what happened to Karen in the improvisation. She stopped appreciating what *was* happening and started worrying about what *should* happen. If she had *been intrigued* by her present situation, this fear (of being stuck) never could have distracted her.

It may seem that in light of these mistakes, the improvisation was a failure. As a theatre piece, maybe it was a failure, but as a learning experience, it was brilliantly successful. It highlighted some of the subtleties of improvisation and taught some valuable lessons about this art form. Everyone has to learn and *understand* these lessons before their improvisations become stageworthy.

You will also find that many (if not all) of the lessons learned through improvisation are applicable to everyday life.

For example, many people feel an exaggerated sense of responsibility in social situations. They feel as if they are personally responsible for the success or failure of these events. Group improvisation teaches that other people are *also* thinking about and contributing to what is going on. You don't have to initiate anything; you don't have to feed anyone the right line or do the right thing. All you have to do is pay attention and let yourself be intrigued. The correct impulses will spring from your curiosity and *presence* of mind.

• • • • • • • • • • • • • • • • •

An Important Thing to Remember

Inspiration is always affirmative. It tells you what to *do*. It's good to know this so that when something tells you what *not* to do, you can recognize this as an impostor. In other words, instead of saying "don't move," inspiration will say, "*stand still, listen, wait.*" Inspiration doesn't say, "*Don't do that.*" It gives you an alternative, "*Do this*" instead.

Ideas for closed, group improvisations are so plentiful that it's no trouble coming up with them. As examples, here are some of the ideas we worked with during our week of improvisation:

Some Ideas for Closed, Group Improvisations

1) Two mourners go to their friend's funeral. In his life, this friend was always clowning around. Now as these mourners approach the coffin to bid farewell, they notice that their friend has requested to be outfitted with his clown nose. The mourners find this hysterically funny. At the same time, they try to act in the manner befitting a funeral.

2) A husband and wife are having breakfast together and as they eat, the audience finds out that this couple is so unhappy together that they actually despise each other. Use typical breakfast objects (sugar bowls, coffee, toast) as vehicles for character development.

3) Death is coming to claim the life of an elderly gentleman. The gentleman tries to convince Death to give him another few years to live. Death has the potential for postponing his claim on the man's life, *if* the man can be convincing enough.

Tony with his part-
ner Fred Garbo in
the mid-1970s.
(Courtesy of the
authors)

Discussion

A Closer Look at the Principles and Subtleties of Improvisation

Starting and Progressing an Improvisation

Starting and progressing an improvisation are two separate problems. The opening of an improvisation is like turning on an electrical switch. You need an extra surge of energy to over-come inertia. Then, to keep the system running, the current must remain constant and uninterrupted.

Translated into improvisation language, this means that the opening of an improvisation requires an extra surge of sensitivity and attention. You may notice that the first word, the first gesture, the first note or whatever, is the most difficult. But remember: The force that overcomes inertia is not willpower; it's not hard, rigid, or blind. It's wide awake, gentle, and powerful—as when a blade of grass breaks through cement.

Once you have gotten over the initial inertia, you must keep your attention fixed and focused on the "here and now." Your attention and your interest must not stutter or drift away from what's actually happening.

For example, suppose you have started an open improvisation. You are sensing and moving with impulses as they first occur to you, and you are paying attention to what you are doing. So far so good. Now you may find yourself picking up a rhythm. Maybe this rhythm reminds you of someone; you're not quite sure *who*.

As soon as you feel a character (or a situation) coming into focus, you may be tempted to get ahead of yourself. You'll be tempted to conceive a full-blown character or situation, prematurely.

Improvisations fail only when *thinking* and *doing* diverge or when your *inside* and your *outside* disagree. In improvisation, thinking and doing should happen simultaneously. The impulse becomes an action before you know what it means. This action then engages your attention and interest. Your attention and interest inspire the next impulse. This way, your thoughts are attached to what you are *doing* and your *doing* inspires your thoughts. Neither activity can go off on its own.

Piano-playing provides a metaphor for improvisation. Consider that everything you know about yourself (your history, your personality, your skills, etc.) are the piano keys and the present moment is a finger hitting the keyboard. The present moment strikes a certain chord (a certain impulse), and you simply listen. Let the note resonate. Let its overtones fill your attention and inspire you. Your experience of that note determines the next note. Do not keep hitting keys in an effort to find the "right note." The note you have hit is the right note. The next note will be right too if it comes from your rapt attention to the first note. There is a profound logic behind the art of improvisation, but this logic is visceral and impulsive as opposed to intellectual.

> "No sooner do I get upon the stage than all my self-protective armour peels away from me and I am a recording instrument as sensitive as a mimosa plant. There is nothing I cannot feel and nothing I do not react to." —Grock[14]

---

[14]Grock, *Life's a Lark* (New York, London: Benjamin Blom, 1969), p. 40.

193

**The Fear of
Moving
Impulsively**

The ability to improvise depends on your ability to follow your impulses, but don't worry if you are the type of person who "clams-up" when asked to move impulsively. This is not your natural state of being and this *unnatural* state can be corrected easily. Here's a typical scenario: I'll ask someone to move "like" a bear. The person, slightly panic-stricken, will look at me and ask, "What should I do?"

I'll say, "Whatever you feel like doing."

"But I don't feel like doing anything."

"That's fine, but if you *had* to move like a bear, what would you do?"

"I wouldn't do anything."

"*But if you had to move* what would you do?"

"I'd do this...(feeble arm gesture)."

"Voilà! That's the beginning."

After that first move, all movement begins.

You will be comforted to find that after the first impulsive move, you haven't exposed anything. You are still safe, "dressed," and decent but you are exposed and vulnerable in the best sense of the word. You have come out of hiding.

Improvisation invites you to look closely at yourself without being afraid of what you will find. Rather than pretend you're *not* afraid, improvisation teaches you to fearlessly accept your fear. You may ask yourself: "What's to be afraid of?" or "*Who* is afraid?" That latter question automatically gives you the upper hand over that timid creature who (you thought) had swallowed you whole.

All of us really *want* to be exposed and vulnerable. We want to see what we do under pressure and how we react to the unknown and the unpredictable. Without these high-risk introspections, something in us dries up. We become petty, cranky, or ineffably sad. Learning the secrets of improvisation frees us from the formidable and elusive fears blocking self-expression. Improvisation is more than a theatrical exercise; it's a way of life.

**The Value of
Waiting**

One sunny afternoon when I lived in upstate New York with my family, I happened to witness the "birth" of a Monarch butterfly. I was walking through our neighbor's garden for one reason or another when, out of the corner of my eye, I saw something move. On closer inspection, I recognized a cocoon and reasoned that the dark, slimy bubble squeezing out of it must be a butterfly.

At that moment, time stopped. I forgot where I was and

what I had set out to do. Nothing was more important than the birth of this butterfly. My family came over and watched with me for a while, but they soon tired of the whole thing and went away. Occasionally someone would check back to see how things were going; "Is he still at it?" He was "at it" for a full forty-five minutes.

For forty-five minutes, this pitiful, greasy creature twitched and struggled and strained to get outside of its jacket. When a crumpled wing would finally jerk itself free and flop down on the leaf, I wasn't sure which one of us—the butterfly or I—felt better at that moment. We both rested as the wing dried and expanded in the sun. Then the agonizing ritual began again with the second wing.

The final break from the cocoon was the most drawn out and painful effort of all. That cocoon wouldn't let go. It stuck to the butterfly's tail with excruciating tenacity. The butterfly pulled away with all its might. Its back contracted and tightened with the effort. It was everything I could do to keep myself from intervening. Then finally, it happened—the butterfly and cocoon snapped apart from each other—forever. And in one luxurious countergesture, the butterfly's back straightened and continued straightening until it arched. It arched and continued arching until the pain of labor was erased by the ecstasy of relief.

Then the butterfly flopped back down again —utterly exhausted—as the sun dried and warmed its wings. I waited until it stood up. I waited for it to find its balance, and I waited for it to leap and become airborne. A beautiful moment.

I've told and retold this story many times to illustrate the value of waiting, the paramount importance of letting the right thing happen at the right time. We start straining and rushing only when we doubt the perfect timing of our most natural impulses. Knowing when to wait is essential to the art of improvisation. If you have no impulses, wait for one. If you don't know what to say, don't say anything. If you don't know what to do, stand still. Notice everything. Stay awake, alert, and sensitive and the right impulses will *occur* to you.

Who or What is in Control?

Everyone is concerned these days with being "in control." Wouldn't it be a good idea to first *define* control before we start looking for it? Don't we have to know what being in control *means* before we start exercising it?

It is impossible to have a good improvisation when the personality is in control. The personality is everything you *know* about yourself and *only* what you know about yourself. It neglects your unexplored aspects, your untapped potential. The personality avoids the unknown and is loath to change its mind. Its hopes and dreams for the future are based on what it already knows. It is suspicious of this nebulous thing called "inspiration," and resists trying new things. In improvisation, when the personality has the center of your attention, you can only fumble and fret. Likewise, in life, when the personality dictates your tastes and decisions, you often feel lost and empty. This is not control.

Real control (on stage or off) is contingent on being aware of the needs of the moment and being free to respond to those needs. When the immediate moment is the center of your attention (when you are impartial and aware of everyone and everything around you) the personality is in its proper place. It is a vehicle and not a driver. This is the essence of real control.

What is the Present Moment?

Many people sing the praises of "being in the present moment." I used to sing this song at regular intervals, too, until I realized that everyone has his own idea about what this means. We *talk* about the present moment, but defining the phrase is not easy. And yet a clear-cut definition is indispensable to understanding the fine art of improvisation.

The "present moment" does not refer to a point in physical space and time. It's not simply *where* (in physical space) you happen to be at a particular moment in time. If this were so, no one would have to talk about "being in the present moment," because all of us would be there all of the time. But "being in the present moment" means something else. It means being in a particular frame of mind.

This particular frame of mind is, paradoxically, when time seems to stop. The succession of seconds and minutes stops, and you are held in rapt attention and interest by one moment or one event. You never know what will happen next, but ideas and insights come to you in a steady, unbroken stream. Your needs and the fulfillment of those needs happen simultaneously. At such times, it seems impossible to make a mistake, fall off balance, or miss a trick. And then for some inexplicable reason, the "present moment" stops unfolding. Time starts ticking away again. That blessed sense of clarity and wonder passes away. Stress, strain, worry, and ennui move in to take their place.

I'm quite sure that we slip in and out of the "present moment" because we don't know how to follow it. Through improvisation, you can learn what "being in the present moment" means and what it feels like. Further, improvisation teaches you how to *stay* present, how to remain in the direct line of inspiration.

Imagine for a minute that you are preparing to improvise in front of a group of people. What are you thinking about right now? Where is your attention? What are you noticing? How are you feeling?

This is your chance to put yourself in the present moment. In this state of mind, your attention is expansive. It fills the room. It embraces you, the people watching you, everything around you. This embrace is so huge that it encompasses the building, the planet, the galaxy. This attention also extends inward—it *inspans* —putting you in touch with everything you know.

As your attention inspans and expands, you find yourself becoming open and receptive. You are so busy waiting and listening for that first impulse, that nothing can distract you. The first impulse may be fully formed: a word, a gesture, a whole scene may unfold immediately in front of your eyes. Or it may be a mere wisp of an idea like a whisper. It can be anything, but one thing for sure, it will take you by surprise. You wouldn't, or *couldn't* predict it. And, once you have received the impulse or inspiration, you have to *show* its effect on you. Respond to your impulses and images as if they were visible, tangible things acting on your visible, tangible body.

•   •   •   •   •   •   •   •   •   •   •   •   •   •   •   •

I remember watching a student struggle with the mime illusion of climbing a ladder. As I watched him, I didn't know what was wrong with his technique or approach. All I knew was that I couldn't *see* a ladder and I couldn't *believe* that he was climbing anything. Then suddenly I knew what was wrong: the student was thinking of himself as a *physical* person climbing an *imaginary* ladder. In other words, the student and his ladder were in two different worlds, composed of two different materials. No wonder the illusion was unclear. Once I had received this insight, I told him; "Let your body become imaginary to match your imaginary ladder." If you think of your images and impulses as dream material, then think of your body as dream material, too. If you insist that your body is a physical, tangible "thing," then treat your images and impulses as physical, tangible things, too.

Once that first impulse occurs, let it occur to *you*. If you hear a word, *say* the word. If you feel a yawing in your chest, go to it. Let it move you. You have to *go to* these impulses (join them!) in order to know what to do next. Your absolute and unabashed *surrender* to your impulses puts you in position to receive the next impulse. It renders you *present* to the moment—present to your source of inspiration.

• • •

Several months after the improvisation week with Jest in Time, Karen asked me to help her with solo improvisations. She had missed several of our sessions and didn't feel she understood the subtle art of improvisation. Karen is a dancer and can improvise with abstract gestures, but the thought of weaving a story or becoming a character was foreign and frightening to her. On this particular day, she decided to "take the bull by the horns" and improvise until she understood the process.

She started out with two or three separate solo improvisations. Both of us knew that she was having trouble grasping the essence of improvisation. Everyone instinctively knows when the improvisation is good, when it flies, or when it is labored and earthbound. I'd stop her after each of these laborious attempts and we'd talk about what she had just done. On the fourth attempt, she had a breakthrough. She understood what I had been trying to teach her.

During this improv, Karen started a rhythmic song from the point of view of a traveler, someone on a path going through forests and trees. As she sang, I could tell that the scene around her was changing and she was experiencing those changes. She sang about a trail of footsteps and a feeling of magic in the air. Her face lit up and she looked like a child going through an enchanted forest. Then her gaze slowly shifted to the right, and I saw that she was genuinely transfixed by something huge and majestic. She stood up slowly and, with reverence and awe, turned to face this "thing." Her song slowed down. Now she sang about a huge mountain looming in the distance. For a few brief moments the sparkle in her eyes expressed the journey-lust inspired by that mountain. But this sparkle slowly gave way to sadness and her chin started to tremble. The final line of her song was, "Far away, far away—I can't—go." As she stressed the last three words of the song, more and more anger, disappointment, and sadness came into her voice until she honestly started crying. Karen was so thoroughly *present* to these emotions, that I felt them too.

The most salient impression she had during this successful improvisation was that she had to "go there." She had to let her impulses lead her away from the studio, away from physical space and time and directly *into* her enchanted forest.

In other words, when you follow your impulses, you have to leave your *physical* surroundings and enter, wholeheartedly, the scenario that is unfolding in front of your mind's eye. The analogy of a hound dog on a fox trail comes to mind. During an improvisation, your attention is fixed to the trail of cues, impulses, and signals. Every impulse takes you further "into the woods" as you close in on your target. You don't know what that target is or where this wayward trail will lead. But if your nose leaves that scent for a second, you might never find the trail again.

• • •

The improviser should not *narrate* what's going on. This happened during Karen's first laborious improvisation. She began by hopping around the room. "I'm a bird," she said. As she continued moving, she told me (the audience) what was happening to her—what she was doing and why. But narrators are usually on the *periphery* of their stories; they're on the outside looking in. This is not "being in the present moment." In improvisation, you should be *in* your story, "present" to it, in its *presence*.

I didn't want Karen to *tell me* what she was doing; I wanted to see it happen. If the bird had to hop because it was injured and couldn't fly, I wanted to see what the bird was going through from the *bird's* point of view.

What unforeseen circumstances would happen to this injured bird and how would the bird (Karen) handle them? Karen could not answer these questions because she "wasn't there"—she wasn't inside the bird's skin. She stood apart from it and relied on preconceptions to guess what would happen next. If you're not present at an event, you have to guess what happened. Likewise in improvisation, if you're not present to your "story," you have to guess what should happen. I explained this to Karen and demonstrated what I meant.

I did an improvisation on an ant. I became the ant. I didn't know what I'd do as an ant. More specifically, I didn't know what would *happen to me* as an ant, but I was willing to find out.

If I had remained a person, I might have started guessing what an ant would do. I might have reasoned that ants carry things and work hard, and I might have carried something or scurried around busily. But nothing would have *happened* to me. Nothing would have taken me by surprise. I had to let the ant get to me. I had to step inside of the ant's skin to see what would happen next.

When I started the improvisation, the first impulse/ impression I had was that my waist was being squeezed into oblivion. I felt this—it *occurred* to me and I reacted just as I would have reacted in real life. As my waist tightened, my chest and hips began to swell. These experiences were *genuine*. I wasn't "making up" anything. The physical distortions were uncomfortable and shocking. I groaned and voiced the thoughts that were coming to me. I can't remember exactly what I said, but I made comments about the size of my chest and hips. All of this *happened* to me, everything took me by surprise.

• • •

If you've never improvised successfully, you may wonder how your own mind can do anything without your consent. It seems impossible that a scene from your own consciousness could have the same element of surprise as a movie you've never seen before. But isn't this what happens in dreams? During a dream, scenes, people, and things come at you out of nowhere. You don't *plan* your dreams or devise clever plots for yourself. The people in your dream appear to have minds of their own. You don't know how they'll answer or what they'll do. And yet aren't all of these people figments of your own imagination? How, then, can they have minds of their own? If the dream happens in your own mind, why is it so unpredictable, so suspenseful, so intriguing?

Those are interesting questions that bear directly on the improvisation experience. Improvising is like entering a dream. You don't know what will happen to you, but you go along with it. Images or impressions may be nebulous. They may be the first wisps of a wind, they may be a name that starts yawing at you from somewhere in your palette. Let these impressions get to you. Your audience may not see the wind or hear the name, but they'll see what these impressions do to you. They'll see you "enter in" and they'll go with you.

You've heard the expression, "You can't judge a man 'til you've walked a mile in his shoes." Improvisation will give you a whole new understanding of this very important saying. You can never really know what it's like to stand in another person's shoes until you've done an improvisation on that character, until that character's life has unfolded in front of you and you've experienced it, second-by-second, through your character's eyes.

As soon as you step into your character's shoes, the character will move. You won't have to grope for ideas and inspiration; the character will know what to do, because you will act as the character's mind. How could your character think for you unless you think for him? How could your character come to life unless you live in his shoes?

When you're in the present moment, there is no such thing as the "other." Your character is not the "other guy;" he or she is you. The middle wall is down. You and your character share the same life. When you're in the present moment, you are the only thing happening. You are the environment, the characters, the event and nothing is predictable. Everything is galvanic, electric, and alive. The audience sits on the edge of their seats because they're in the present moment, too. There's only one present moment and we're all in it. Therefore, when one performer is really centered in the stream of inspiration, he pulls the audience in with him. They see one life (their own life) unfold in front of their eyes.

Is improvisation a scary lurch into oblivion? Could you venture out and not come back? No. The very fact that you are capable of starting out indicates that you are in full control of "going out and coming in." Just as a good parent does not allow a child to leave home until that child knows how to return safely, you cannot go *into* an improvisation unless you possess the skill to come back from it.

Another definition of the present moment is the intersection of body, mind, and spirit.

Body, Mind, Spirit

In everyday life, we often do things without thinking or think without doing. To *do* without *thinking* means to misplace keys and telephone numbers because you weren't "present" at the moment you handled those keys or wrote down those numbers. To *think* without *doing* means to entertain thoughts, dreams, and visions without ever acting on them. These common occurrences in everyday life indicate a schism between body, mind, and spirit. They indicate a disagreement between the inside and the outside, cause and effect.

In improvisation however, your rapt attention to the present moment unifies inspiration, thought, and action (i.e., spirit, mind, and body). You notice everything you do, and "do" (or reveal) everything you notice. Your mind thereby reinstates the vital and harmonic relationship between the outside realm of expression (body) and the inside realm of *inform-ation* (spirit). This is what it means to be in the present moment.

Questions Most Often Asked about Improvisation

During my career as a teacher, I've answered dozens of questions about improvisation. But two questions in particular come up in *every* class, and I assume every student of improvisation asks these two questions at one time or another. Therefore, in anticipation of your curiosity regarding these issues, I thought I'd answer those questions right now.

Question 1) "Why is it so scary to improvise?"

Improvising is scary because you have to lean *unreservedly* on extremely *subtle* cues or impulses.

In this society we are not trained to trust subtle things. The "cues" we generally follow in life are solid and intellectual. We typically depend on strong physical forces and sensations to tell us where we are and how we feel; or we trust an aloof and callous intellect to tell us "what's going on" and what we should or shouldn't do about it.

In improvisation, you must leave these "dependable" but impersonal signposts and lean, *wholeheartedly*, on a series of evanescent impulses. These impulses are deliciously palpable, but they're so subtle that you've probably never noticed them before. Improvising sometimes feels like stepping out on a bridge made of cobwebs.

Now that you know this, I hope you'll have more courage to trust those gossamer highways. You'll discover that they're more substantial than cement and they'll never let you down.

Question 2) "How do you *do* that?"

Students ask me this after I show them what I would have done with *their* improvisations. This happened at my latest workshop.

Suzy started skipping around the room. We watched *intently* for a few seconds until it became obvious she was groping for ideas. When people start groping, their motor goes on idle and they repeat the same action over and over again with only minor variations. After Suzy had skipped for a minute or so I said, "OK now evolve this." This little nudge worked. Suzy saw "Mary" up ahead and expressed genuine delight to see her friend. She waved and yelled, "Hi Mary!" She skipped faster, then stumbled, fell, and began to cry. The improvisation was good up until then, it had started and evolved. But the third component was missing—the ending or the resolution.

Every improvisation has three distinct parts: a beginning, an escalation (or a complication), and a resolution. There is *no* exception to this. Every improvisation naturally yields these three components.

We discussed the three components of an improvisation, but even after the discussion, the concept of "resolution" seemed unclear to people. So I got up to *show* them what I was talking about.

I did everything Suzy did and I honestly experienced the story as if it were happening to *me* for the first time. I skipped around, saw Mary, experienced honest and unfeigned delight, waved, and accelerated my skip in Mary's direction. Right before I reached her, I tripped. Since I was smack-dab in the middle of the story, I had no idea what would happen *after* I fell. I had to wait and *see* what would happen. I had to *be there.*

As I fell, I experienced a little fear, then I began blubbering as a natural recourse to pain and bungled intentions. And then suddenly I was really ticked off at Mary! My face twisted into an ugly scowl and through my tears, I yelled at my friend. This was the denouement. To cover my pain and embarrassment, I blamed Mary for my fall. This reaction, revealed a petty side of my nature that no one had seen before. Now my "outside was looking like my inside." (See page 175)

An entire event had happened. A situation had unfolded and a character had been revealed. Everyone watching the improvisation recognized this as the "resolution" I had been talking about. Then Suzy looked at me incredulously and asked, "How did you *do* that?" She had experienced the beginning and middle of the improvisation, but a resolution had not "occurred" to her.

My answer to that question is that I am able to "*do that*" because I yield to each instant in the unfoldment of the improvisation. I am always right square in the middle of every impulse. I do not preconceive my impulses before they *happen*, and I don't decide which impulses to follow. I follow every impulse as it occurs to me. In doing this, my story gradually unfolds and makes its own sense.

"Buy It"

I use the phrase "Buy It" in all of my classes whether I'm talking about premise work, mime illusions, or improvisation. And I'm grateful to the consumer business for making the meaning of this phrase almost self-explanatory.

In consumer terms, when you buy something, you pay for it and it's yours. You must have needed it, otherwise you

wouldn't have bought it. And once you've made the invest-
ment, you are bound and determined to make it work for you.
The only time you may have to buy something you *don't* need
is when you inadvertently knock a knickknack off the shelf.
In which case, "you break it, you buy it."

The phrase "buy it" is applied to movement the same way it
is applied to merchandise. You must take responsibility for
and *use* everything you do and everything that happens to you.
You can't ignore, neglect, or miss anything. If you're in the
middle of a dance maneuver and you fall, you have to "buy it"
the same way you had to buy that knickknack you inadvertently dropped in the gift shop.

Through premise work, you learn that cause and effect are
viscerally connected to each other. This understanding carries
over to improvisation. When you "buy something" in improvisation, you experience both cause and effect. Both the *need* for
the thing and the *use* of the thing happen at the same time.
"Buying a gesture" means finding a psychological or emotional
need for that gesture. "Buying an impulse" means *using* or
expressing that impulse. Effect evokes cause and cause evokes
effect, instantly.

If, while you're improvising, you do something inadvertently, you won't ignore this in an effort to get back to "adver-
tent" behavior. You will *buy* what you just did. You will buy
the gesture *as well as* the emotional and psychological cause of
that gesture even if that means changing your own emotional
or psychological base in order to *justify* what you just did.

**"Buying It"
in Group
Improvisa-
tions**

In solo improvisations, you must buy your *own* gestures and
impulses. In group improvisations, you have to buy everyone
else's gestures and impulses as well as your own. The unique
challenge of group improvisations is that you can't know the
cause of your partners' movements. You can't read their minds
or feel their impulses. Therefore, you must be especially adept
at reading and *buying* their physical effects: their words, movements, facial expressions, etc.

Since cause and effect are *viscerally* connected, it is possible
to see your partners' gesture and know, immediately, the
emotional or psychological *cause* of that gesture. This will not
be an intellectual knowledge, but a *visceral* understanding. It
also doesn't take *time* to figure out where your partner is coming from. Buying your partners' behavior is an instantaneous,
gut instinct, a product of the empathic sense.

You can't ignore or reject *anything* your partners do. Their gestures are just as valid, real, and motivated as your own. If there are three people in your group improvisation, you have to think of yourself as being three people: one mind inspiring, moving, and using all three of you. You have to buy the gestures and decisions of all of your "selves."

If one person in the improvisation suddenly turns to you and says, "Mary! What are you doing?" you have to *hear* the question, *use* it, and *blend* it with your own scenario. You have to buy it.

You don't necessarily have to *respond* to it, but you do have to acknowledge it. It happened and it cannot *unhappen*; therefore you must admit its definitive role in your evolving environment. You have to let it change your understanding of *who* you are, *where* you are, and *what* you are doing.

Notice the tone of voice. Is Mary a little girl being scolded or is she a woman being caught red-handed? Maybe Mary is an adult doing something stupid? If the tone of voice indicates that Mary is a little girl, then you would not respond as a grown woman unless you said something like, "Why are you talking to me as if I were a child?" This response indicates that you have "bought" your partner's tone of voice. You haven't ignored it or thrown it away.

Your response should further *define* your relationship to your partner. You and your partner are setting up the logic of your situation and defining each of your individual characters. Mary is someone who doesn't like being addressed as a child and the other person is Mary's adversary. This adversarial relationship has been established twice: once when the question was forcefully posed, and again when the question was rebuffed. This adversarial relationship will not *change*, it will *develop*. Nothing will change unless there is a very good *reason* for it to do so. The audience will need to see and believe those reasons before they will accept (buy!) any changes in this already established order.

This precise question ("Mary! What are you doing?") was actually posed to me by my good friend Bernie Kramer during one of our improvisations together. When Bernie and I improvise, we often throw curves at each other to see how quickly and spontaneously the other will justify and deal with those curves. In this particular improvisation (an open improvisation), I began feeling burley and tough. I picked up a "shovel" and began digging. Suddenly, Bernie came at me with, "Mary! What are you doing?" Without a second thought, I pursed my lips, glared at him and lisped emphatically, "Shhh! The others don't know yet!"

I had instantly transformed myself from a macho to a closet homosexual. My behavior did not seem comical (at least not to me); it felt natural. It was my personal and spontaneous response to Bernie's curve. I had instantly *bought* Bernie's question and *blended* it with my own impulses and my own gestures.

I also *assumed* that Bernie's question was valid. Not for an instant did I entertain the notion that he had made a mistake. I assumed that Bernie had seen my burley, tough character and that his question had taken that into account. The instant I heard Bernie's question, I experienced the visceral *cause* of that question. I honestly *felt* my insides become soft and feminine even as my burley, tough exterior remained intact.

Curve throwing in improvisation can create bizarre and absurd situations. I recommend curve throwing only as a game for advanced improvisers. If you want to throw your partners a curve, make sure it's *intentional* and not simply the result of not paying attention.

Fear of Literal Themes

In this day and age, many choreographers shy away from stories and narration. They tend toward more abstract themes—the sometimes obscure juxtaposition of certain words, ideas, and shapes, a personal depiction of a life cycle or the human condition, a study of textures, dynamics, and atmospheres. Abstract themes can create wonderful theatre. But I feel that most performers tend toward the abstract because they're afraid of the literal. It is more challenging to commit to a situation, a character, and a plot than it is to move abstractly.

Abstract themes welcome the free associative processes. They are arbitrary and easily manipulated. You can put a shape here and a shape there and these shapes *will* relate to each other in some inexplicable way. That's a fairly safe bet. It's also easy to *escape* from the abstract themes. You can stop your sketch anytime you want. On the other hand, narrative themes are much more demanding. You can't do whatever you want; you have to *adhere* to the logic of your characters and story. Literal themes create high expectations in the audience and these expectations must pay off. The plot must evolve. The characters and situations must fill out, become more intriguing, more real, accessible, and interesting. You have to resolve tension and create tension.

Literal themes pose many problems, but your understanding of yourself evolves with each problem you solve. Developing a literal theme is certainly a soul-searching exercise.

The avoidance of literal themes and the tendency toward abstract themes indicates (in some way) a fear of commitment. Following an improvisation into the intrigue of character development and story line means abandoning the intellect and the personality to explore a higher *relevance* to your thoughts and impulses.

I love the moments in improvisation when something makes perfect sense to me but I'm not quite sure what that sense is, yet. At such times the impulsive, abstract gesture contains an inherent, literal meaning.

The Perfect Balance Between the Abstract and the Literal

For example, I remember one improv session in which we worked with the theme of prison. At one point, the improviser (Gretchen Berg) grasped an imaginary bar coming out of her head.

This impulsive and immediate response to the word *prison* illustrated a feeling rather than a story, a mood rather than a plot. We, the audience, didn't see the word itself; we saw what the word *did* to Gretchen. And this is what the audience *should* always see during an improvisation: what the word, story, mood, situation *does* to the improviser.

When I thought about it later, I realized the prison bar was a metaphor for the real captivity. Gretchen's intensity as she grabbed and struggled with the bar suggested that the real prison is a state of mind rather than a physical locality. All of us saw the prison bar coming out of the head, but the precise *meaning* of this metaphor was an individual and private issue.

As you become more versed in the art of improvisation, you will find that every improvisation yields a perfect blend of abstract and literal gestures and themes. In improvisation, when the first dawning of an impulse translates *immediately* into physical space, it often doesn't make any literal *sense*. You haven't given it a *chance* to make literal sense; you've expressed it before you know what it means.

But once an impulse takes a physical shape, you have to *use* it. You have to discover the visceral *logic* of what you've just done and act on that. This rule of improvisation practically guarantees that your improvisation will take on some literal meaning.

In life, elemental substances evolve concrete things. Likewise in improvisation, elemental impulses evolve literal situations (*if* you have followed the rules of improvisation and *lived* those impulses). If you are truly vulnerable and present to the immediate impulses, your improvisation *will* become more intriguing, mature, and meaningful for you as well as your audience.

The only difference between an improvisation exercise and normal day-to-day existence is that during improvisation you are revealing impulses *before* they make any conventional sense. Whereas in everyday existence, elemental impulses are usually disguised in conventional ways. For example, if you feel uptight and anxious in everyday life, you might take a walk, go to a movie, call a friend, have a glass of wine. These are conventional ways of dealing with nebulous, elemental, inexplicable feelings.

In improvisation, however, you physicalize those nebulous impulses *before* they branch off into conventional patterns. In so doing, you will unearth some brash, unconventional, and *abstract* shards of self-expression (as when Gretchen, in the above example instinctively grabbed and grappled with an imaginary prison bar coming out of her head).

• • •

Improvisation teaches that literal reality is composed of abstract impulses. The object of improvisation is to make those abstract, invisible, inexplicable impulses visible. You want to detect those raw, unadulterated impulses and physicalize them before they manifest themselves in conventional ways. *That's* the creative process.

Paradoxically, even though viewers may not literally understand the improviser's opening moves, they will "recognize" them. The word "abstract" does not properly mean abstruse. If the abstract gesture is properly exposed and presented, its *meaning* will be absolutely apparent to the audience. This meaning will be viscerally (as opposed to intellectually) known. Gretchen didn't have to *explain* the bar coming out of her head. The audience understood what it meant. We were not puzzled. This indicates a perfect balance between the literal and the abstract: something that eludes the rational mind for a second, but which makes perfect sense on a deeper, gut level. I also think that the masterful blending of abstract and literal should, ideally, incite the rational mind to understand itself a little better.

A Few Great Improvisers from History

Closed, group improvisations were the *modus operandi* for the Commedia dell'Arte (see pages 17-18). The Commedia dell'Arte consisted of a group of stock characters: Pierrot, Arlecchino, Pantalone, Scaramouche, Franceschina, and so forth. These characters were archetypes. They had specific personalities and predictable behavior patterns. The audience "knew" these characters in the same way audiences today know the characters from soap operas or situation comedies on television.

Today, actors have scripts to follow. In the sixteenth century, the actor/mimes from the Commedia were given certain situations ("scenarios") to act out, but they made up their own scripts as they went along. For example, Arlecchino was a master of disguise. In a typical scenario he might dress up as a maid to gain entrance into Columbine's house. The actors would be given a short synopsis of the scene that might read:

> Arlecchino (disguised as Maid) enters Columbine's house. Bumps into Pantalone (Columbine's father). Pantalone falls in love with "Maid." Grabs her passionately. "Maid" resists and defends herself. Dress rips off. Pantalone recognizes Arlecchino. Chase.

The language of these scripts is not exactly as I've outlined, but mine gives the gist of how the Commedia dell'Arte operated. The players enjoyed infinite freedom within this scenario to add their own inspired comments, gestures, or gags.

The Italian word for trick or gag is *lazzi* and the Commedia dell'Arte developed and perfected dozens of them. For example, Arlecchino was always running away from irate fathers or jealous husbands and his classic lazzi would be to change into a statue. He'd freeze and his pursuers would stop short. They'd look like bewildered hound dogs outwitted by the fox. Arlecchino, trying to escape, is forced to freeze every time one of his pursuers turns to face him. He freezes in some ridiculous poses, each one more ridiculous than the last. In the meantime, the statue becomes the scapegoat for the assailants' frustration. They kick it or strike it in fury.

Arlecchino was free to use this lazzi when the scenario called for it. The other players knew the gist of the lazzi, so they were always ready to play along should Arlecchino lead them into it. This type of theatre would be hugely popular today if a few players had the courage and the heart to perfect the art of true improvisation.

Charles Chaplin

Charlie Chaplin performed in the spirit of the Commedia. He used some of the old lazzis and created many new ones. Whether they were old or new, all of them were unique expressions of Chaplin himself. Everything he did had an urgency about it. Some of his routines may have been "old," but his *reasons* for doing them were always new and fresh. He never appeared to be copying anyone.

I've heard many people praise the work of Charlie Chaplin. His sensitivity as a performer and his conscience as a upright citizen of the world made him a model for just about everyone. Anyone familiar with the work of Chaplin describes his genius in his/her own way. I have praised Chaplin hundreds of times and *each* time I say something different about him. What I say depends on the context of the conversation. In this chapter on improvisation, it is fitting to say that Chaplin was a master improviser. And a book on mime wouldn't be complete without an accolade of this *physically eloquent* man.

Early Hollywood

Early Hollywood fostered the spirit of improvisation. Buster Keaton, Stan Laurel, Oliver Hardy, Bud Abbot, Lou Costello, Red Skelton, and The Ritz Brothers are just a few of the great improvisers to have appeared on television and in the early films. Danny Kaye and Dick Van Dyke came a little later but they had the unique, improvisational flare of those early physical comedians.

I once read that the directors who worked with the Ritz Brothers learned to have cameras on these characters at all times. The three brothers would improvise with each other whether they were being filmed or not, and often the *off*-camera improvs were just as masterful as the on-camera ones.

Today there are great improvisers working in Hollywood but very few of them can work brilliantly with each other or in groups. (Or maybe they *do* work brilliantly in groups, but I just haven't seen them.) The art of group improvisations is on the decline at the moment. But it's bound to make a comeback.

Anyone interested in the art of mime and improvisation (the two arts are inseparable) should watch the above-mentioned artists in the early films. There's a stellar performance by Buster Keaton and Charlie Chaplin in the movie *Limelight*. The Ritz Brothers are harder to track down, but we saw them in *Kentucky Moonlight* the other day and there are a couple of routines in this movie that I recommend seeing.

Watching these master improvisers at work, you will sense a sweetness about them. They are wonderful performers but their art goes deeper than that. Below their diligence and discipline as performers, one senses a sincere and kind heart. I think this may be the result of *paying attention*, of perfecting the skill of watching, listening, waiting for the right impulses to come at the right time. Improvising with other people develops an appreciation and respect for another person's timing, tastes, and decisions.

This is what I love about the Keaton/Chaplin routine from *Limelight*. Each of these artists has a tacit respect for the other's work. They sense and support each other. The audience, in turn, senses this intimacy and basks in the atmosphere of true improvisation.

• • • • • • • • • • • • • • • • • •

The more adept you become at group improvisations, the more you will understand the value of supporting your partners, of doing whatever you can to develop and underscore their decisions. There are no "stars" in group improvisation. The group fails or succeeds depending on the sensitivity, acuity, and flexibility of its individual members.

The Celebration Theatre Ensemble. From left to right: Jackie Reifer, Frans Rijnsbout, Shelley Wallace, John Saccone. (Photo by Al Fisher)

8

CREATING
SKETCHES

The "Celebration Mime Theatre" in the late 1970s. Top row: Brian Meehl, Bob Berky, Benny Reehl, Fateh Azzam. Bottom row: Billy Fink, Sarah Durkee, Bob Dillard, George Sand, Denise Reehl. (Courtesy of the authors)

The Essentials of a Sketch

The economy of creating sketches consists of *justifying* everything you do. The trick, then, is knowing what's justified and what's not. Here are a few indispensable guidelines for designing a mime sketch and deciding how a sketch should start and progress. If you follow these basic rules, you will find that your sketch holds together (i.e., it holds the audience's attention) while affording you unlimited possibilities within its structure.

Guideline 1) Design your sketch from the audience's perspective.

Designing a sketch is an exercise in empathy. When the curtain goes up, your audience is in the dark. They have no idea what you're up to, but they are ready, willing, and anxious to follow you. They desperately *want* to understand and appreciate your work. In return for their goodwill, you must understand and appreciate them. You must sense what your audience is seeing and make sure that this corresponds to your intentions. Give them enough information so that they won't have to speculate or strain to understand what you're doing. But once they understand, you have their imagination on your side and you can—to a certain extent!—abridge your explanations.

Guideline 2) Remember that at the opening of your sketch, your audience has absolutely no idea what your sketch is about or what kind of character you are playing.

It may seem that this fact is too obvious to warrant special mention, but I've had to repeat this several times in every mime class I've taught! Beginning mimes often assume that their intentions are immediately clear to the audience. They assume that their audience already knows the character, the setting, and the predicament. But this is not so; audiences start at zero. As far as they are concerned, when you assume your opening position on stage, you could be a fly on a picnic or Queen Victoria mourning the death of her husband.

Therefore, everything you do in the beginning of a sketch should be chosen for the purpose of setting your scene and revealing your character. Don't expect your opening moves to reveal *everything*, though. Your character and situation should emerge one step at a time.

The role of Hamlet can be intimidating to an amateur actor if he mistakenly believes that he should be Hamlet all at once. The young actor is expecting too much from his acting ability. No one (not even Lawrence Olivier) expects to reveal Hamlet all at once. The great actors take it easy; they let the play reveal Hamlet a little at a time. The responsibility of the classic "To be or not to be" soliloquy is heavy only if you use it to establish the entire character of Hamlet. In the play, however, the speech occurs *after* the character of Hamlet has been revealed. The actor can relax into the lines knowing that the previous scenes have already justified those lines.

Guideline 3) Remember to subject your talents to the demands of your sketch.

The performance is not a showcase for your skills. Your skills should *serve* your performance. *Use* them to reveal characters, moods, situations. When your talents *serve* the sketch, *you* look better.

Guideline 4) A sketch must reveal something new to the audience, something the audience doesn't already know.

The most intriguing aspect of a sketch is *your* role in it. An individual's selection and treatment of a subject will always be the most fascinating aspect of a sketch because each individual is unique. Therefore, the most captivating and original sketches are those that reveal the performer's personal connection to the subject matter.

I know that my strength as a performer lies in my empathic sense for both my character(s) and the audience. When I step inside of my character's shoes, I show the audience how everything affects me personally. At the same time, I keep track of my audience to be sure that they are always intrigued but never confused by my character's behavior.

In my "Golf" sketch, I play an over-anxious, inexperienced golf enthusiast who is eager to make a good impression on the course. When I enter the stage, I'm aware of the fact that the audience doesn't know what kind of a golfer I am. They know I'm a golfer because I've already announced the sketch ("The Golfer"), but they don't know what *kind* of a golfer I am. Everything I do in the opening of the sketch must establish my character so that the gags (the highlights of the sketch) are justified.

The audience first sees my arm emerge from behind the backdrop. It soon becomes clear that I'm having a great deal of difficulty maneuvering my golf bag. It's throwing me off balance and making me stagger a bit. This entrance prepares the audience for a farce, and they wonder what will happen next. I'm setting them up. My treatment of my golf bag has already revealed the cracks in my veneer as an experienced golfer. Now the audience is eager to see the next step in my character development.

The next thing I do is defer to my fellow golfers by letting them tee-up first. I know that my character is doing this because he wants to postpone making a fool out of himself, but the audience may not know this yet. They may think that my character is simply being polite. But after he badly botches his first shot, the audience understands *why* he urged the other golfers to go first; he thought he'd draw less attention to himself if he went last. (I call this retroactive mime. A character's behavior will be justified later, after the plot has revealed more of that character's true colors.)

In the opening of my "Golf" sketch, the audience is getting to know my golfer gradually, through the process of elimination. The first thing I do on the golf course *limits* the type of person I could be, but it doesn't *complete* my character.

With everything I do, my character becomes more specific, more complete. I have to be careful not to contradict myself and turn into another type of character *unless* I reveal a *reason* for this transformation. This *reason* must also be in keeping with the main thrust of the sketch. For example, my golfer sometimes behaves like a gentleman, but his *reasons* for behaving this way are in keeping with his pettiness.

It's a fact of life that the less noble one's intentions, the more readily that person, if provoked, submits to undignified behavior. This fact of life justifies the end of the sketch when my character, in a fit of rage, drops to his hands and knees on the putting green, manually stuffs the ball into the hole, buries it, and then breaks the clubs over his knee. Here is a man who began his golf game with largess and calm, but finished it with pettiness and rage.

Audiences love this sketch. They may not realize it, but they appreciate my character because everything he does and everything he feels affects me personally. His feelings are my feelings, his reactions are my reactions. It's easy to become petty and aggravated when "objects" don't obey me.

Guideline 5) Your sketch must *escalate* or *accumulate*.

This is very important. Each movement must evolve out of the movement that preceded it. Every situation must progress naturally out of the situation before it. The audience's attention and imagination must be scrupulously directed to some conclusion or climax.

Even a sketch or a piece of choreography that is deliberately repetitious must hold the audience's attention. The audience must become increasingly aware of the choreographer's theme or *reason* for writing the sketch even if that theme is the depiction of futility.

Guideline 6) While you perform or rehearse, be aware of the undercurrent of "causes." Don't merely jump from effect to effect.

As I have said before, every effect (every gesture or facial expression) has an invisible cause—a psychological or emotional *base*. I trust, then, that you are beginning to sense this invisible "foundation" behind everything you do. In consonance with the theme of invisible causes, it is also important to know that during every action sequence, the next action sequence is gathering impulse and information. In other words, there is an overlapping of cause and effect. Effects (gestures and facial expressions) are occurring *while* the causes of the next effect are accumulating.

I remember watching ballet dancers performing a mime scene from one of the classical ballets. They were supposed to be jovial villagers or some such thing. All I can remember is that their facial expressions and gestures were changing every split second. They were rushing from effect to effect without motivating those effects. The audience couldn't see their *minds* working. We could see their reactions, but we couldn't see the mental and emotional cause of those reactions.

Guideline 7) Honor your transitions.

Often a mime sketch begins with several good ideas that relate to each other in some remote way. The next step is deciding your strategy: how to turn *several* good ideas into *one* coherent sketch. This brings up the subject of transitions.

The transitions in a sketch are sometimes more critical than the actual situations, and the strength of your sketch depends on the cleverness with which those transitions are formulated.

In one of my classes a student, Motoko Dworkin, wanted to show a woman grieving the death of her husband. Further, she wanted to relay this message using only an ironing board and a sheet.

She had collected several funereal images using these two props. At one point, the ironing board became a person lying in a coffin. When Motoko draped the sheet over the narrow end of the board, the audience saw a woman pulling a cloth over the head of a corpse. She also discovered that the ironing board could look like a tombstone when it stood on its end. These images were clear and poignant, but when she performed her sketch in front of the class, all we saw was a "slide show" of separate images and positions. The transitions between the images were not "justified."

To solve this problem, we looked at what needed to be done, logistically, to progress from one image to another. To progress from the "head covering" to the tombstone image, the ironing board had to be lifted and lowered on its end. How to perform this maneuver appropriately? How to make this transition compatible to the theme of the sketch?

It didn't take us long to justify Motoko's transitions. Lifting one end of the board could easily represent lifting one end of a coffin. It didn't matter that only one end of the coffin was lifted; the gravity of the coffin and the weight of sorrow colored Motoko's actions and maintained the dynamic tension of the sketch.

When the ironing board needed to be lowered on its end to create the image of the tombstone, Motoko carried in her mind the image of someone lowering a coffin into the grave. After the tombstone image was in place, the next transition was returning the ironing board to its original position, standing on its legs.

Since the woman was mourning the death of her husband, we justified this transition by treating the upright tombstone as if it were a person. The woman embraced the tombstone and tenderly lowered the "person" into a lying position. This maneuver could have been interpreted in different ways, but tenderness and amorous affection colored Motoko's movements and the audience reasoned that the woman was very much in love with this person.

By solving the problem of transitions, we discovered more values and dynamics in the sketch. These transitions became vehicles for revealing the woman's feelings toward her husband and toward his death. They became opportunities to bring more images into the sketch, making the end product more poignant and striking.

Guideline 8) Listen to your character's internal dialogue while you are performing.

When I perform or rehearse a mime sketch, I can hear my character's thoughts. For instance, when Karen and I perform a duet about flirtation, I often look at her and think; "Hey, you're kinda cute." On stage, I think these thoughts silently but when I'm rehearsing, I often think aloud. (I wasn't aware of the fact that I was thinking aloud until Karen pointed this out to me one day.)

It is important to watch your thoughts while you are on stage. You don't want to be consumed by self-consciousness and worry. Think your *character's* thoughts and allow every action to evolve naturally and sincerely out of your character's internal dialogue. This will insure a good sense of timing, too.

Guideline 9) Don't belabor the mime illusions.

Choose only those gestures and illusions that *serve* your theme and nothing else. If you are showing a disgruntled husband, you don't need to show him tying a tie unless the tie can be used as a vehicle for character development or unless this action is an indispensable part of your plot.

This is one of the most common mistakes in mime: The

mime often deliberates over an illusion and forgets the *reason* for performing it. The illusion must develop a plot or reveal character. Otherwise it is superfluous.

I'm not saying that you should *never* deliberate over an illusion, but the time for deliberation is in the studio, not on stage. In preparation for stage, you must minimize the illusions as you weave them into context (into the sketch). Your illusions *serve* your theme. They should not attract undue attention to themselves. (See Guideline 3.)

Guideline 10) Don't be afraid to throw away good material for the sake of the overall sketch.

Once you have determined what is essential to your sketch, you have to forget your personal attachments as you strip away the unessential.

Bearing in mind that your sketch must escalate and progress, you will probably find that certain movements and segments are unnecessary and/or monotonous. Karen and I had to strip away quite a bit of dance choreography when we were working on our sketch "The Spider and the Fly." She resisted this at first because the steps were good from a dance perspective, but this sketch was not a dance, it was a story. We

Karen and Tony in "The Spider and the Fly," 1993. (Photo by C.C. Church)

didn't want to show interesting steps for their own sake. The choreography had to reveal character and plot, nothing more.

Guideline 11) Be conscious of the tempo and dynamics.

Very often beginning mimes and storytellers adopt one speed and stick to it. This makes their sketches monotonous.

In life, we're always doing things at different speeds and dynamics. This fact of life should carry over into the mime performance, but many mime students give all of their gestures equal weight and emphasis. They lift pianos as if they were picking up kittens or they jump out of burning buildings as if they had all the time in the world. (Unlikely tempos and dynamics are fine for certain comic effects, but make sure that they are intentional.) Tempo and dynamic changes determine the credibility of your performance.

Guideline 12) Beware of antics or pieces of choreography that do not conform to the "bell curve" of action.

All sketches have a beginning, middle, and end. They gradually accumulate information as they accelerate in intrigue and tension. The height of tension is the climax or the peak of the bell curve. This is followed by gradual or abrupt descent. (An example of an abrupt descent would be the punch line of a joke.) Beware of action that does not fit in with this bell curve. For example, if your sketch is building in tension, make sure that each sequence of events is more exciting than the last. Don't let your audience down until it's appropriate to do so.

Guideline 13) Don't belabor a point if your audience has already "gotten it." This advice pertains to long, drawn-out action sequences and repeated "phrases."

Suppose your character is getting ready for a date. He must get dressed to make an impression. Don't show the generic illusion of putting on clothes. Remember the audience already knows the mechanics of putting on clothes. They want to know something new.

Twice during my "Golf" sketch, the golfer has to walk a great distance across the course. After the first time he does this, the audience has already seen my "time-lapse" walk showing progressive fatigue. I don't need to show them as much as I showed them the first time. Therefore, instead of taking six steps, I take only three. I can abridge my first walk because the audience already knows that I'm walking a long distance and getting tired. I don't need to belabor the point.

In most cases, storytellers would do well to abridge repeated action sequences in their stories. For example, if

Johnny has to go over the river and through the woods and encounter a witch and a goblin before he gets to his destination, and if he has to follow this path several times throughout the course of the story, it's a good idea to abridge this narration in an imaginative way so as to spare your audience the tedium of hearing the same old spiel over again.

Guideline 14) Practice empathy when you *create* sketches (as well as when you perform them).

If you are angry with the world and you want to make a scathing comment about human nature, make sure that you don't approach your audience as if they were the culprits. The audience will sense that you are blaming them and they will resent it. Beware of that pedantic tyrant (he's in all of us) who wants to point a finger at "them" and say, "It's all *your* fault."

Always remember that the audience is a highly intelligent, well-meaning, and *empathic* entity. It will graciously accept your message as long as it is tactfully and skillfully presented. Simply *present the facts* to your audience; don't *interpret* those facts for them. The audience is intelligent enough to form its own opinions.

• • •

The preceding guidelines serve the purpose of bringing the audience and the performer together in one event.

The most common mistake in creating and performing is this: Performers often *think* they are doing one thing, while the audience *sees* another thing. The audience is never at fault here. It is the performers' job to *know* what the audience is seeing and to reach them.

Summary: Success in creating sketches is contingent on two basic skills:

1) The ability to understand and follow through on the cause of your actions and;

2) Empathy for your subject matter as well as for your audience.

The Secrets of a Gesture

Creating sketches is an exercise in premise work. The *theme* of your sketch is the central reason or premise behind everything you do. This premise or theme remains constant and unbroken through all the various states and stages of the sketch.

Although there is one premise governing the construction of your sketch, there are countless sub-premises governing the authenticity of each gesture *within* that sketch. I call these sub-premises "secrets" because they are the *invisible* reasons for visible behavior.

Keeping track of your premises and sub-premises is not a formidable task. As a matter of fact, a major premise always takes care of the sub-premises that serve it.

Here's a story to illustrate what I mean. Karen and I do a tug-o-war sketch in our show. In the beginning of the sketch, we are at opposite ends of the stage facing each other. Each of us is holding an end of the "rope."

She has just played a trick on me and I'm mad. I jerk the rope as if to say, "Take that! You bully." She, on the other hand, is still a bit playful, not expecting my belligerence. However, when she feels my jerk, she snaps out of her good mood and bristles, prepared to fight. She jerks the rope back at me. Now we're both ready for war. We yank our ends of the rope at the same time causing a slight whiplash effect to reverberate through both of our bodies. We yank again and the whiplash is even stronger, lifting both of us off the floor. The audience giggles and the tug-o-war breaks out in earnest.

After years of performing this mime successfully, we realized something interesting about those initial jerks. When I yank the rope the first time, I'm yanking it away from Karen. We noticed that only Karen's *arms* move in response to that tug (i.e., she stood still and her arms lurched toward me). But when she yanks me back, my *whole body* lurches toward her.

After some discussion, we figured out *why* these two effects were different and *why* this progression of effects was correct. When the sketch opens (before either of us has yanked the rope), my character is antagonistic. I am defensive, ready to fight. I jerk the rope.

Karen's character is initially playful, her body is lanky and pliable. Therefore, when she receives my yank, her peripheral joints (shoulders and elbows) "give in" to it and her body is unaffected. However, when she feels my antagonism, her mood changes, her shoulders and elbows tighten, and she returns an antagonistic jerk. My body is already tight with antagonism. Her jerk, therefore, affects my *chest* because my arms and shoulders are tense, resisting her yank.

After we have provoked each other, we are both in the same mood, our bodies are equally taut, and we both do the same thing at the same time. We yank the rope simultaneously and our bodies rebound with equal force and rigidity .

We did not *choreograph* our arm and chest movements per se and yet, each of our gestures was accurate and logical. This

221

is an example of a major premise (the theme of the sketch) accommodating all of the sub-premises that serve it. We had wanted to show the progression from play to provocation to "war." This was the theme of our sketch, our premise. That theme dictated the mind set of each character within the sketch. In turn, each *character's* mind set automatically took care of the sub-premise behind each gesture. For example, my character was antagonistic and this "solidified" the appropriate joints in my body without my having to think about it. Karen's character was initially playful and her state of mind produced the appropriately relaxed body.

Mimes are insatiably curious people. They instinctively seek out the "whys" behind the "whats." This is because our careers depend on the credibility of our movements. And the credibility of our movements depends on our understanding of causes.

As I said earlier, I went to Paris in 1957 to study with Marcel Marceau on scholarship. While I was over there, I also studied with Marceau's teacher, Etienne Decroux. Decroux was constantly probing beneath the surface appearance of things to discern the cause of those appearances. Consequently, he had developed a keen sense of causality. He could tell immediately whether his students' gestures were caused or contrived.

I remember doing his exercise called "Goalie" in class one day. During this exercise, each student had to get up in front of the class and do a mime of a soccer goalie. Through the mime's (the goalie's) gestures and expressions, the rest of the class had to "see" what was happening on the soccer field. The mime had to "narrate" the entire game from the goalie's point of view using only his actions and expressions (i.e., sudden looks where the ball was, relaxed stance when timeouts were called, tension and anticipation when the referee was making a decision, decrease in tension when the ball was far away, increase in tension when it was kicked closer to your end of the field, etc.). It was a brilliant exercise.

When it was my turn to do the exercise, the first thing I did was wave to some friends. Big mistake. *"Qu'est-ce que tu fait?!"* Decroux yelled. ("What are you doing?!") He thought I was being a wise-guy. In French he asked me, "What's all this waving?!"

"I'm waving to my friends in the stands." I said.

"What is this—an American comedy? You're supposed to be a goalie, not a clown!! Now play soccer!"

I sobered up a bit and went back to work. I stood there and

waited. The game was about to start. My body tensed up. Then I relaxed to show that the ball was far away. The ball moved in closer. I became more and more tense and prepared to defend my goal. Now, I watched the ball closely and when I saw it being kicked, my head jerked slightly before my gaze followed the flight of the ball.

That sudden jerk of my head was the ball being kicked. Every time one of the players would kick the ball, my head would jerk slightly before I'd watch the ball fly through the air.

Decroux stopped me again. "Wait! What's that?!" His tone was a bit different than it had been the first time he stopped me. "What's that sudden movement of your head?!"

"That's the ball being kicked," I said.

"You actually *see* the ball being kicked and then you do that with your head?"

"Yes," I said, "that's the impact of the ball being kicked."

Decroux was silent for a second and then he said, "*Profundomento*" (a French/Italian word meaning, "That's profound").

Decroux liked me a lot, but he didn't like to compliment me. "It's only because you're Italian that you did that with your head. You Italians are tremendous mimes, but you're lazy. You'll never go anywhere because you don't work!" (He was right to a certain extent. I never did push my career. As soon as I had made enough money to support my family, I cooled off and played chess or planted trees or something.)

Anyway after the class was over, I recalled that months before, I had seen a slow-motion film of a ball being kicked. The ball literally *bent* around the foot.

The film showed how the stationary ball first becomes grossly misshapen as it absorbs the impact of the foot. But, then the ball's natural imperative to maintain its shape *causes* it to fly off the foot with a tremendous amount of speed as it recovers its original shape.

The ball goes through a brief moment of stress and release. While it is enduring stress, it is stationary. The moment of release is the most violent moment of the kick—the ball "pushes" itself into flight.

The jerk of my head telegraphed this event. It revealed the brief moment when the ball is stationary (receiving the impact of the kick), followed by a violent release of tension. This stress-and-release event is too fast for the naked eye to see. But my head gesture looked right because it telegraphed a real event. It represented something essential in the natural process of a ball being kicked. Decroux noticed an authenticity about this gesture that excited him.

This is another example of a major premise engaging the minor premises (or sub-premises) that serve it. In this case, my major premise was the goalie's objective: keep your eye on the ball. This, in turn, served to call up the memory of my sub-premise (the *reason* a kicked-ball behaves as it does).

Premise work is powerful because it automatically taps into your storehouse of information and unearths any insights you've collected that now *serve* that premise. All I had to do was keep my attention on the goalie's premise, and this called forth my memory of that slow-motion film. That memory, in turn, instantly inspired the appropriate gestures.

Graphics: "Little Choreographic Victories"

I did not *invent* graphics. Many choreographers use them, but I did *define* the term and give it an honored position in my choreographic vocabulary. There are several ways to define graphics.

1) Graphics are movements or poses that make literal sense in an abstract way.

2) In graphics, a gesture relays many aspects of a thing or an event. A graphic is an objective "thing" that makes subjective sense. It represents a concrete object (or event) *and* what this object (or event) *does* to people—how it affects them.

Examples of Graphics:

1) Fingers draped over the forehead to symbolize hair. The way the fingers *behave* when they are "combed" becomes a vehicle for character development. For example, perhaps the hair will not cooperate with the comb. Maybe the groomer has very bad taste in hair styles. In this graphic, the fingers show two things: hair and what hair reveals about the person. The fingers are an abstract representation of a literal thing.

2) During one of my workshops, Karen created a sketch about Vincent van Gogh. At one point during the sketch, the palm of her hand became a palette and the other hand became the paint brush. She was painting a "canvas" in front of her and after she had done a few strokes on the canvas, her movements became more urgent and impassioned. She began smearing paint all over her face. This forceful application of paint to her own face distorted her expression.

This was a graphic. The painting of the face was suggestive of a self-portrait. The distortion of the face revealed the artist's mental anguish. These movements revealed a thing (a painting, a self-portrait) and they revealed van Gogh's *feelings* about himself and his work.

3) My first mime troupe came up with a delightful graphic of a campfire. Several people sat in a circle on the floor. Their legs were straight out in front of them so that everyone's toes converged in the center of the circle. This place where their toes converged became the campfire and the wiggling toes symbolized the fluttering of the flames. (Everyone was barefoot, of course.)

Here, the toes symbolized many aspects of a camp fire: the fluttering flames, the warming of the tootsies, the gathering of many people together in one spot. This graphic sometimes elicited applause from the audience.

This is why I call graphics a choreographic victory. The audience is *thrilled* to recognize so many things in one simple gesture. This recognition is especially gratifying when what they see is nothing like the original. A bunch of toes wiggling simultaneously doesn't look anything like a *real* campfire, yet the meaning is absolutely clear. The great thing about graphics is the audience doesn't have to *work* to recognize these images, and they are positively delighted to recognize something whose meaning eludes the physical senses.

4) The "idea!!" Imagine someone holding his head as if in deep, troubled thought and then suddenly opening his fingers to symbolize a moment of clarity, a light going on. That's a graphic.

5) There's a graphic in the "Rose Adagio" from the ballet *Sleeping Beauty*. When Aurora stays on *pointe* while one suitor after another takes her around in a promenade (see postscript, page 247), this *pointe* of the foot becomes symbolic of the *point*-of-indecision. This dance step, the promenade, is befitting a courtship. It also reveals Aurora's *feelings* about the courtship; she is delicately poised on the brink of decision and indecision.

6) I mention a graphic in "Turning Rounds into Choreography" (next section). Specifically, I describe a moment from a sketch about the Cathedral of Notre Dame in which one person symbolizes many things: *First* Antonio is the piece of furniture that the confessor kneels on, and then he becomes Jackie's temptation. This is a graphic—one pose, one gesture revealing many aspects of a thing or an event.

7) The word "graphic" also refers to any movement in which a person becomes something other than a person. A certain pose may be a graphic for a tree. A particular movement may look like a door opening or closing. A bunch of people may

move together in such a way as to portray a ship sailing across the wide open ocean. All of these are graphics. Of course, people do not look like trees or doors or ships, but the audience will "see" trees, doors, and ships if the graphic is done well.

To my way of thinking, the abstract and literal are improperly united when the eyes recognize what they see but the mind is confused. When abstract and literal work *against* each other, the images are clear but they don't make easy and immediate sense. On the other hand, abstract and literal are triumphantly united when the eyes are confused but the mind is sharp, when the audience *recognizes* what they see, but don't know why or how they recognize it. Graphics achieve the latter effect.

Turning Rounds into Choreography   In Volume II of my video book *Mime Spoken Here*, twelve professional mimes demonstrate how Closed Rounds and Group Rounds (see pages 151-152) transit into choreography and stageworthy sketches. Here, the theme of the Rounds was the Cathedral of Notre Dame.

I divided the class into two groups of six people. These two groups went off on their own and performed Closed Rounds (and Group Rounds) on the theme of Notre Dame. After an hour or so, each group had collected its own series of physical impressions of the Cathedral. The next step was to select and assemble these impressions, to string them together into a collage format.

The end product was two very different "collages" or sketches. Many impressions were common to both, but each group had discovered its own unique way of graphically illustrating these impressions. For example, bells figured in both sketches. But the first group illustrated bells by holding a person upside down and swinging her back and forth. The other group became six individual bells. They used their arms to indicate the shape of the bell while their lower bodies swayed back and forth and "clapped" against the arms.

Each sketch consisted of a variety of images. There were crucifixes, gargoyles, tourists, candles, worshippers, the Stations of the Cross, confessions. The beautiful thing about these collages was that you saw the Cathedral from the players' point of view. You didn't see a photograph of a building, you saw what the Cathedral *means* to people. This is, I think, the real value of any sketch—what that sketch reveals about humanity.

For example, on this tape, you see an impression of a confession. Jackie plays the part of the confessor, Rick plays the priest, and Antonio plays many parts. First, Antonio is the piece of furniture that the confessor kneels on. He is facing Jackie in a seated kneeling position. His thighs are the platform that Jackie kneels on. Antonio's arms become the platform for her elbows. Both Jackie and Antonio are profile to the audience. The priest (Rick) is facing the audience kneeling behind Antonio. It is obvious that Jackie cannot see Rick even though there is no visible barrier separating the priest from the confessor.

While Jackie is in a prayerful position (elbows resting on Antonio's arms) she begins her confession. We don't hear her speaking but we know she's confessing. Her face reflects guilt and concern as she mouths a plea for forgiveness. Rick's expression reflects beatific boredom.

As Jackie recalls the cause of her guilt, a transition takes place. Antonio slowly "becomes" her temptation. His arms wrap around her waist. Jackie begins caressing his head. Rick sits up straight, his boredom giving way to consternation. Suddenly Jackie's conscience returns; Antonio snaps back to his original position (as a piece of furniture), and Jackie returns to her petition. Rick relaxes. But within a few seconds the pastoral calm is again shattered by another rapturous confession. In a fluster, Rick makes a quick sign of the cross and dismisses Jackie with a brisk wave of his hands.

The audience immediately recognizes what's going on. They see more than the outward appearance of a confession. They see what the confession *means* to people. They see the internal struggle between conscience and temptation and they understand the difficulty, on the part of the priest, of maintaining equanimity in certain situations.

In Rounds, you let the theme "get to you." Then you move honestly and impulsively as you hold that theme in mind. The theme itself may be common knowledge (i.e., everybody knows what the Cathedral of Notre Dame is), but your impulsive and personal interpretation of that theme is uniquely your own. You cannot hope to reveal something new to your audience unless everything you do reveals something new about you to *you*. This is the science of theatre.

The only thing going on in life, in rehearsal, and on stage is self-revelation. We design sketches in order to see how certain themes affect us. We perform in front of an audience to see what *this* does to us, how we handle the distinctive pressures of performing.

Sometimes we forget that the primary motive for doing

anything is to learn more about ourselves. Other objectives (i.e., creating sketches, receiving ovations, getting good reviews) vie for our attention. But if the performer forgets the paramount value of self-revelation, his/her work will miss the mark; it will fail to reveal anything new or interesting to the audience.

Rounds: Overcoming Obstacles

Expectations often block the flow of inspiration. Setting your sights on what you *want* to happen, you may lose touch with what *is* happening. Aiming for an *effect* (i.e., success), you may miss the *cause* of success (inspiration).

Rounds provides an ideal atmosphere in which to stay focused on the inspiration and free of distractions. Judgments, opinions, expectations, and deadlines count for nothing in an environment where one hundred percent of everyone's attention is absorbed by a visceral, spontaneous impression of a theme.

I have often told people not to *think* during Rounds. This is not quite accurate. Of course you *think* during Rounds. What I mean is: don't let thinking *stop* you from doing anything.

Analytical thinking has gotten a lot of bad press among performing artists only because it often acts as an unsuspecting haven for the fear of failure. When the fear of failure governs your thought process, then thinking is an obstacle. But it is the *fear of failure* that is inimical to success; not *analytical thinking*. Analytical thinking, by itself, is an indispensable tool for understanding. (We couldn't dispense with this tool even if we tried.)

Rounds unobtrusively defuses the fear of failure. People often worry about being "caught short" (unprepared); I tell students *not* to prepare their moves. People often shy away from their own vague and unclear impulses; I tell students be as vague and unclear as possible. Sometime I tell students to deliberately *fail* in the Rounds. Once students *indulge* in the very thing they've dreaded and avoided for so long, they soon realize that their fears were unjustified. They also realize that those previously dreaded scenarios (of being unprepared and uncertain) are more interesting, more tantalizing, and more fruitful than their former mode of action.

The fear of failure is far worse than failure itself. Failure is part of getting better. The latent fear-of-failure blocks progress and discovery. In the same way a dog senses fear and growls in its presence, so an audience senses the fear of failure and remains subtly "on edge." Even if the performer is "succeeding" and doing impressive things at the moment, the latent fear of failure hangs in the air and blocks the organic and edifying exchange between the audience and the performer.

To engage in the Rounds exercise is to find yourself suddenly free of a slew of unconscious fears. You see for yourself that inspiration is constantly available and that a wellspring of insight and information is stored in the obscure recesses of your own consciousness.

Appointing a Director for Your Sketch

There is another unforeseen benefit of using Rounds as a springboard for choreography: A director emerges from the group without anyone's conscious effort to appoint the most worthy candidate.

I have found, without exception, that every group yields its own director. One person does not monopolize the directorship position. Rather, one person naturally begins to direct and organize the inflow of good ideas coming from the group.

In other words, Rounds act to establish the group mind. This mind works unobtrusively to accumulate whatever it needs to complete its mission successfully.

This is a variation on premise work. We learned earlier that a premise naturally produces its own conclusions. Likewise, Rounds teach that a theme naturally produces its own sketch.

Crosses and premise work pertain to the individual. Rounds pertain to groups of people, but the phenomenon is still the same. In Rounds as well as in Crosses, ideas (premises and themes) are the conducting forces. Individuals are simply the vehicles for whatever needs to be done.

Tony, with Leland Faulkner and Shelley Wallace. (Photo by William D. Leitzinger)

• • •

When Rounds yield a sketch, the performers all have a vested interest in the sketch as a whole. Each individual feels personally attached to the entire sketch since each individual acted as a director, a rehearsal coach, and a writer at one time or another.

I have been the director of two mime troupes, but whenever we did Rounds, I joined the group and followed the rules. Often another member of the troupe would come up with a strong "directorial sense" for the sketch. I would then step back and silently monitor the process. I'd know when to lead and when to let someone else lead. The Rounds would tell me (and everyone else) *what* to do and *when*.

This is the secret of true collaboration. Most performing companies are governed by a board of directors, and strictly delineated duties. Consequently, most employees have blinders on. They attend to their own tasks and trust that the other employees will uphold their individual ends of the bargain. Many wonderful productions have come out of this arrangement. But I think that the *modus operandi* of successful businesses and performing groups may be changing, and this promises to yield even greater results than before. Certainly an arrangement in which each individual takes a vested interest in the success of the company is preferable to the "I just work here" attitude.

A Final Note about Creating Sketches

I've already told you the story of how I once spent a full forty-five minutes watching a Monarch butterfly being "born" (see pages 194-195). A few years later, my mime troupe and I created a sketch entitled "Insects."

This sketch evolved the way all of our other sketches evolved: through the process of Rounds (see pages 146-154). In other words, each member of the troupe contributed to the process of creating this sketch. After an hour or so of Rounds, we had collected hundreds of images, dynamics, shapes, and movements that suggested and developed the theme of insects. We were then able to construct and choreograph a sketch using these images.

During the Rounds, I recalled the birth of that butterfly. I recalled how *I felt* watching its struggle and its final release from captivity. My memory of this event affected my timing, my dynamics, my feelings, and sensibilities. All of this came up during the Rounds.

Whenever you watch something happening in nature—whenever you watch something with rapt attention—it happens to *you*. It affects your own dynamics and feelings. When "my" butterfly finally broke away from its cocoon, I felt the *correctness* of this moment. As he arched his back slowly and luxuriously, I relished a sense of freedom.

If suddenly this natural unfoldment of events had been interrupted, I would have sensed something was wrong. I would have been frustrated if that butterfly had not arched its back to the extent it did. You will find that you understand the *rightness* of nature's timing. The discovery of the natural tempo with which life unfolds is a type of *self*-discovery.

In light of this fact, you may now understand why developing your power of observation is essential to creating sketches and developing stage presence. An understanding of nature's tempos improves your own sense of timing. And a good sense of timing on stage means a riveting performance.

9

THE SUBTLETIES
OF PERFORMING

Manne af Klintberg, "Manne Clownen." (Photo by Ellinor "Tusse" Hogrell)

The Difference Between Class, Rehearsal, and Performance

The difference between class, rehearsal, and performance is obvious. Class is devoted to exercises and drills, and rehearsals are preparation for performances.

In mime, however, several factors come into play that make it difficult to separate these three occupations. First of all, mimes have to write their own material. No one hands them a script or a score and it's rare to perform another mime's material on stage. There are a few exceptions to this, but in general, mimes must conceive, create, and polish their own material.

Another fact about mime that blurs the distinction between class, rehearsal, and performance is that most of the time you are your own teacher and director. Today, the majority of mimes work solo and the few mime troupes in this country are democracies (that is, everyone has a shot at playing director and/or choreographer at one time or another).

Since mimes have to write their own material and direct themselves, it is important to have some guidelines as to how to work and how to judge whether something is ready for stage or not.

During my first few years as a professional mime, I found it increasingly difficult to go to my studio and work. My attitude toward rehearsals worsened through the years until finally I avoided the studio altogether; my career consisted solely of performing and traveling.

Predictably, I noticed my creativity waning. I was unable to create mime sketches. I dried up. But rather than resign myself to this "fate," I resolved to find and correct this problem. I suspected that my drop in creativity was somehow linked to my drop in studio work.

Just when I was feeling the most unproductive, I had to teach my summer workshop. Something happened in that workshop that gave me an insight into why mimes avoid private studio time.

I tried a slightly new approach to teaching. I divided the class time into what I called drill time, process time, and scene-study time. I kept these sections separate; not allowing anyone to mix up or blend the three. I noticed that the scene studies improved dramatically.

It was obvious that everyone looked forward to working when their "duties" were clearly delineated and enforced. This discovery shed light on my own predicament. My *purpose* for going to the studio had been the problem. I had been going there to "write masterpieces." What a formidable task! No wonder I avoided the studio—the *void*. I was approaching the studio as if it were the stage. I was expecting to perform there.

The key to a successful work regime is to be constantly interested in what you're doing, whether you're rolling across the floor in a crescent shape or perfecting a simple isolation exercise. Masterpieces evolve from interest, not from ambition. They are byproducts of a good work ethic. In other words, the ethic comes first, the masterpiece second.

If you're still tense and frustrated about studio work, analyze your reasons for working. You might find that the desire to impress people has become more important to you than your genuine interest in what you're doing.

**Being
Prepared
vs. Being
Over-
Rehearsed**

"Being in control" on stage means only that you are prepared. You are comfortable enough with your material to respond to the unique contingencies of performing without losing your bearings.

Rehearsals cannot make perfection automatic. Automatic means static, dead. Perfection is alive, flexible, dynamic, and spontaneous. If the intent of rehearsals is rigid perfection, the results will be rigid performers who have lost the ability to deal with contingencies on (or off) stage.

The stage stories that survive are those recounting a performer's spontaneity or presence of mind. Karen's grandmother went to see a play performed by a prestigious theatre company. For this production, the scene designers had rigged up an elaborate contraption whereby the actors would appear to be stranded in a boat in the middle of the ocean.

A large piece of sea-green material covered the stage and stagehands stood under the material waving it furiously to create the effect of a turbulent ocean. Three actors sat in a boat above the billowing waves and performed the scene.

As the scene progressed, the storm intensified, the waves became more and more ferocious and the actors began to shout above the roar. The effect was stunning. Then suddenly in the middle of the action, the cloth-ocean ripped and the top half of a stagehand popped out from under the material. Without missing a beat, the actor yelled, "*Man overboard!* "

The actors hauled the stagehand into the boat and the scene continued uninterrupted.

• • •

The above story reveals how presence of mind responds to contingencies. Presence of mind also responds readily to inspiration.

In the early part of my career, I was on stage performing my "Gymnasium" sketch. In this sketch, I play an elderly gentleman who attempts to build his body about thirty years too late. In the crowning moment of the sketch, the man has finally managed to "muscle" a set of barbells over his head. But his joy is short lived—the barbells sway too far behind him and he is forced to crumple backwards under the weight.

During this performance, I had reached the point where the barbells are lofted over my head and I'm feeling proud. Then, for some reason, I waited a few seconds longer than usual before I let the barbells force me backwards. In this space of time something happened. I heard someone out in the audience giggle. When I heard this, I realized my character was in a comic predicament that I hadn't planned.

Now, it's a fact of life that this is a potentially dangerous moment. The weight lifter is standing directly under a tremendous amount of weight. This moment is more dangerous than the actual lifting. He could suffer a hernia on the way up, but he could break his neck on the way down. (My character certainly didn't know how to lower his barbells correctly.)

It's also a fact of life that pride is a temporary state of being. When my character first brought the barbells over his head, he was proud. But he couldn't stay proud forever; he'd have to lower the bells and get on with life. These facts of life produced the comical moment when pride faded into the feeling of, "Uh-oh.... Now what?"

Someone in the audience had seen my character's predicament even before *I* had. This audience member sensed that the man was in trouble, not because I had *shown* her this, but because she knew the facts of life and understood what the man was going through. I had not produced the comedy of the situation. (That would have been too much of a responsibility.) The facts of life produced the folly.

•   •   •   •   •   •   •   •   •   •   •   •   •   •   •

The audience must know the facts of life that are acting on your character, otherwise the comedy is lost. I wouldn't perform my baseball sketch in Germany, for instance, because the German public is not familiar (yet) with the facts of life for a baseball player.

Since my attention was centered on my character's thoughts, I was not trying to be funny. I was not "going for" an effect. I knew that my character was funny by himself; I was simply seeing life from my character's point of view. Consequently, my character's point of view became the focal point of *everyone's* attention. His perspective became our perspective. His thoughts became our thoughts. One of us just realized the comedy of this situation before the rest of us. In this particular case, an audience member caught on before I did. But once I heard the giggle, I instantly knew *what* was funny and could then expound on the folly of the situation.

As the saying goes in showbiz, "I kept it in the act." This moment when pride fades into panic became the high point of the sketch.

The above stories illustrate the invaluable pay-off of working with presence of mind. Make sure that your rehearsals are geared toward sharpening your mind rather than automating your movements.

Cause and Effect of Comedy

I made the point earlier that the desire to achieve certain *effects* (the desire to be funny) often interferes with your performance. Your expectations then block you from experiencing the inherent wit and wisdom of the present moment.

Adopting "funny" as your premise means focusing your attention on the *cause* of humor. You will notice the little comic incongruities that occur naturally in life. You must *discover* humor; you don't create it.

A high point in comedy is that suspenseful moment when the *cause* for comedy is apparent before the *effects* of comedy appear. When the audience recognizes the *cause* for comedy, they know that the *effects* are soon to follow. The anticipation of comedy greatly enhances the overall comic effect.

When the elderly gentleman in my "Gymnasium" sketch found himself stranded, the audience *caught* the humor. They had "seen" the humor before anything *showed*. My facial expressions and gestures were particularly funny then because they were inevitable—the audience anticipated them. And yet, I had not tried to *be funny*; I simply reacted honestly and sincerely to my humorous predicament.

• • •

Comedians know how to find comedy. They know how to set up a comic situation and let that *situation* produce the humor. Several years ago, Karen and I were invited to Sweden for the Midsummer Celebration. We were the guests of my friend, Manne af Klintberg, who is one of Sweden's top clowns. In the middle of a huge celebration dinner, Manne broke into the theme song from one of Humphrey Bogart's movies, "You must remember this...."

Manne began singing with absolute sincerity. We all turned to look at him and admire his artistic rendering of the song. He was thoroughly absorbed in what he was doing—singing to a dear friend and recalling a treasure of shared memories. "You must remember this...."

He paused to take a breath before the next phrase. Our ears were primed—we waited for " ...a kiss is just a kiss...." Silence.

We looked at Manne closely. Something was "happening"; our expectations had not been met and we wondered why. The minute we looked at Manne's face, we understood what went wrong. Manne's eyes still had that far-away look of someone reminiscing, but now we realized he was no longer recalling treasured memories, he was searching for the next line of the song.

At precisely the right time, his face slumped into perplexity as if to say, "Hmmm, I know this song like the back of my hand...."

He collected himself, sat upright, and that nostalgic look returned to his eyes: "You must remember this ...."

Another silence. Again, the bliss of nostalgia turned to perplexity. More racking of the brain and then, the predicted face slump ("Now *how* could I forget that line?"). We were in hysterics by now.

At different times during the evening, Manne broke into his song. He must have done this about eight or nine times in the space of two hours, and each time it produced gales of laughter.

Manne was not trying to *be* funny. That was probably his original intention, but when he *performed* he was too busy experiencing his character's situation to worry about our reaction. Manne's character was sincere and earnest. For a few seconds, he honestly forgot the words to "You Must Remember This." Manne put himself in a comic situation and let the *situation* make us laugh.

• • • • • • • • • • • • • • • • • •

What stands in your way is that you have a much too willful will. You think that what you do not do yourself does not happen.
—Eugen Herrigel, *Zen and the Art of Archery*

Letting Life Happen on Stage

After forty-five years of teaching, directing, and performing, I have come to the realization that one misconception, alone, is responsible for both laborious rehearsals and lifeless performances. This misconception is that work is an interruption of life and that one has to stop living in order to work and stop working in order to live.

A consequence of this misconception is that the performer concentrates intensely on stage and spaces out (sometimes due to sheer exhaustion) offstage. In fact, being offstage is no different from being on stage. Life is unfolding in both places, and the only thing the performer must *do* to bring life to a performance is *be there.*

Life *on* stage and life *off* stage are the same life. It follows that the life of your subject matter is your own life. Empathy is the realization that life is a unified whole—a shared experience.

Practiced offstage, empathy leads to an intimate, visceral understanding of your subject matter. Practiced on stage, empathy means drawing your audience into your world. They are "taken-in" by your honesty and presence of mind. The

237

audience doesn't necessarily want to see a flawless performance; they can go to a movie for that. The audience wants to watch life happening to you.

Stage Nerves

Performing may be scary or exhilarating, frustrating or satisfying, but always it is a confrontation with the unknown.

Heading over to the theatre for an eight-o'clock curtain, you can never be quite sure how the next few hours will unfold. Your nerves are on edge. Nowhere and at no time is the novelty of every moment more apparent than when you take your place on stage and wait for the curtain to go up. At this moment, you are keenly aware of the "unseen" and the "unforeseen." And the minute you step out on stage, you are almost bowled over by the power of that moment, the thrill of being the center of attention. Everyone, the audience as well as the performers, feels the significance and the intensity of this moment.

So what do you do if you are petrified? What do you do if your confidence is on low ebb that night? Or if your energy level is waning? These are questions every performer asks at one time or another.

When I remember my reasons for performing, much of the fear of taking center stage turns into excitement. Performing is a lesson in living. All of life is *new* every second. The unseen and the unforeseen surrounds us every second of the day. Therefore, when you go on stage, you should know that you are confronting *reality*. The intensity of this moment on stage will (if you *let* it) reveal you to you. This should be your *reason* for performing. You are learning about yourself and how you articulate with the world. The audience is a metaphor for the rest of humanity.

One of the most formidable jobs that a performer imposes upon him/herself is the job of "getting psyched up" for a performance. Beginners at the art of performing are particularly susceptible to the misconception that they have to be in a certain mood before a performance. I urge my students to get rid of this notion as soon as possible.

The most important thing during a performance is that you pay attention to the present moment. If you are trying to relive a previous "high," then you can't be paying attention to *now*. If you are laboring to change your feelings, then you can't be using and exploiting those feelings during a performance.

Many performers hate to be tense before a performance. As soon as they feel the first hint of nerves they do everything they can to get rid of those feelings. Paradoxically, they promote their own tension by paying so much attention to it. Stage nerves need to be put into perspective. If you're nervous say, "OK, I'm nervous, but *what else* is going on."

Whether you are angry, sad, happy, or scared, every mood may be *used* on stage. Revealing your moods on stage doesn't mean divulging your life's secrets to the audience. On stage, your moods are simply dynamics, qualities, textures. They add color and vitality to your performance.

• • • • • • • • • • • • • • • • • •

"It's a good idea to allow some small piece of unhappiness from your life to be a part of your work every night. It gives your singing depth."

—Mel Tormé

Finding "Absolute Zero" or the "Common Ground"

In all walks of life, people are besieged by the fear of "other." (The "other" is anyone or anything that threatens your sense of well-being.) Psychotherapy, meditation, and self-help treatments are primarily geared toward reinstating a person's sense of ease within the environment and this sense of ease comes when the fear of "other" has been overcome.

Performing artists are no different from the rest of humanity. We also experience the fear of "other," but for us this fear takes on certain characteristics unique to our profession. Performing artists deal with at least three variations on this basic fear.

1) The fear of the audience. We're afraid of being defaced or attacked. Our stomachs leap into our mouths when we hear there's a critic in the audience. Beginning mime students experience this fear as the fear of embarrassment or of being ridiculed by the other students.

2) The fear of losing ourselves in our work. Many performers (actors in particular) are afraid that their characters might "take them over" completely. I guess, in some remote way, this is the fear of insanity.

3) Finally, if the subject matter of the performance happens to be controversial, performing artists may be afraid of offending someone in the audience.

All of these fears are variations on the basic and ubiquitous fear of "other." Everyone devises his or her own way of dealing effectively (or ineffectively?) with this fear. Many people simply avoid confrontations with strangers and the unknown.

Tony, with Michael
Henry in
"Scrapbook of a
Dictator."
(Courtesy of
Michael Henry)

But the performing artist cannot avoid such confrontations.
Therefore, I want to share one of the ways I have overcome
these fears.

Many years ago, I discovered what I now call "absolute
zero." I have coined the term "zero" to refer to that state of neutrality where nothing can unnerve you. In this state, I don't
feel that I am male or female, rich or poor, happy or sad. I don't
have interests, opinions, strengths, or weaknesses. I have no
history, no friends, no enemies, no profession. I simply *am*.

From this state of awareness, I experience an exhilarating

fearlessness because I have attained the *common ground* that I share with the rest of humanity. Here, no one is different from anyone else. There are no advantages or disadvantages. There is one mind, one life, and one ego.

A knowledge of this place within myself settles all of my fears. The inclination to be afraid of my critics is erased because there are no critics and no performers in absolute zero. The fear of being overtaken by another personality is also erased because there is no such thing as multiple personalities: there is only one ego. And, finally, the chance of offending your audience is reduced to nothing. There are no *partisan* interests at "absolute zero."

People often remark on my ease in front of people. I have no problem standing up in front of huge crowds and talking to them extemporaneously, as if we are old friends. I am often asked to speak at graduations, Rotary Club meetings, business meetings, etc. These engagements are a special pleasure for me because I can follow my intuition. I sense my audience and I speak directly to their sense of humor, their needs, and their reasons for being there. I am able to do this because I honestly feel that there is no separation between my audience and me. I sense our common ancestry.

Attaining a sense of absolute zero is the antithesis of "going numb." Zero is a state of mindfulness rather than mindlessness. It is a dynamic, vital state of awareness rather than a senseless stupor.

It is not difficult to attain zero. As a matter of fact, the common ground between people is always there; we simply need to turn our attention to it in order to feel at peace with the world, our work, and our situation. This is why it is such a useful tool for performing artists. You don't have to deliberately deny or accentuate any aspect of your own personality in order to overcome fear. Simply locate that place in your own psyche where you are neutral—without needs, without hope, without a care in the world. Here, you will discover that you are fundamentally and basically fearless.

The Past, Present, and Future of Theatre

If you trace the arts back to their origins, you'll find that they began either as forms of worship or as ways to honor and celebrate the sense of community.

In the early days, art was simply self-expression and it was such an intrinsic part of social and religious ritual that there was never a need to give "art" a special name. The specific forms of self-expression (mime, dance, song, etc.) were simply channels for the sentiments inspired by those ritualistic gatherings.

In those days, there was no separation between the performers, the spectators, and the performance. Everyone participated in the event and everyone was equally responsible for the arousal and expression of feelings.

This scenario has changed quite a bit over the ages. Now self-expression is called "art" and art is a business, a way to make money. This means that artists and spectators have diverged into two distinct groups: those who *make* money and those who *spend* money. (Usually, the artist spends more money than the spectator, but that's another issue altogether.) Art, too, becomes a thing unto itself—a *commodity* just like anything else on the market—often distinct from the sensibilities of both artist and "consumer."

At the moment, the performing art scene is characterized by a huge rift between performer, spectator, and subject matter. A live performance is no longer a *community* event nor is it the soul-searching, soul-satisfying occupation it used to be. (This is a huge generalization, of course. There are still extremely exciting things going on in the performing arts, but in general, the original spirit of live theatre is suffering under mercenary rule.)

The good side of this story is that many artists and art appreciators are trying to figure out how to make things better, how to make the arts more accessible and the public more responsive. I think the solution is to reinstate the ritual. Not that we have to go back to the altars and the funeral pyres to reignite a tribal furor, but that every performance should be a celebration of our common ancestry.

Today, the most memorable performances still reinstate the sense of community. At such times, there seems to be no barrier between the artist, the audience, and the subject matter. Everyone in the theatre feels personally and intimately touched by what's going on. It's important now to analyze these events, to find out why some performances have this effect and why some do not.

I hope this book will be a step toward understanding what works on stage and why. Mime is an ideal art form from which to approach these questions because mime is the study of life. It's the study of what makes a performance come to life and breathe. Mime does not lean on special effects or superhuman techniques. It's an exercise in subtlety, clarity, and the economy of movement. It's the practice of empathy, honesty, imagination, observation, and believing.

Treat your work as an exercise in self-revelation and reinstate the art of true improvisation into everything you do.
Then you will discover for yourself that there really is no separation between you, your subject matter, and the audience.

I danced professionally for almost ten years before meeting
Tony. My career was an emotional roller coaster, a mixture of
thrilling highs and devastating lows. While on tour with the
Ohio Ballet, I remember thinking that this was the happiest
time of my life. Being on the road, wearing pointe shoes eight
or nine hours a day, tackling challenging roles was my idea of
utopia. After a full day of class, rehearsal, and performance, I'd
go to the hotel room and stretch for another hour. I knew that
this extra hour of work was accelerating my progress.

Then everything I had been raised to believe in started

**Postscript:
To the Ballet
Dancer, by
Karen**

Karen and Tony on
tour in Germany,
1992.
(Photo by Christa
Engelhardt)

betraying me. I had been raised to believe that "practice makes perfect." But the more I worked, the more I ached and the more depressed I became. My back started to hurt, but I kept dancing. After months of ultrasound treatment and megadoses of arthritis-strength aspirin, I was diagnosed with a stress fracture of the spine. I was in a back brace for a year before resuming my position with the Ohio Ballet. For years after that, my dance career was plagued with injuries. While working in Germany, I had to have surgery on both feet. By now, I thought that injuries and pain were synonymous with dancing.

Each injury felt like a rebuke from the Universe. I changed my religion several times during my career hoping to correct whatever mistakes I had made. I prayed fervently to know what I should do. Finally, a friend of mine told me to stop taking my injuries so seriously; "An injury simply means that you're working incorrectly." It was a great relief to hear my spiritual crisis translated into such simple terms. But these words of wisdom didn't usher in the correct way of working. The injuries, frustration, and introspection continued.

By the time I met Tony, I had every intent of finding another career for myself. I was intensely interested in medicine and the philosophy of science and thought I'd enter academia. Instead, I landed under Tony's tutelage.

When I first saw Tony perform, I couldn't believe what I was seeing. Trying to analyze his genius later, I remember telling my mother that he moved with impeccable economy. "Not even a little finger moves if it doesn't have to." Tony's work reminded me of Michael Jackson's dancing. This comparison has nothing to do with the actual subject matter of their performances; it has to do with the eloquence, power, and clarity of their gestures. It seemed to me that Tony and Michael knew the secret of dance and I wanted to know this too.

It took me a few years to appreciate the science behind Tony's method of teaching. In the beginning of our work together, I was too overwhelmed by the novelty of it to fully appreciate what I was learning. The tug-o-war illusion was one of the first things Tony and I did together on stage. I remember performing it several times before I finally felt like a victim caught off-guard by my opponent's "tug." Dancers are never caught off-guard. We are never clumsy or awkward on stage. Now, in the tug-o-war, I had to stumble and stagger and more importantly, I had to "give in" to these awkward moves in order to make my victimization look authentic.

It was here that I began to suspect a built-in hypocrisy in

traditional ballet training. Ballet is concerned with flexibility. And yet ballet dancers often become so *inflexible* in their way of working and thinking about things. We tend to have very strong opinions about what's right and what's wrong. We tend to be set in our ways. If someone asks us to do something awkward, we resist or complain. This is not flexibility.

Ballet dancers are also trained to believe that muscles and willpower move the body—that all the forces acting on the body come from *within* that body. One of the most astounding things I discovered while learning mime from Tony is that there are, indeed, forces acting on the physical body from the outside. In the tug-o-war, you are not supposed to move until you feel your opponent's tug. The logical question is: How can you "feel" your opponent's tug when there is no physical opponent and no physical rope?

Tony's answer to that question is: "through believing." If you *believe* that you have a real opponent and a real rope, then you *will* experience a force acting on you from the outside. This force takes you by surprise. It yanks and jerks you off-balance; and yet this force does not *begin* in the physical body or in physical space, it begins in the mind, in the belief system.

This is the point of departure between *Tony's* way of teaching and the *traditional* ways of teaching an art form. Most technique classes are training for the body. Tony's classes are training for the mind. When you work strictly on the body day in and day out, the mind tends to be excluded from this work. You may do a thousand *relevés* while your mind wanders all over the place. But if your attention is absent from your work, can you really improve?

I cannot overestimate the value of premise work for the ballet dancer. A couple of years ago, I was doing the crescent roll in the studio (see pages 33-36). I had done the crescent roll many times before and thought I had pretty well mastered the exercise. I wasn't paying too much attention to what I was doing. But then for some reason, I *tuned in* to the premise. Epiphany!

At that moment, I experienced a startling difference between the mind and the body, the premise and the conclusion. I was in the crescent shape and I turned 100% of my attention to the premise. I wasn't thinking about my body, I was paying exclusive attention to the premise. When my attention turned away from the physical plane and toward the premise, I experienced a profound sense of clarity. Tension drained out of my body as if someone had released a plug. I knew that this mental clarity was being reflected by the body.

I also noticed that at specific points during the roll, this sense of clarity was eclipsed by a distraction, a blunt sense of confusion. It was almost as if a dense cloud had come between me and my premise. I knew my body was in the right position but my mind was unclear. For example, just as I rolled from my side onto my back, the idea of crescent was no longer perfectly clear in my mind. I knew too that the integrity of my movement was lost at those moments (even though the body was still in the correct position!).

Once I had noticed these things, it was very easy to correct myself. I simply recovered the idea of crescent and held onto that sense of clarity with all the mental strength I could muster. As I rolled onto my back, I made sure that the only impression in my mind was that clear sense of crescent. The fact that my clarity was continuous at all times during the roll created a remarkable physical effect.

This experience changed my approach to dance for good. I understood that dancing is not a *physical* exercise. It is purely mental and spiritual. Success in dancing is not a question of what your *body* is doing, it's a question of where your attention is. For example, I often ask my students to stand in *plié* in fifth position and prepare for a *relevé, passé,* balance. Right before they actually move, I ask them to tell me what they're thinking about. At first they say that they're thinking about heel positions, hip positions, attack, or some physical correction that (they hope) will work for them. Then I ask them to look a little deeper into their thoughts. Inevitably, they admit that in the back of their minds is a slight misgiving, a subtle fear of failure. They believe they're dealing with chance and that the odds are against them.

I now believe that it's more important to address this subtle fear of failure than it is to address the issue of hip placement. Hip placement is obvious—easy to detect and correct—but fear and doubt are subliminal and often go unnoticed through an entire career. And I believe that these subliminal thought forces are responsible for injuries, insecurity, and aborted careers.

It's crucially important for dancers to probe their thoughts—their background perceptions—because ultimately their state of mind determines their ability to assimilate and apply corrections. It also determines their temperament and the artistic credibility of their dancing.

To shift one's attention from the body to one's state of mind has a remarkably positive effect on one's dancing. For example, it used to be that my "turn-out" was automatic, something I no longer needed to think about. Now as I dance, I have a constant *awareness* of the turn-out. The turn-out is not a physical "thing" to me anymore; it is a dynamic interplay of forces. I find that while my mind is attentive to forces, I am at the *origin* of the movement and I enjoy a much more dependable and consistent sense of control. While my mind is attentive to the *cause* of movement, I can often stop mistakes *before* they happen.

Two parallel stories about Margot Fonteyn in *Sleeping Beauty* serve to illustrate this point. The part of Aurora is one of the most technically demanding roles in the repertoire of classical ballet. At one point in the ballet, many prospective suitors have come to the palace to ask for Aurora's hand in marriage. Classical ballet lends itself beautifully to storytelling here. Aurora takes a *piqué attitude* and gives her hand to the first suitor. The suitor then takes her around in a *promenade*. (The ballerina pivots on one foot while her partner walks around her.) Then, when the promenade is completed, she lets go of his hand, brings her hand up over her head and *balances* (as if on the point of indecision) while the next suitor steps in. She politely gives her hand to the second suitor, and he takes her into the second promenade. This happens *four* times. The ballerina is on one leg, one *pointe*, the whole time. The promenade itself is difficult enough, the balance at the end of the promenade is practically impossible. And in *Sleeping Beauty*, the ballerina has to repeat this maneuver no less than four times!

At this difficult section of the ballet, the audience typically holds its breath. The storyline is completely forgotten; everyone is wondering whether the ballerina will "pull it off" tonight or not.

This, however, was not the case when Margot Fonteyn danced. I read one particular review of Fonteyn in which the critic commented that Fonteyn's interpretation of this role was far superior to any other he had seen. He said that lesser dancers perform this difficult promenade section as if they are saying, "Look Mom! No hands." But when Fonteyn performed it, the audience saw a sixteen-year-old princess on the point of indecision. When she balanced between each promenade, the audience didn't see a technical feat; they saw a shy and delicate princess trying to decide which suitor to marry.

The other story about Fonteyn dancing this role was told to

me by Roxanne Rigoloso, one of my ballet teachers. Roxanne was one of Fonteyn's greatest fans, and she had the good fortune to be in the audience during one of Fonteyn's performances of Aurora. During this particular performance, Fonteyn was part of the way through the promenade section when, in the middle of a balance, she slowly began to tip backwards. This is not "supposed" to happen. It usually means that the ballerina is losing her balance and that she'll have to come off *pointe* (horrors!) in order to recover herself. But Fonteyn never came off *pointe*.

The audience watched in rapt disbelief as Fonteyn's weight shifted precariously backwards. She seemed to reach the point of no return—if the body were simply governed by muscles and bones, she would certainly have toppled over. But she did not topple over. Instead, she began to come back up! Slowly and miraculously, she recovered the *attitude* position. Finally, she was back in a perfect position, and she had never once come off pointe. Roxanne said that the audience practically came out of their chairs with rapture and amazement.

I always tell these two stories (the one about the review and Roxanne's story) together because they prove an important point: how the mind absolutely governs the body. This is an example of premise at work. The ballerina's premise during this promenade section should be her feelings about her suitors and marriage. The storyline and Aurora's feelings are the *cause* of the promenade—the *reason* for it. Margot Fonteyn's attention was tuned to *why* she stood in an attitude balance. She didn't take the *balance* in order to impress anyone, she took the balance in order to tell a story—Aurora's story. While her attention was tuned to the emotional cause of her balance, she was at the *origin* of that balance. She was not lost in physical effects, she was "on top" of them. And she corrected a faulty heel and shoulder position the way a puppeteer corrects a puppet.

If she had been concentrating on a heel position or a shoulder position as she was losing her balance, she never could have recovered herself. Instead, she never really *lost* her balance. The effects started drifting in the direction of error, but her attentiveness to the premise never wavered. Her mind was never lost *in* the physical body (i.e., the error). The mind was always tuned to the premise, and the premise controlled the entire situation—heels, hips, shoulders, etc.

Premise work is scary in the beginning. You are abandoning a former sense of control (based on brute strength and willpower) for a new and improved sense of control. In the beginning, this *improved* sense feels more like abandonment.

The most scary thing about premise work is that you don't experience any resistance from the body! This was disconcerting at first. I had grown to depend on that sense of resistance from the body. Strong physical sensations *grounded* me. They told me where I was and what I was doing. But these were crutches. Strong physical sensations may have identified me for a while, but depending on them was not teaching me how to *dance*.

I have found that the power of assumption is much more effective than muscular power. It is amazing how easily the hips stay in place simply by *assuming* that they are in place and that nothing can change this fact. If you use muscular power (as opposed to mental power) to put your hips in the right place, then you are admitting that the correct position is *unnatural* and that you have to strain to achieve it. But by "becoming the person for whom correct hip placement is *natural*" (see page 184), you spare yourself a lot of sweat and strain.

Working with Tony has also taught me that every position of the body means something. Now when I have to learn a dance, I watch the choreographer closely and ask myself: "What feeling do I need to have in order to make those steps *inevitable?*" Even when the actual steps are unclear, the choreographers *intentions* are always crystal clear. This clarity is more *visceral* than intellectual. If you watch and empathize with your choreographer's state of mind, then learning the steps is much easier.

Premise work is the search for meaning. The search for meaning has many applications to dance. I have often heard older dancers complain that they used to be able to do phenomenal things and now they can't do them anymore. Usually these phenomenal things were meaningless; there was no real reason for them. *Why* would anyone have to jump 5,000 times in the space of a few minutes?!

Improvisation is another invaluable tool for the ballet dancer. I advise all ballet dancers to read the chapters on improvisation in this book and get together for a few improv sessions. It won't take you long to realize that all dancing is an improvisation whether you are dancing old choreography or creating new things. No matter how many times you have danced a role, each time will be different because you are different. You have acquired new thoughts, new experiences, new insights, and all of this will affect how you dance and how you feel at the moment.

Ballet has infinite potential when it is approached as a mental, spiritual exercise rather than a physical one. This does not mean that you have to accept and live with physical shortcomings, either. On the contrary, when your intention and your attention are in the right place, there is nothing about your body or the physical world that can hold you back.

—Karen Hurll Montanaro

BIBLIOGRAPHY
AND RELATED
READING

Aubert, Charles. *The Art of Pantomime*. Translated by Edith Sears. New York: Henry Holt and Company, 1927.

Balliett, Whitney. "Profiles: Mel Torme." *The New Yorker*, 16 March 1981, pp. 49-50.

Chekhov, Michael. *To the Actor*. New York: Harper Collins Publishers, Inc., 1985.

Deburau, Gaspard and Charles. *Pantomimes de Gaspard et Charles Deburau*. Traduction par M. Émile Goby. Paris, France: Libraire de la Société des Gens de Lettres, 1889. (In French.)

Decroux, Etienne. *Paroles sur le mime*. France: Gallimard, 1963. (In French.)

Delsarte System of Oratory. 4th ed. New York: Edgar S. Werner, 1893.

Duchartre, Pierre-Louis. *La Commedia Dell'Arte: Et Ses Enfants*. Paris, France: Éditions D'Art Et Industrie, 1955. (In French.)

Fajikura, Takeo and Yoshiko. Kanjiyama Mime. *Oshaberina Pantomime*. Tokyo, Japan: Ohtsuki Shoten Publisher, 1994. (In Japanese. This is the first mime book ever to appear in Japanese. It was written by two of my protégées. The title in English means "The Talkative Mime.")

Gordon, Jan. *A Stepladder to Painting*. 2nd ed. Revised by Colin Hayes. London: Faber and Faber, 1962. (Mr. Gordon teaches his readers how to develop their power of observation. For this reason, I think every mime should read this book. See the bottom of page 166 and top of 167 for the author's comments on empathy; specifically, the painter's empathy for his/her subject matter even if that subject matter is a bunch of carrots.)

Grock. *Life's a Lark*. Translated by Madge Pemberton. Edited by Eduard Behrens. New York/London: Benjamin Blom, 1931 and 1969.

Guitry, Sacha. *Deburau*. Translated by H. Granville Barker. New York, London: G.P. Putnam's Sons, 1921.

Hacks, Charles. *Le Geste*. Paris, France: Librairie Marpon et Flammarion, 1892. (In French.)

Harmonic Gymnastics and Pantomimic Expression. Boston: Marion Lowell, 1895. (This book is a description of Harmonic Gymnastics as taught by François Delsarte in France in the mid 1800s. Ted Shawn writes: "In book dealer catalogs, this book is listed as the work of Steele Mackaye. But in the book itself, neither the name of Steele Mackaye nor even the name of Delsarte is mentioned! However, it seems to me quite obvious that this book is the work of a student of Steele Mackaye, and one who attended a great many of this classes and lectures and made very careful and complete notes.")

Haskell, Arnold L., and Nouvel, Walter. *Diaghileff: His Artistic and Private Life*. New York: Simon and Schuster, 1935. (Pages 105-106 and 109-110 contain entertaining and insightful comments about the role of mime in ballet.)

Kipnis, Claude. *The Mime Book*. New York, Hagerstown, San Francisco, London: Harper & Row, Publishers, 1974.

Kisselgoff, Anna. "How Realism in Mime and Romantic Ballet Began." *The New York Times*, Sunday, 5 May 1985, p. H8.

Leabhart, Thomas. *Modern and Post-Modern Mime*. New York: St. Martin Press, Inc., 1989.

Leabhart, Thomas et al. *Words on Decroux*. Edited by Thomas Leabhart. Mime Journal Series. Claremont, California: Pomona College, 1993.

Loeschke, Maravene S. *All About Mime: Understanding and Performing the Expressive Silence*. Englewood Cliff, New Jersey: Prentice-Hall, Inc., 1982.

Martin, Ben. *Marcel Marceau: Master of Mime*. New York and London: Paddington Press Ltd., 1978.

Montanaro, Tony. *Mime Spoken Here, Vol. 1, Illusions*. Produced, directed and performed by Tony Montanaro. 2 hrs., 1991. Videocassette. (In this tape, I demonstrate and explain 19 of the most widely used mime illusions.) $57

Montanaro, Tony. *Mime Spoken Here, Vol. 2, Spontaneity and Invention*. Produced and directed by Tony Montanaro. 1 hr. 49 min., 1992. Videocassette. (Twelve professional mimes join me in this demonstration of exercises designed to develop spontaneity, improvisational skills, and choreographic abilities.) $57, or $100 plus $3.50 S & H for both tapes. Order from Tony Montanaro, P.O. Box 1054, Portland, ME 04104.

Perugini, Mark. *The Art of Ballet*. London: Martin Secker, 1915. (This book provides a thorough and erudite account of early mime history. One of the best I've read.)

Rolfe, Bari. *Actions Speak Louder: A Workbook for Actors*. Berkeley, California: Personabooks, 1992.

Rolfe, Bari. *Mimes on Miming: An Anthology of Writings on the Art of Mime*. North Hollywood, California: Panjandrum Books, 1980.

Scenarios of the Commedia dell'Arte: Flaminio Scala's Il Teatro delle Favole Rappresentative. Translated by Henry F. Salerno. New York: New York University Press and London: University of London Press Limited, 1967.

Shawn, Ted. *Every Little Movement*. Pittsfield, Massachusetts: The Eagle Printing and Binding Company, 1954. (An invaluable source book for anyone interested in the work of François Delsarte.)

Shepard, Richmond. *Mime: The Technique. An Illustrated Workbook*. 2nd ed. New York: Drama Book Specialists, 1971.

Stanislavski, Constantin. *An Actor Prepares*. Translated by Elizabeth Reynolds Hapgood. New York: Theatre Arts Books, 1983. (I especially admire Stanislavski's study and use of the imagination.)

Stebbins, Genevieve. *Delsarte System of Expression*. 6th ed. New York: Dance Horizons, 1977.

Storey, Robert F. *Pierrot: A Critical History of a Mask*. Princeton, N.J.: Princeton University Press, 1978.

Whone, Herbert. *The Hidden Face of Music*. New York: The Garden Studio, 1978. (Another book to prove the universality of certain principles of art.)

Wylie, Kathryn. *Satyric and Heroic Mimes: Attitude as the Way of the Mime in Ritual and Beyond*. Jefferson, North Carolina, and London: McFarland & Co., Inc., Publishers, 1994.

INDEX

(Note: Page numbers for illustrations are in itallics.)